PENGUIN BOOKS

Public Spending

Evan Davis is the Economics Correspondent for the BBC's *Newsnight* programme. He is also a member of the advisory council of the Social Market Foundation, the London based think-tank, and was the 1996 Gatsby Visiting Research Fellow at the Foundation. He studied at St John's College, Oxford, and at the Kennedy School of Government at Harvard University. Prior to his current post he worked at the Institute for Fiscal Studies and the London Business School. He is co-author of the *Penguin Dictionary of Economics*.

Public Spending

Evan Davis

PENGUIN BOOKS

PENGUIN BOOKS

Published by the Penguin Group
Penguin Books Ltd, 27 Wrights Lane, London w8 5tz, England
Penguin Putnam Inc., 375 Hudson Street, New York, New York 10014, USA
Penguin Books Australia Ltd, Ringwood, Victoria, Australia
Penguin Books Canada Ltd, 10 Alcorn Avenue, Toronto, Ontario, Canada m4v 3b2
Penguin Books (NZ) Ltd, 182 – 190 Wairau Road, Auckland 10, New Zealand

Penguin Books Ltd, Registered Offices: Harmondsworth, Middlesex, England

First published 1998
10 9 8 7 6 5 4 3 2 1

Copyright © Evan Davis, 1998
All rights reserved

The moral right of the author has been asserted

Set in 10/12.25 pt Monotype Bembo
Typeset by Rowland Phototypesetting Ltd, Bury St Edmunds, Suffolk
Printed in England by Clays Ltd, St Ives plc

Except in the United States of America, this book is sold subject
to the condition that it shall not, by way of trade or otherwise, be lent,
re-sold, hired out, or otherwise circulated without the publisher's
prior consent in any form of binding or cover other than that in
which it is published and without a similar condition including this
condition being imposed on the subsequent purchaser

Contents

CONTENTS

Preface

It may not be an exciting title, but public spending is an exciting topic – and rarely has it been more so than today. The combination of tax-weary politicians; endless pressures on spending; and a government determined both to deliver strong public services and prudent finances has led to a good deal of fresh thinking on the state and its role. Rarely have governments been more aware of the problems they face in this area, rarely have they been aware of more possibilities for overcoming them.

This book aims both to summarize and to contribute to some of the new thinking on those problems and possibilities. It outlines some of the economic principles that govern public spending; it takes an updated look at some old arguments about the state; it briefly describes the salient features of public spending in the UK. At the same time, given that a lot of recent debate on the state's role has revolved around the use of market-type mechanisms in the delivery of services, the book focuses on reforms of this category. In particular, several chapters broadly support the idea that government should run fewer services itself, and instead buy more of them in – the so-called purchaser–provider split. This is an idea of tremendous importance, often discussed in different guises for different services, but as a general approach to reform it is not one that has been written up or appraised in enough textbooks.

Although this book does have a point of view, nowhere does it purport to offer easy solutions to the problems governments have, nor does it promote the idea of the purchaser–provider split without highlighting the difficulties inherent in that route. Nowhere does it present a blueprint for reform, and although there are plenty of ideas within the book, there is no department-by-department guide as to what ministers should do. It is not a manifesto.

As for its structure, the book attempts to take a look at public spending in general rather than as a series of unrelated departmental decisions. It offers principles and examples, not a systematic audit of what the government does.

It should be useful for several groups of readers. For a start, it has been written so that the average − well-motivated − reader of a broadsheet newspaper could follow the argument. It is not an academic book, stuffed with unsightly references. (Writings referred to in the text and not footnoted, and some other relevant texts, are listed in unambiguously identifiable form in the 'Additional Reading' sections at the end of each chapter.)

For those who start with some knowledge of the economics of public spending, or who work within the environs of Whitehall, or who are doing politics or economics courses, it should serve as something of a crash course on the subject. For those already expert in the subject of public spending, it is hopefully a fresh enough account, with sufficient new content, to add some value to what is − at the academic level − a crowded market.

Many thanks are due. Probably the second most important acknowledgement must go to the BBC − particularly Martin Leeburn, Peter Jay and colleagues at *Newsnight* − for allowing me time off to write this book. And the first must go to the Social Market Foundation who kindly paid me to do so. The SMF's generosity was only possible on account of the support of the Gatsby Charitable Foundation, to whom I am also obviously indebted.

For motivation, stimulation and general support, it is the SMF which again merits thanks. Robert Skidelsky, Roderick Nye and former director Danny Finkelstein have all agreed with enough of what I say to be supportive, while disagreeing with enough of it for us to have interesting and helpful conversations. Alastair Kilmarnock, Stephen Pollard, Marc Shaw, Katharine Raymond, Susan Foulis and Helen Brown all provided generous help with great patience.

Many of the other people who have helped develop the thoughts outlined here are probably unaware of their complicity: participants in seminars at the Social Market Foundation and the Institute for Fiscal Studies; the members of the two SMF public spending study groups; and friends and colleagues who have found themselves arguing or agreeing with me on the claims made here − Alan Kemp, Neil Buckley,

Christopher Exeter, Steve Richards, Peter Boone and Peter Taylor Gooby. Jill Rutter and Stanley Wright deserve very special thanks for extensive suggestions made from an early manuscript.

I am also grateful to the excellent press offices at the OECD in Paris and at the Office for National Statistics in London, to Robin Bew, Tony Hockley and the Chelsea & Westminster Hospital Trust for providing specific pieces of useful information. And to the Shepperton Women's Cricket Team who helpfully spent an evening with me downloading their views on public services.

For all this help, however, I simply could not have completed the book without research assistance. Joseph Thomas gave up weeks of a lucrative summer job to help me and is responsible for some of the most complicated tables. Ben Harnwell and Jaime Powell collected, compiled and processed large amounts of information on disparate topics at my request — without reward — while never complaining. Graeme Tennyson saved me days of library work by educating me in crucial areas of existing literature.

Finally, some thanks to friends and family for provoking me into starting a book — and indeed finishing it. Leandro Lonzetti Fontana in particular was a source of constant support. And there should be a special acknowledgement for my father, who not only provided comments on an early version of the text, but who has always graciously indulged my interest in current affairs and who attempted to imbue all of us with a sense of the value of logical thinking.

Part One
Public Spending and the Public Sector

Public Spending, Public Disquiet

Why is the Department of Social Security not as effective at being a social security department as First Direct is at being a bank? Why when the comedian Julian Clary shuts up an interrupting heckler by asking, 'Who cuts your hair? The council?', does the audience not sit bemused and puzzled, but laughs? (Presumably nobody sees anything to laugh at in the fact that it's the council that teaches their children.) Why has Camden Council had a policy of closing most of its public swimming pools on bank holidays when people might want to use them? Why does passport control at Heathrow Terminals 3 and 4 set itself 'customer service' targets under which it is acceptable for 15 per cent of passengers to wait more than half an hour in a queue? Why does the overseas aid budget – some £2bn in 1996–7 – have no discernible long-term effect in aiding the world's poor? Why, at the European level, do farmers receive cheques for an average of £13,766, often more if they agree not to grow things?[1]

Most books on public spending are rather dry, but these questions demonstrate the subject need not be. This book is about these kinds of issues; about the way in which we spend public money, and the way we deliver public services. It looks at what government does, what is wrong with what government does, and at some routes for reforming what government does. It is not a textbook, or an academic treatise; but nor is it a simplistic proclamation of a single point of view. It covers a wide range of topics, and it often reaches no very strong conclusion on them.

This book is based on the simple premise that the public wants good schools, it wants decent health care and pensions, it by and large supports

1. This figure for 1996 was calculated by the OECD in 1997.

the notion of a secure state in which the unfortunate are helped by the fortunate; and it is willing to pay for these things. But at the same time, it has lost faith in the state as a vehicle for delivering them. Polls show people are more impressed by the quality of service they get on package holidays than that which they get from the NHS. They might be willing to pay higher taxes for services, but not so willing that many mainstream politicians have felt inclined to ask them to do so. This is not – as some appear to believe – merely a public relations problem, that can be willed away if only people can have the truth explained. Poor public perceptions were not invented by tabloid newspapers or devious politicians. You can't fool the public into believing schools are bad if they are good, any more than you can trick them into believing they are good when they are bad. Quite simply, public aspirations for standards of service and quality have risen faster than the standards they associated with public services.

There is nothing new in the observation that the state hasn't always been effective in what it does, nor in the idea the public have grown disillusioned with it. Those on the right and the left ends of British politics – in other words those who had no intellectual stake in the middle-of-the-road post-war political settlement – noticed it years ago. And they responded.

The left saw that bold change was needed in the way services were delivered. Its most successful response to the gathering clouds of public disquiet was personified by Ken Livingstone at the Greater London Council in 1981. His answer was to boldly spend more. No national government, with responsibility for really large budgets, has emulated his approach.

As for the right, it joined and then overtook the public in its disquiet. Margaret Thatcher didn't listen to what people actually said about the state, or what they told opinion polls. She simply guessed that she would not be punished at the polls if she erred on the side of tax cuts rather than spending increases. Her risk paid off, but ultimately she didn't solve the problem that the public actually wants higher quality services, and requires some government lead in finding a means of paying for them.

So, suddenly – since the mid-1990s – debate over the state has become exciting again. Intellectuals, 'policy wonks' and politicians are once more arguing about the state of the state. Public spending and taxation are fashionable subjects – fashionable here and around the world, particularly in Anglo-Saxon countries. Britain is at the front of that debate. Plots are being hatched at think-tanks around the capital, schemes are being devised at universities around the country. The debate over the state in the twenty-first century is under way.

New Thinking on Public Spending

There are two main approaches to the problems identified with the public sector and public discontent, and this book discusses both of them. They can loosely be described as applying to the *demand* for services and to the *supply* of them.

The demand-side agenda is about the way we pay for services. In its most usual guise, it is about cutting the tax burden and making people pay for things more directly. Under this approach, the state would buy rather less for us all than it does at the moment. The demand for services would be privatized. While this is the agenda of the 'smaller state' brigade, there is no need for it to be exclusively theirs. After all, even if you support a Swedish-size state, as long as you want the public to smile as they pay taxes for services they want, you'd better make sure that you are not taxing them for services they don't want. For people anywhere on the political spectrum, therefore, cutting certain pieces of nonsensical spending should be a priority. And in some areas, the public may need to end up making a direct financial contribution towards services which they pay for today entirely in taxes.

But this is not the only show in town. For those who believe a strong state can promote a gentle society, there is a second, complementary route of reform, working on the *supply* of public services and improving the quality of delivery of the things taxes pay for. This is the route on which this book places most emphasis. It has to involve reforms in public services that go much further than those we have seen so far – the Citizens' Charter, contracting out, the Private Finance Initiative and internal markets – and in particular it involves making a distinction that recurs as a great theme of this book: the distinction between the state as the provider of services, and the state as purchaser of them.

One of the best ways for the state to improve the supply of public services, perhaps the biggest policy idea of our time, is for government to hire private service companies – or more likely public service organizations run on more or less private lines – to supply them. You can *pay* for schools without *running* them, for example, and it is important to understand the advantages and disadvantages of doing so. This route is much discussed within these pages. The argument of the book is that the public sector can benefit from new and more commercial styles of management, because over time the pressures applied to the private sector have demonstrated themselves as more effective in obtaining adaptable and responsive services than the pressures applied to the traditional public sector. Following such a route requires us to sort out the treatment of capital, capacity, investment, and profit within the public sector. Those are subjects that merit far more attention than they generally obtain, and this book only modestly rectifies that deficiency.

The supply-side route is attractive for a number of reasons. It is an approach that won't get the state share of spending in GDP down very much, but it will get the state's share of the economy down; it's a public service revolution based on the slogan 'Down with the public sector; long live public spending'. If it does achieve better value for money over the long term, it could reinstate public confidence in public services and increase public willingness to pay for them.

Both the supply-side and demand-side agendas have the potential to solve some problems in public spending, and the mismatch between resources and aspirations. Neither approach is straightforward, which is indeed one reason for there to be this book at all, and for it to devote so much space to analysing the problems they solve, and the principles of their implementation.

Later in the book, in Part Two, we can look at those problems in full, and at the costs of making decisions in the public rather than the private domain. Part Three is about reform – some reforms that have occurred, and the reforms that could occur – on the supply-side and the demand-side. But before you can get to the problems or solutions, it is wise to have a very clear idea about the background.

So Part One simply collates some facts, and rehearses some basic arguments about the size of the state. Chapter 1 looks at the size of government, measured both in terms of its role as a purchaser and as a provider. Chapter 2 looks at the arguments for a large public sector and at whether our traditional model of public sector delivery in everything from schools to hospitals can be justified by the values that motivated its inception, and concludes that it cannot be. Chapter 3 looks at the arguments for public spending, rather than a large public sector. And Chapter 4 focuses on what we know about the public's willingness to pay for services.

I   The Size Question

The background facts

MAYOR QUIMBY: Are these morons getting dumber or just louder?
AIDE: Dumber, sir. They won't give up the Bear Patrol, but they won't pay taxes for it either.

> Episode 3F20 of *The Simpsons*, in which an escaped
> bear in the town of Springfield creates a demand for a Bear Patrol,
> and a subsequent tax revolt.

The Weekly Shopping

Suppose for a moment that we are in a country rather different from our country: a country where our existing levels of government services like schools, health care, defence and social security are not delivered to us by government, ready-made and already paid for. Instead, we are compelled to visit the shops each week, or perhaps a post office, and pay a separate fee for each government function.

How many of us do you think have any idea of how much we would be paying? What, for example, does the average household spend each week on defence? Is it more than we spend maintaining our homes and gardens, for example? How much do we each pay on our subscription to the National Health Service? Is it as much as we pay for electricity and gas? Or do we spend as much on overseas aid as we do on newspapers?

Few of us have any idea of the answers to these questions. Of course in practice the questions are complicated by the fact that we are a varied bunch of people, and the answers really depend on who we are. But accepting that the 'average household' does not really represent any particular household, it is still interesting to look at the answers to these questions averaged over households. In 1996–7, the average household in Britain spent about £309 a week, around 95 per cent of its disposable income. But how much do you think the government spent each week, per household, on our behalf? How much on defence, the NHS or overseas aid? On roads and education? Table 1 gives the answers, expressed as the average household weekly bill, simply calculated as total spending divided evenly across an assumed 24 million households in the country. It is laid out in a manner that juxtaposes public spending with comparable private items where possible.

In answer to the questions posed above, the table shows that we spend over twice as much on defence – about £17 a week – as we do on maintaining and decorating our home. We spend £33 a week on the NHS, which is two-and-a-half times as much as we spend on power and fuel, and about ten times as much as we spend on medical care ourselves. We spend a little under £2 a week on overseas aid, which is, incidentally, about a third of what we give to charity, and about two-thirds of what we spend on newspapers and magazines.

Schools cost us all £16.80 each week, and higher education costs us another £10.43 – far more than the £4.55 we spend privately educating ourselves. The government buys us 74p's worth of public library services each week – two-thirds as much as we spend on books, diaries and maps privately. The Department of Culture, Media and Sport spends more each week than we do ourselves on going to movies and the theatre (even when you subtract the department's library and sports budgets). On public transport, the government spends about as much on our behalf as we spend ourselves. The police cost us a mere £6.68 a week – a bargain you might think. But prisons and courts cost £4.53, which may seem like quite a lot. In total, we spend about the same on all the so-called 'protective' services as we do on holidays – the equivalent of about £13 a week. On the other hand, for every pound we spend on holidays, we spend 7p on the Foreign Office.

Finally, what about the European Union? The full cost of EU membership is not always borne in the form of budget levies – the agriculture programme can simply mean we pay higher than necessary food prices with no money passing through the hands of government at all – but in terms of direct contributions to the explicit EU budget, each household paid a little over a pound a week in 1996–7. In fact, that was an unusually modest contribution – the EU levy varies a lot

Table 1: Weekly Household Expenditure

£ per week, 1996–7

Privately purchased goods/services[1]		Publicly purchased goods/services	
Food and non-alcoholic drinks	39.94	Agricultural support[2]	3.08
Food purchased away from the home	15.21	Other agriculture, fisheries and food	1.86
		Forests	0.04
Beer and cider	7.18		
Wines	2.82		
Spirits, liqueurs and other drinks	2.41		
Cigarettes, tobacco and tobacco products	6.07		
Men's clothing	4.45		
Women's clothing	7.40		
Children's clothing	2.59		
Footwear and accessories	3.83		
Housing: mortgage and rent	41.59	Housing	3.20
Repairs, maintenance and decorations	7.51	Other environmental services	7.86
Electricity, gas and other fuels	13.35	Energy, trade and industry	4.04
Furniture, furnishings, durables	19.08		
Other household goods	4.88		
Pets and pet food	2.78		
House insurance	1.63	Defence	16.98
Telephone, postage	6.03		
Other household services	8.70	Police	6.68
		Fire service	1.32
		Prisons and courts	4.53
		Other 'protective services'	0.66

Table 1 (cont.)

£ per week, 1996–7

Privately purchased goods/services		Publicly purchased goods/services	
Medical care	3.37	Health	32.99
Other personal goods and services, cosmetics	8.27	Personal social services	8.11
Motoring	41.20	Transport: roads, national and local	4.63
Public transport	2.67	National rail services	1.51
		Local transport	1.45
Air travel	0.74	Marine support and civil aviation	0.10
Other forms of transport	4.05	Other transport	−0.49
Books, maps and diaries	1.14	Libraries	0.74
Newspapers, magazines and periodicals	2.85		
TV, video, audio, computer purchases, rental and subscriptions	9.34		
Educational and training expenses	4.55	Education: schools	16.80
		Education: further/higher	10.43
		Employment and training	3.54
		Education: other (e.g., admin & research)	2.34
Cinema and theatre	0.87	Nat. Heritage, except libraries and sport	0.88
Sports (passive and active)	2.85	Sport and recreation	0.63
		Lottery spending	0.48
Holiday	13.23	Overseas services, excluding aid	0.97
		Overseas aid	1.76
		EU contribution	1.12
Gambling payments	3.82		
Cash gifts and donations	5.00		

Table 1 (cont.)

£ per week, 1996–7

Privately purchased goods/services		Publicly purchased goods/services	
Other leisure expenditure	5.48	Miscellaneous expenditures	4.02
Miscellaneous	2.21	Administration of social security	2.84
Total	**309.09**	**Total**	**145.10**
Total Spending	**454.19**		
Public Spending Proportion	**32%**		

Memo items

Life assurance/pension fund contributions	18.90	*Social security payments*	75.35
Insurance premiums (medical and other)	1.64	*Debt interest*	17.65

1. These numbers are gross of VAT and other taxes, thus inflating the true cost of these particular items relative to the public services which, by and large, do not have tax applied to them. The message is not to attach too much weight to the precision of the figures, as opposed to the general picture.

2. Comprises market supports under the Common Agricultural Policy of the EU.

Source: *Family Expenditure Survey 1996/97*: and author's estimates drawn from *Public Expenditure Statistical Analysis*, March 1997. Estimates based on UK population in 1996, at FES average household size of 2.5 people.

year by year, if only because the EU financial calendar runs from January to December, rather than April to March as the UK one does, so the timing of payments relative to the UK year sometimes alters. The average contribution to the EU for the last five years or so has been about 40p more than for 1996–7; even so, that makes our entire contribution to the EU budget less than three times the size of our bilateral contribution to the Commonwealth via the overseas aid budget – some £700m in 1995–6.

All in all, government ends up spending some £145 a week on our behalf – almost exactly a third of the total of private and public spending. In other words, a third of what we buy comes from a shop called Her Majesty's Government. Of that third, just over a third is delivered to us by local government, and just under two-thirds comes from the branch in Whitehall. (The bit that comes from the branch in Brussels gets lost in the rounding.) And as for how we paid for it all? Of the money raised, 93 per cent of it was collected by central government.

In addition to all the items mentioned in the table, there are two other major areas of public spending. In 1996–7, the government was spending over £78 a week for each household on social security (broadly defined as including all state benefits). Some £75 of that has been included as a memo item at the bottom of Table 1 for the simple reason that it is both a source of income and a source of spending by households: on average, the extra £3 – the difference between what government gives out and what we receive – is the cost of administering the system. Only that is actually a net burden on spending by households.

The other big item is debt interest: again, this is paid out and also received as income by some households, so is included as a memo item. But the fact that each household spends £17.65 on merely maintaining the national debt – each week – may come as a shock to those who never miss a payment on their credit card to avoid incurring interest charges.

This view of public spending as part of our weekly shopping basket may appear a bit trite. For those who find it easier to digest information in the form of annual billions of pounds, Table 2 offers much the same information in that more conventional form. But presenting public spending as in Table 1 is designed to clarify, rather than shock or amuse; to alert us to the trade-offs between private and public forms of consumption. That trade-off looms over every British election, but it tends to do so in a rather obscure form. Clear exposition of the real choices – choices about the marginal benefits of spending privately and publicly – is usually absent.

This is a pity. Such is the complexity of a modern economy, that quite simple arrangements become quite obscure to people, and costs and benefits of the kind presented in the table become hard to trace. One apparent item on a New York City TV news programme featured a man suing the local authorities for $6m in compensation after falling

Table 2: Public Expenditure in the UK, 1996–7
£ billion

Defence	21.2
Overseas services, overseas aid	3.4
Agriculture, fisheries, food and forestry	6.2
Trade, industry and energy	5.0
Employment and training	4.4
Transport	9.0
Housing	4.0
Other environmental services	9.8
Law, order and protective services	16.5
Education	36.9
Culture, media and sport	2.8
Health	41.1
Personal social services	10.1
Social security	97.5
EU contribution	1.4
Miscellaneous expenditure	5.0
Debt interest	22.0

Source: *Public Expenditure Statistical Analysis*, March 1997, estimated out-turn.

on poorly laid paving stones. When asked whether he thought it fair for taxpayers to bear such a large cost for the minor injuries sustained, he said he didn't want the taxpayer to suffer at all; it was the city itself which ought to pay.

Confusions of this kind are apparent in the UK, for example when people in London carelessly complain that they have the 'worst and most expensive public transport system in Europe'. It is of course far from obvious that our underground really is expensive; it just seems expensive because we pay more at the ticket barrier than the populations of most other European capitals. We pay less for it out of our payslips.

The Size and Shape of Government

So far we have seen the services on which government spends its money. But to get a better view of the size and shape of government, we need to dissect the forms of spending that occur in a rather different way. The starting point is Table 3, which provides a close examination of government spending – local authorities and central government taken together – in five sample years spanning four decades, all expressed as a percentage of the total economy.[1] A full version of the table, for each year since 1961, is carried in the Appendix.

Unfortunately, there are many ways of counting public spending, so any figures on this subject are always subject to some detailed debate which probably should not concern the average citizen: do we use current or historic cost depreciation? Do we measure GDP at market prices or factor cost? Do we count government sales or purchases of private company shares as spending? And what about government loans to the nationalized industries? As these kinds of rather technical decisions can make a significant difference to the numbers, one should not treat the absolute magnitudes of the figures listed with any reverence. They are primarily indicative.

The top line of the table looks at the crude measure of spending – it says total spending represented some 46.4 per cent of GDP in 1996. This is rather higher than the figure most often quoted – which is about 40 per cent – primarily because of the less favourable effect of the particular measure of GDP selected.[2] Neither this number nor the

1. The table covers what statisticians call 'general government'. It excludes public corporations, like the Post Office and the BBC, which are counted as part of the public sector, but not part of general government. In practice, there are bits of the broader public sector which are rather government-like in their outlook, and ideally, these would be included in this statistical study. Unfortunately, there are also bits of the broader public sector, like British Nuclear Fuels, which are rather private-sector-like in their governance which we would not include. For all statistical purposes, though, you have to actually make a choice – taking either the whole public sector, or general government.

2. Table 3 also refrains from using the government's preferred measure of spending, so-called GGE(X), which quite unjustifiably strips lottery spending out of the total, and counts government interest and dividend receipts as negative spending.

Table 3: The Development of Public Spending and the Public Sector

all figures are percentage of GDP

	1961	1966	1976	1986	1996
Crude total of government spending	36.2	38.4	46.9	48.1	46.4
minus *capital spending*	3.6	4.8	4.5	2.2	1.5
minus *debt interest*	4.3	4.2	4.4	5.0	4.1
plus *'fictitious charge' for use of capital assets*	4.3	4.5	6.1	4.9	3.8
Current spending by government	32.5	34.0	44.0	45.9	44.5
minus *basic state pension*	3.0	3.6	4.6	5.2	4.7
minus *core social security*	3.7	4.0	5.5	9.1	10.0
minus *peripheral social security (subsidies etc.)*	2.6	2.1	3.9	2.6	1.9
Current spending by government on goods and services	23.2	24.2	30.1	29.0	27.8
minus *purchases from the private sector*	7.9	7.8	8.4	9.2	13.4
General government value added	15.3	16.4	21.6	19.8	14.4
Wages	9.9	10.8	14.1	13.5	9.3
Capital – return and depreciation	4.9	5.1	6.9	5.7	4.3
Payments overseas	0.5	0.5	0.6	0.6	0.7

Source: author's estimates based on ONS United Kingdom National Accounts 'Blue Book' data. See Appendix for details.

oft-quoted 40 per cent is very meaningful for a number of reasons. So let us break it down into parts, to better understand truly how big government is relative to the economy as a whole.

Capital and Investment

One cannot properly look at the size of government in the economy, the burden it represents (or even the way it should be reformed) without looking at government's treatment of capital and investment. The state owns more assets than anyone else in the country, with the possible exception of the Creator. Each year its capital spending is equivalent to the cost of two Channel Tunnels; and each week the government spends nearly £18 for each household in the country on servicing the national debt. The government's capital account – its balance sheet and the changes that occur to it year after year – are important in determining the true burden of government in the UK.

The crude measure of government spending in national accounts is not a good measure of the burden of government *today*. To get that, we might subtract government investment from the total (1.5 per cent of GDP) as it is really spending on the future, rather than on today. In looking at the size of government today, it should be disregarded therefore. Secondly, we should subtract government debt interest (4.1 per cent), which is a legacy of spending decisions made in the past, rather than a reflection of decisions made today, or of services being offered to existing taxpayers.

At the same time, thirdly, we have to add to the current spending total the value government today draws from spending decisions of old. This is the value government draws from all the capital assets it owns, but which today's taxpayers have not paid for. For example, take the headquarters of the Treasury in Parliament Street. We think this a piece of real estate worth something close to £200m. It is owned by government, and put to essential use (assuming you think accommodating the Treasury is essential). Yet it was paid for by taxpayers who have gone before us, and although we do not have to pay a rent to those old taxpayers (they gave it to us), as a result we save the cost of having to rent equivalent accommodation for our most important government department. The property clearly adds to the productive power of the economy, and it is government that absorbs its potential. To value the contribution of that resource over, say, a year, we want to take into account not the £200m total value of the building, nor the repair cost of the building; but the rent the government would pay, were it required to do so. Given the level of market rents as about 10 per cent of capital value, that might work out as £20m a year.

The same argument applies to all government assets. In a world of clear accounting, to measure how much of the economy government absorbs, we would charge government a fictitious rent on the assets it owns. The rent should reflect what government would have to pay if it did not own the asset itself. That gives us an idea of how much government is relying on the capital stock of the nation to deliver services to us in addition to the day-to-day revenues raised.

It is not possible to get an accurate measure of this fictitious, or implicit, capital return, although the government is in the midst of reforming its accounting procedures to obtain one. That is to be welcomed, as clear accounting can enhance our understanding of what government does. For example, government has a valuable stock of residential property, on which it does not always charge market rents. It chooses to forgo the income it could earn to help low-paid council tenants. Forgone rents do not show up as spending, but that is exactly what they are. Indeed, if it is true that council rents today are closer to market levels than a decade ago, and if it is true that instead of offering subsidized rents we today pay out more in housing benefit, then the crude figures which count housing benefit as spending, but exclude forgone rents, may give the false impression that help to the poor has increased, when it has not. Or it may give the false impression that social security has grown (housing benefit is one of those that has exhibited the apparently 'explosive' tendency of social security to grow out of control) when in fact, we have merely switched from a benefit-in-kind, to a benefit-in-cash.[1]

Table 3 attempts to adapt the published spending figures for the last three decades and account for capital more effectively. After the three adjustments for capital,[2] the government ends up absorbing just under

1. The statisticians do make up a charge – an imputed charge – which they take as equivalent to the depreciation of the government's assets. But it is far lower than a private company would charge for use of such assets as it does not take into account the cost of the capital used in providing them – i.e. the cost of paying interest on the capital invested.

2. The capital stock referred to in the table is that of fixed assets – it includes tangible assets with a life over one year, and certain intangible assets with a clear market value (like a patent). All the valuations in the table are based on what statisticians think is their current cost – how much you pay for them, not how much government paid for them at the time they were bought. Current cost accounts are more useful than historic cost ones, but are also more tenuous. The list does not include the so-called 'heritage assets' (like the Tower of London) except in as far as they yield a commercial service.

To impute a regular return on government assets, the table assumes that all assets yield 7 per cent a year. That is fairly modest. It is true that in the NHS today, government asks all trusts to budget for an even more modest 6 per cent return on their capital. In the private sector, assets are often expected to yield in excess of 10 per cent. In the real estate market, rents do average about 10 per cent a year. All in all, 7 per cent seems reasonable, if anything rather conservative. The total imputed return on this figure amounts to about 4 per cent of GDP.

45 per cent of GDP. It is marginally smaller than the crude figure, primarily because government is spending more on debt interest than it earns on its capital stock under the assumptions used in the table.

There are other messages from the table: the growth in government between the 1960s and the 1980s on the crude measure would have been worse, but for a substantial drop in spending on new government investment – from about 4 per cent of GDP, to less than 2 per cent. About a quarter of the fall in government spending in the latter half of the 1980s relative to the early 1980s was simply the result of lower investment spending and debt interest payments. (Much of the rest, of course, was down to the boom conditions in the economy.)

It also happens to be true that government owns a smaller proportion of the nation's capital than it used to (and this does *not* take into account the sell-off of the broad public sector assets in the form of privatization – we are truly talking about government here). At the same time, the government's capital stock has become *more* residential in complexion in recent decades, despite the fact that about a third of the council house stock was transferred to the private sector between 1981 and 1991. The increase in house prices left a more valuable housing stock in public hands. Despite that development, government's capital stock has become more concentrated in central government hands, although most capital is still local. Government has become altogether less capital intensive as a provider of services. A look at the ratio of government capital costs to government wage costs shows a modest fall.

Some of these findings are dependent on the assumptions used in Table 3, so none of the data should be interpreted very precisely. Even the figures lifted directly from the Office of National Statistics tables should be treated as illustrative. But they do give a more meaningful picture of the accounts than the raw spending figures.

Social Security

After these adjustments, we have a better measure of the resources that government uses from day to day – still over 40 per cent. But the figure still needs further dismantling, and in particular we need to sort out the treatment of social security, which is both a form of spending for government, and a form of income for the private sector, so is not a true 'burden of government' at all. (After all, the private sector spends some 75 per cent of GDP, and according to the table, government spends 40, adding up to a total of 115 per cent of GDP. The discrepancy needs explaining.) So the next adjustment to make is for these 'transfer payments'.

First, it is sensible to remove the basic pension pay-outs – the basic state pension – which amount to a little short of 5 per cent of GDP. These are a little different to other payments by government, being governed by a pseudo-contract based on National Insurance. In principle, in offering the basic state pension to the public, government is acting as a banker – running a savings scheme under which we pay money in for one period when we work, and then draw it out later. It is not remotely a burden on the economy, or even on the individual, assuming that we would have saved that money for a pension anyway.

Once this pensions provider function of government is out of the way, we can look at the rest of social security. The formal social security budget – on top of the pensions already covered – is about 10 per cent of GDP.

However, that is not all of it, because government hands out a lot more to the private sector, which it just avoids calling social security. In particular, it hands out all sorts of money to private companies to create jobs or to lower prices. These hand-outs account for another 1.6 per cent of GDP, and are all really forms of social security, just as much as child benefit is, although they are not conventionally described as such. They were far higher in the 1970s.

How about trends in social security? Most of the growth in government spending has occurred in the field of social security, and this is where most of the concern about large government spending arises today. *Since 1966, social security – broadly defined – has risen from just under 10 per cent of GDP to about 16.6 per cent.* However, before you join the already very large queue of those panicking about the 'explosion' in welfare benefits, remember that 1.7 per cent of that is growth of the basic pension. And it is helpful to make a comparison with the 1970s. In 1976, social security was 14 per cent. In other words, since then, the 'explosion' has seen social security absorb about an extra 0.1 per cent of GDP a year, about one-twentieth of the economic growth that occurs each year. Even this is an overestimate, as it does not count changes in subsidized rents to council tenants, cuts in which have not been included in social security spending here. The growth is not negligible, but it is not catastrophic either. The most worrying aspect of this figure is that social security has grown at all as a proportion of the economy, while benefit levels have remained as parsimonious as they have.

Now many people will give you alternative figures for the growth of social security since the 1970s that seem more worrying than those presented here. The reason is the inclusion here of peripheral grants and subsidies in the social security category. These have been dramatically cut back, and replaced with explicit cash benefits, thus enhancing the apparent burden of social security in the past relative to the present. The fact that we do not have the same level of industrial support we enjoyed in, say, 1975 is one reason why we have needed to expand the explicit benefits that comprise the core social security budget.

After all these transfer payments of one kind or another have been taken into account, the government's remaining consumption absorbs a little over a quarter of the economy.

Value Added and Turnover

We are not finished yet: there is still another important distinction to make, and one which recurs in discussion of reforms of the state around the purchaser–provider split model. It is the distinction – very familiar to accountants and Customs and Excise – between turnover and value added. Sainsbury's illustrates the difference well: it had a turnover in the financial year ending in 1996 of about £12.6 billion. That is how much it sold. But of course most of what it sells, it buys. It doesn't itself create that value – it acts as a middleman or a broker. So, of the revenue Sainsbury's takes in, how much is actually really a revenue for Sainsbury's, as opposed to revenue that Sainsbury's passes on to manufacturers? It is just what Sainsbury's sells, minus what it buys from other companies. In the case of Sainsbury's, the amount it actually creates itself amounts to about £2.5bn. That is its value added.

We can do the same exercise for government. The 27.8 per cent of GDP spent on goods and services mixes up two different categories: what government *buys* and what it *produces*. It is vital to distinguish between government as a purchaser (an agent with a fat chequebook), and government as an actual provider of services (a large company with a lot of employees actually delivering the services the public wants), because different potential diagnoses of the faults of government tell you different things about which of these roles needs to be examined. If you are someone who thinks the public sector is inherently inefficient, for example, you should surely worry more about what it is that government is doing, than what it is buying.

The distinction between the purchasing role and the providing role was never really made until the 1980s. Then, confronted with the difficulty of trimming the government's purchasing role, the Conservatives discovered reforms which trimmed its provider role. So for example, contracting out services that were previously provided by government employees meant government still spent roughly the same amount of money it always did, but it was nevertheless a very much smaller government than it once was.

When we look at what government buys in from outside, we see that it is 14.4 per cent of GDP. That includes all the things government buys from private companies – from stationery to missile systems – plus a number of things government buys from what one might call the arm's-length public sector – public organizations which are statistically defined as outside government but are rather like government in behaviour. The two that are most prominent are trust hospitals and universities.

That means what is left is what we might call government value added – the proportion of the output of the economy that government itself produces – and that amounts to about 15 per cent of GDP. That 15 per cent is a measure of the output of government. It includes defence, schools and a large number of health services for example. It includes local authority employees, passport officers and driving test examiners as well, of course, as civil servants.

Most interesting is that if we look at government value added as a proportion of GDP, it has apparently declined even from the 1960s levels. In effect, government has apparently done what a lot of private firms have done – it has concentrated more on core functions, buying in from outside services less central to its role. Or to make the comparison with the 1970s, although overall government spending on goods and

Table 4: Government Employees
Millions

	1961	1971	1981	1991	1996
General government employees	3.7	4.6	5.3	5.1	3.6
General government employees, including NHS Trust Hospitals	3.7	4.6	5.3	5.2	4.7
Public sector employees	5.9	6.6	7.2	5.8	5.1

Source: *Economic Trends*, March 1997.

services has not risen since 1976, buying of services from external suppliers has jumped by five percentage points of GDP. In the terms of business accountants, HMG has become a less vertically integrated operation over the last few years.

In fact, a lot of this is statistical illusion, attributable to the statistical treatment of trust hospitals, which on becoming trusts were defined out of the general government sector to the broader public sector. They are now supposedly at arm's-length from HMG, and their services are considered to be 'bought in'. Between 1990 and 1996, there was a transfer of over 888,000 full-time equivalent employees from one sector to the other. That did not really represent a shrinking of the state at all as trusts are still run as though they were in the core government sector. If this effect was removed, we would probably see more like 19 per cent of the economy as government value added: still down on the 1976 and 1986 levels, but still well up on 1966.

The story of the shrinking state – in terms of its provider role – is borne out by other figures on the number of government employees. These are in Table 4. The number of general government employees in 1996 was back at its 1961 level. Add in the effect of NHS trusts, and it was well above the 1961 level, at more like the 1971 level. Nevertheless, even with this taken into account, the state was a great deal smaller than at its peak; and the number of *public sector* employees – including everyone employed by nationalized industries – was well below the 1961 level.

To complete the dismantling of the government accounts, you may finally want to know how government added that kind of value, or what resources government employed to add it. What 'inputs' corresponded to the 15 per cent of GDP that was government's output? The breakdown is given at the bottom of Table 3. The bulk of value added was paid out in wages – a return to labour, which is not surprising given that labour is the single most important factor of production in the economy. Most of the remainder is the government use of its own capital.

All these statistics are a little more approximate than the decimal-point specification of them implies. GDP itself is not measured that accurately – it skips the government's return on capital as I have already mentioned – and other pieces of the equation are rougher still. Nevertheless, this breakdown gives us a neat starting point for considering what has recently been going on as regards the way and extent government spends money.

Public versus Private

There is one last way in which it is useful to break government spending down: on the basis of the level at which a service is consumed. To understand the distinction, imagine a society where it is not just health, education, defence and the like that are provided free to the user and are paid for out of taxation; but cars too are purchased by the government on behalf of the public. As you would expect, every household gets the same car so that complicated decisions in allocating better or worse cars are avoided. Everybody is given a Ford Escort, paid for out of taxation. Of course taxes have to be high to pay for all the Ford Escorts the government buys – but at least in this country you don't have to spend your own money on a car.

The example is an extreme one to illustrate the idea that government spending in principle can be devoted to either public consumption – services like defence which are consumed by society as a whole – or private consumption. In practice, would any government really pay for private consumption out of public money? The answer is yes. Some 60 per cent of government spending (net of social security), it could reasonably be argued, is *primarily* private – such that the chief beneficiary is the person to whom the service is directly delivered. Table 5 outlines some of spending headings and the weight they account for in govern-

Table 5: Public Provision of Private Goods
percentage of government spending devoted to different categories of service

Primarily private		Primarily public	
Housing	2	Agriculture, fisheries, food	4
Health	23	Environmental services	6
Personal social services	6	Energy, trade and industry	3
Transport	5	Defence	12
Education	21	Law and order	9
Employment and training	2	Foreign office/overseas aid	2
Culture, media and sport	2	Miscellaneous	3
Total	**61**		**39**

Source: based on Table 2.

ment spending on goods and services. It is pretty clear that more than half of government spending is devoted to items which are best defined as narrowly private; or to put it another way, about a quarter of our total private consumption is actually private consumption that is purchased by government. All this is quite independent of the social security system. As for the traditional role of government as the provider of *public* goods, things we can only practically buy if we all buy them together, just under 10 per cent of GDP (39 per cent of government consumption) appears to be spent on those.

The big private items purchased by government come in two broad forms with a blurred boundary between them: the first, and smaller category, are those items like housing, free school meals and subsidized arts, which are distributed selectively. Only the needy are meant to get subsidized housing; only those with a certain type of taste, and a large wallet, enjoy most of the arts subsidy. The second category, much larger and the one to be discussed here, is the delivery of private goods on a uniform and universal basis. In this category one can most obviously find health and education. These have of course some public element to them – I benefit from you being healthy (because I am less likely to catch your diseases) and I benefit from you being educated (because you contribute more to society if you are clever) – but are still primarily private.

The Growth of Government

Some History

Taking all these facts and figures together, the first and most striking trend is growth in the total crude measure of the size of government spending – from 36 per cent of GDP in the early 1960s, to more like 46 per cent today. Even if value added has shrunk in recent years, and even if spending has flattened out, it has shown a dramatic rise in the post-war era.

That growth was, however, all concentrated in the first decade after the 1960s – by 1975, most measures of the size of government had peaked and flattened: the crude spending total; spending on goods and services; value added. All were bigger twenty years ago as a proportion of GDP than they are today. A measure of the size of the broader public sector, including the nationalized industries, would have provided an even more extreme contrast between the 1970s and today as most of the big public enterprises have been sold off.

But still, one should not underestimate the growth of government that has occurred, and been sustained, and the growth of spending net of defence is considerable: defence has been trimmed from almost 10 per cent of GDP in the mid-1950s, to less than 3 per cent today. Other headings have taken up the slack. The growth of government in the 1960s and 70s, and the end of the growth of government in the 1980s and 90s are undoubtedly important developments by the standards of the twentieth century.

Table 6 takes the crude measure of government spending back a hundred years or so. The statistical series are not always comparable – the latest consistent series all started in the early 1960s – but even if direct matching to recent figures is not possible, it is indicative to look at the trends that occur from 1890 onwards. Because that pattern is so dominated by military activity, the figures for 'defence' are given in a separate column.

If government has grown over the century, it has primarily done so in three big jumps: one in the aftermath of the First World War; another in the aftermath of the Second World War; and one in the 1960s and

Table 6: Public Expenditure – the Long Run Record
percentage of GNP

	Total government expenditure	Military expenditure	Government net of military (first minus second column)
1890	8.9	2.4	6.5
1895	10.4	2.9	7.5
1900	14.4	6.9	7.5
1905	12.3	3.2	9.1
1910	12.7	3.5	9.2
memo 1913	*12.4*	*3.7*	*8.7*
1915	35.0	26.2	8.8
memo 1918	*51.7*	*41.7*	*10.0*
1920	26.2	8.6	17.6
1925	24.2	3.0	21.2
1930	26.1	2.7	23.4
1935	24.4	3.1	21.3
memo 1938	*30.0*	*8.9*	*21.1*
1940	60.1	n.a.	n.a.
memo 1944	*72.6*	*n.a.*	*n.a.*
1945	66.0	n.a.	n.a.
1950	39.0	7.2	31.8
1955	36.6	9.6	27.0

Source: Peacock and Wiseman, 1961. Table A6 (at current prices). Table A17.

70s. Each jump saw non-military spending rise by about 10 per cent of GDP. The Liberal government of the 1900s – although a reforming government – did not in fact lead to as large an expansion of government spending – as a proportion of GDP – as the Wilson government of the 1960s. The question that arises out of all this is why has government grown so much over the last century?

A number of reasons have been described and tested in economic and historical literature. One main category of explanations essentially argues that government has grown as a result of what one might call political processes – processes which one might think of as irrational, such as the power of interest groups; the tendency for bureaucrats to fight for increased resources; the ability of politicians to disguise their taxes from the public. In contrast, another category of explanations describes events in terms consistent with economics, or with processes that one might describe as rational decision-making.

Growth Attributable to Political Processes

Theories of the irrational then, which are described more fully in Chapter 5, are about how the incentives and desires of interest groups, bureaucrats, and politicians lead to behaviour that expands government spending at the expense of the population, and expands it to a level, or in areas, even when an informed population would rather spend the money in different ways.

Of course, it is interesting and surely not fortuitous that the century of big government coincides with the century of emerging worldwide democracy, and yet the theories of irrational government argue that the population of taxpayers has been 'ripped off' by this development. These accounts are thus a little incomplete unless they can explain why the public do not vote for politicians who refrain from ripping them off. Maybe the public are themselves irrational and vote for the wrong parties; maybe it could be argued the public have – at last – voted for tax-cutting politicians in the form of Reagan, Thatcher and the like, and the end of the era of big government has thus now arrived.

On the irrational, however, it is worth mentioning here the thoughts of the most noted scholars of this subject, Alan Peacock and Jack Wiseman, who documented the statistics on the subject meticulously and spawned the whole study of the size of government in the UK. They noted the connection between growth of big government and the occurrence of wars, and explained the connection by reference to the notion of tax tolerance. In normal years, the public will not tolerate higher taxes: government spending is thus restrained, and stable. During periods of extreme upheaval, such as major wars to see off brutal dictators bent on world domination, the public's tolerance of taxation naturally rises dramatically. Come the end of those periods of upheaval, the public are habituated to higher taxes, so they are more tolerant of tax than before the upheaval, so spending ratchets upwards.

Table 6 makes the point (as indeed it ought to, as it is drawn from

Peacock and Wiseman's work). During the wars, military spending soars and other government spending falls back. After the wars, military spending collapses and other government spending increases. It uses up some of the slack left by military cuts, to finish at a level higher than where it started. Compare 1910, 1915 and 1920 to see the effect. A similar pattern occurred in the Second World War.

This account – which leaves open exactly how you measure government spending (is it in real terms, or is it as a per cent of GNP, or is it as a growth rate?) – was put together in 1961 and thereafter suffered an immediate blow as there was no war in which Britain was involved in the 1960s to explain the surge in government spending which occurred then. Nevertheless, it could be argued the 1960s was a decade of great social upheaval, with the emergence of television as a familiar source of popular entertainment, men on the moon, the decline of Britain as a major power, and a dramatic change in social attitudes towards personal permissiveness. The Peacock–Wiseman theory anyway scores 'two out of three' in explaining the great surges in spending through the century.

Growth Attributable to Economic Factors

It is worth considering the alternative categories of explanation, in which the growth of government is considered to reflect the underlying preferences of the population, and to be the outcome of processes one might describe as rational.

Here there are several important accounts for the growth of government. One is that as we get richer, we want more and more of the kinds of things government provides. This is the idea that public goods are 'luxuries', so that when our income rises by say 1 per cent, our demand for public goods rises by more than 1 per cent. Over time, therefore, you would expect a rational system to deliver an increasing proportion of spending on publicly provided goods.

This is an argument associated with a German political economist, Adolf Wagner, who died in 1917. He noted that social progress would place disproportionate demands on the state. He based this finding on several factors: that as we get richer, we would seek a more redistributive state (charity to others is a luxury we will support only when we are rich enough to afford it); that progressive economic activities would require huge investment, best provided by the public sector; and most importantly, that certain public services would grow too.[1]

While there is some debate as to exactly how we should interpret what Wagner himself actually meant, it is common to assert that public services are special luxuries for which demand grows more than proportionately as our incomes grow over time. Unfortunately, the proposition is hard to establish. After all, for government to grow as a proportion of GDP, we need to establish not just the plausible idea that we want more schools and hospitals as we get richer; we have to establish that our increase in demand for schools and hospitals is greater than our increase in demand for, say, cars, books and television – all the private goods at our disposal. It is far from obvious that this is the case. Those who have looked at the evidence, such as economist Norman Gemmell, conclude that the idea that demand for public goods rises with income at a disproportionate rate cannot yet be said to have been demonstrated.

As for the idea that as we get richer, we want more and more redistribution and equality, this too is far from obvious. It may have looked that way, because over most of the century we have seen states engage in more redistribution, and we have seen them get richer. But the two events may not be causally related. For example, after wide extensions of the electoral franchise, one might not be surprised to find a big kick towards redistribution. However, that could be a one-off process, resulting from the introduction of democracy and a corresponding re-weighting of the interests of different groups in society. At some stage, the process would complete itself, and thereafter no more redistribution would necessarily follow. This convergence towards the desired level of redistribution would take time, and may give the phoney appearance of being causally related to growing incomes.

Even without this account, there is a second 'rational' explanation

---

1. Some have helpfully caricatured Wagner's findings in the language of modern economics. His most important view could be interpreted as being that the demand for public goods has an income elasticity in excess of one; or to put it more simply, any proportionate change in income leads to a more than proportionate change in the demand for public goods.

for much of the rise in public spending that relates not to an increase in the demand for services, but to a change in the cost of supplying them. This account is by far the most technical and least sociological on offer, and it is certainly the least likely to lend itself to wild political rhetoric on the problems of government. It is the effect of changing relative prices, and the fact that the costs of government tend to rise more quickly than other costs in the economy.

Suppose that the cost of teaching, or hospital services, rises faster than costs in the economy generally; we can then measure growth in the amount hospitals and schools take up in the economy in two different ways: we can look at the amount we spend on these kinds of services; or we can look at the amount we get for our spending. Our spending will appear to rise fast; what we get for our spending will not be rising as fast. It would not be impossible for us to spend a growing proportion of GDP to buy a fixed, constant amount of certain services.

This is a plausible account because relative costs in the public sector do appear to rise more quickly than those elsewhere. The reason is simple: there is less growth in productivity there. In general in the economy, higher wages are paid for by higher productivity. So even though wages rise more quickly than prices, overall costs simply rise at the same rate as prices generally. But in the public sector, when wages rise faster than prices − as they will to keep pace with private sector wages − there is less productivity gain to pay for the wage rise, so costs rise faster than in other sectors. In short, if there is no productivity gain, higher wages simply translate into higher costs. As a result, the relative costs of public outputs rises.

There may be less of a productivity gain in the public sector for bad reasons (that the public sector is badly run and can't extract better productivity) or for good reasons (that human-intensive services, from teaching to prostitution, are likely not to enjoy big helpful changes in technology to engender productivity growth, and these services are more predominant in the public rather than the private sector). Either way, if you measure how big the economy is on the basis of real outputs for each sector, rather than the money spent on them, the government sector would be exposed as not growing nearly as fast as you would think.

This is not some minor statistical detail. Norman Gemmell's Social

Table 7: The Cost of Government

Inflation rates applicable to government spending and the economy overall – annual percentage rates

	General govt. consumption	GDP
1975	30.7	27.4
1976	15.8	15.0
1977	10.5	14.0
1978	10.8	11.4
1979	14.0	14.5
1980	24.1	19.4
1981	12.7	11.5
1982	8.1	7.5
1983	6.8	5.3
1984	5.1	4.5
1985	5.8	5.7
1986	5.7	3.3
1987	6.6	5.1
1988	6.8	6.0
1989	7.2	7.1
1990	8.2	6.4
1991	7.1	6.5
1992	6.3	4.6
1993	4.5	3.2
1994	2.4	1.9
1995	2.5	2.3
1996	1.9	3.0
Average	9.1%	8.3%

Source: ONS United Kingdom National Accounts 'Blue Book' 1997.

Market Foundation monograph, *Taxing and Spending Dilemmas*, estimates that a little more than half the total apparent increase in government expenditure as a proportion of the whole economy between 1960 and 1994 can be explained this way. Table 7 lists inflation in the government sector, as opposed to the economy taken as a whole. It has averaged a little under 1 per cent higher over the last two decades.

Finally, one other 'rational' explanation for the growth of government is that the population has shifted towards those who consume public services most heavily, away from those who consume them least. This is the demographic explanation for the growth of government. In practice, the big users are primarily old people – who get pensions and need lots of health care. Young people – who receive education and occasionally go to jail[1] – are also big users of government services, but not as big as old people.

Since 1961, there has in fact been a shift from the relatively young to the relatively old. This has an effect: in 1961, the state was spending 2.6 per cent of GDP on contributory pensions, with 14.6 per cent of the population of pensionable age. Today, the state is spending about 4 per cent of GDP on contributory pensions – an obvious growth – but now 18 per cent of the population is of pensionable age. So, about half the rise in spending on contributory pensions can simply be explained by the increasing number of recipients – not by any extension of generosity to pensioners.

Overall, then, much of the recent growth of the state can be explained by – in reverse order of likely importance – the effect of growing incomes on demand for public services, demographics and cost effects. Together, these 'mechanical' explanations for the increased proportion of the economy absorbed by government spending have been estimated by Thomas Borcherding – a government sceptic – as explaining just over half the increase in spending in the US. Of course, the rest of the increase in spending might be interpreted in more or less benign ways, so Borcherding's estimate gives us a neat starting point for the range of views one might hold: anything from zero to half the increase in government spending can be explained by factors we might want to call irrational.

Rational or irrational, Britain has not been alone in allowing government spending to grow. Table 8 provides some grounds for comparison. Indeed, as we end the century, it is clear that in the league tables of big government measured in terms of crude spending totals, Britain lies at

---

1. In Britain in 1995, there were more than seven times as many 18–20-year-old men in jail, as there were men over sixty.

Table 8: Public Expenditure Internationally
percentage of GDP

	1980	1996
Sweden	60.1	64.7
Denmark	56.2	61.5
Finland	38.1	57.4
France	46.1	54.5
Belgium	57.8	54.3
Italy	42.1	52.9
Austria	48.1	51.7
Netherlands	55.8	49.9
Germany	47.9	49.0
New Zealand	n.a.	47.1
Portugal	23.6	47.0
Greece	30.4	44.7
Canada	38.8	44.7
Spain	32.2	43.3
UK	43.0	41.9
Iceland	32.5	38.1
Ireland	48.2	37.6
Australia	31.4	36.6
Japan	32.0	36.2
US	31.4	33.3

Source: *OECD Economic Outlook*, June 1997.

the bottom of the first division: now smaller than continental Europe, bigger than the US and Japan.

This table looks only at the crude spending total in each country; but it is important to reiterate that government size can be measured not just in terms of spending totals, but also in terms of government activity, or production. Why is government not just a big spender, but also a big producer? Should it be a big producer and should it be a big spender? These are the subjects of the next two chapters.

Additional Reading

Borcherding, Thomas E. (1977), 'The Sources of Growth of Public Expenditures in the United States, 1902–1970' in Thomas Borcherding (ed.), *Budgets and Bureaucrats: The Sources of Government Growth*, Duke University Press, Durham, North Carolina.

Cocks, Richard and Roger Bentley (1996), *£300 billion: Government Spending, The Facts*, Data books, Reading.

Gemmell, Norman (ed.) (1993), *The Growth of the Public Sector: Theories and International Evidence*, Edward Elgar, Aldershot.

Gemmell, Norman (1997), *Taxing and Spending Dilemmas*, Social Market Foundation.

Jones, Rowan and Maurice Pendlebury (1992), *Public Sector Accounting* (second edition), Pitman Publishing, London.

Musgrave, R.A. (1981), 'Leviathan Cometh – or does he?' in H.F. Ladd and T.N. Teidman (eds), *Tax and Expenditure Limitations*, Urban Institute Press, Washington DC.

Peacock, Alan and Jack Wiseman (1961), *The Growth of Public Expenditure in the United Kingdom*, Princeton University Press, Princeton NJ (second edition, 1967).

2 Do We Need a Public Sector?

Public services, the public sector, and the public service ethos

> It is a Socialist idea that making profits is a vice; I consider the real vice
> is making losses.
>
> SIR WINSTON CHURCHILL

Having looked at the size, shape and some history of public spending
and the public sector, let us now add another two phrases beginning
with the word 'public' to our consideration: public services and the
public service ethos. There is a funny old relationship between these
four concepts. They are all connected to each other, but not in any
necessary way. Most public spending is on things that we might call
public services, but not all of it (agricultural subsidies would hardly
fall into this category). Most 'public services' are financed by public
spending, but not all of them (water and the postal services, for example).
Most public services are in the public sector, but not all (local authority
cleaning and dental services). And most of the public sector delivers
public services, but not all (British Nuclear Fuels does not).

And then what about that fourth phrase – the 'public service ethos'.
That is important as it effectively explains why we have a public sector.
The public service ethos can be found in public services and in the
public sector, but, it should be said, it is not necessarily found in either,
and it can be found elsewhere.

This may sound confusing, but we are in an era of unparalleled
complexity in the relationship between these concepts. In our political
system, the looseness of the relationship between public spending,
public services, the public sector and even the public service ethos,
has only been observed relatively recently. For most of the post-war
period, the four concepts were so intertwined, people almost came to

think of them as one and the same. A public problem merited public spending to deliver a public service. A public service was automatically delivered by the public sector. Why? Because then it would be governed by the public service ethos rather than by a profit-maximizing private company. Private firms were not considered to have been blessed with a 'public service outlook', and the public sector was thus the appropriate vehicle for delivering public services, all financed by public spending.

This view of the world gave rise to what might be called the traditional public sector model:

Public services: the abandonment of normal commercial activity for a broad category of 'special' services, particularly those in which universal coverage is considered important.

Public sector: services provided through organizations owned by and accountable to government rather than shareholders.

Public spending: financing of services through taxation, and access to services separated from ability or willingness to pay for them.

Public service ethos: conduct of public services based on a set of principles designed to maximize social welfare.

The model aimed to provide economic efficiency and social justice. It was a rather monolithic model, but it dominated the delivery of services from roads to public libraries, to terrestrial television, to health and education, law and order and defence. Indeed, in many cases it was almost impossible to conceive of alternative models. In the aftermath of the Second World War, it was simply not on the agenda to, say, use private companies listed on the stock market to provide education, any more than it was on the agenda to reinstate the army of the East India Company to maintain control over the colonies; it was not on the agenda to make working people pay private insurance companies to cover their medical needs, any more than it was on the agenda to launch pop radio stations financed by advertising. The idea that the general good – the public service ethos – should prevail seemed self-evident, and it seemed self-evident that it would prevail, if only we avoided employing profit-maximizing private companies to run the services we wanted taxation to finance.

The characteristics of the old public sector model were deemed so attractive that even in those areas where the fully fledged version was considered unsuitable – transport, energy and communications, for example, where users would still have to pay for their service through charges rather than through taxation – even in these cases, pieces of the model were taken on board. That gave rise to the very large public sector that existed outside the area of central and local government.

In Britain, it was really after the election of the Conservative government in 1979 that the relationship between the four 'publics' began to be questioned. Margaret Thatcher promoted the view that the public sector was not necessarily governed by the pure motives of the public-service ethic, as people had supposed. The idea that private firms could perform public services was injected into the political psyche. And the non-public-service elements of the public sector were gently removed into the profit-maximizing sector of the economy, offering everybody a clear view of what alternative mechanisms of corporate governance could achieve. It is true that the concept of lowering taxes and letting consumers buy for themselves what government had previously bought for them did not get far – dentists are perhaps the best example of the principle being applied – but the idea certainly came to the fore of political discussion.

But why did it take so long for the relationship between public services, the public sector and public spending to break down? Why was the traditional model so seductive? Why indeed do we need a public sector at all? To answer these questions, we need to look more carefully at the public service ethos and the values behind it.

The Public Service Ethos

Here are eight examples of commercial or social situations, designed to infuriate you:

The chief executive of a large airline gets an annual salary of £700,000, while planning 5,000 redundancies among staff.

An ambulance transferring a patient from one hospital to another says it cannot proceed until it has been paid for the journey by the patient's relatives.

A mother lets her child eat sweets all day, and doesn't take him to the dentist because it costs a few pounds which she prefers to spend on other things.

BAA – a company with monopoly control of Britain's biggest airports – crams its available terminal space with shops, leaving little room for the travelling public, and causing generalized discomfort to passengers. It does so because it can make money out of shops, but comfortable passengers have no way of expressing their comfort with extra cash.

The ticket-seller at the railway station at Gatwick airport sells a hapless foreign tourist the ticket for the most expensive train to central London, even when he suspects the person would rather take a slower train at a much cheaper fare. The ticket-seller, incidentally, works for the company providing the most expensive service.

Hospital wards are cleaned by contract staff – hired on extremely low wages – who are treated as a commodity and who never last more than a couple of weeks in the job, and hence have no sense of commitment to what they are doing.

A company manufacturing artificial limbs for the NHS and its patients puts up its prices to a level well in excess of its costs, and it says it will withhold the supply of limbs unless the NHS agrees to pay the higher prices.

The traveller, with a rail ticket from London to Southend on the London, Tilbury and Southend line, catches a train from London to Southend on the Great Eastern Line, and finds he has to buy a whole new ticket for the journey as the two different companies running the two different services will not co-operate in sharing revenues.

These are plausible accounts of commercial life as it exists in the newly privatized transport sector, and in the relationship between private and public producers in the health sector. Most of us would consider them somewhat undesirable features of a society, or of an industrial structure. In several cases they represent economic madness. In addition in the cases relating to health, most of us would have an extra moral repugnance. Certain practices that may be all right in industries providing baked beans or even transport – practices like demanding payment from a vulnerable client and profiteering – are not considered all right in health.

The concern of these eight scenes is the system of values that pervades the traditional public sector. These scenes describe the absence of certain values which we might loosely call the 'public service ethos'[1] and each case represents the absence of one strand of that ethos. It is a belief in those values that explains the decision of many Western governments to make the government a provider of services. We value the ethos highly in this country, and it has been employed to govern something between 15 and 35 per cent of economic activity over the last few decades.[2]

So what are these values? The eight stories at the opening of the chapter each related to a different component of the public service ethic – giving eight different separable elements to the concept. These are the fundamental features the old monolithic model of public sector organization was implicitly designed to deliver, and which were thus incorporated into the behaviour governing that model:

A fair, and reasonably egalitarian, distribution of income: everybody's standard of living is adequate to allow them dignity and self-esteem, and obscene social inequalities are outlawed.

Equality of access to services: the supply of services is offered to everyone with equal enthusiasm, regardless of income.

Discrimination in favour of meritorious activity: consumption of certain special services is promoted, as they are considered especially deserving.

Non-profit-oriented decision-making: corporate policy is not conducted to maximize the surplus paid out to shareholders, but to maximize the welfare of society generally.

---

1. People mean many different things by that phrase – sometimes the attitudes of employees within the public sector, sometimes the goals of public sector organizations. I treat the public service ethos as being a loosely defined bundle of values.
2. At a minimum, one supposes that the public service ethos governs the portion of GDP actually produced by government (i.e. government value added, as discussed in Chapter 1); at a maximum, it would represent the total proportion of GDP spent on goods and services by government (about 25 per cent, again taken from the figures in Chapter 1), plus the proportion of GDP not spent by government, but in the public sector. That was 11 per cent of GDP in 1979.

Dealings with customers based on the customer's interest, not the commercial interest of the supplier: service is provided on the basis of a customer's interest, without abuse or exploitation, particularly where the agent providing the service is more expert about it than the customer.

'Stakeholder type' personnel policies: staff are treated as adults, are well trained and well motivated; they have responsibility and as a result are customer-conscious.

Non-payment of profit: services do not provide for an explicit return on capital.

Co-operative industry relationships: within industries (be they health, education, public transport or public libraries), suppliers co-ordinate their activities rather than compete for business.

Before we take a close look at each of the values themselves, it is worth noting that our views towards the so-called 'public service ethos' appear to exhibit a curious combination of both depth and superficiality. There is depth in the sense that the views are held strongly, are held more or less consistently across a wide variety of social groups and, most importantly, are not inclined to be generally abandoned with impunity. We are almost uniformly suspicious of the idea of allowing profit-maximizing private firms in certain sectors. These views even appear to be strongly held by those who are willing to take private medical insurance for example. We know what we think, and we appear to carry on thinking it despite the testimony of opposing experts.

But there is superficiality in our views in the sense that many of them do not withstand much in the way of rigorous criticism. We suffer all sorts of apparent contradictions: water, for example, is at least sometimes held to be one of those items from which no supplier should make a profit, whereas food and food retailing are very clearly held to be appropriate for the normal profit-maximizing sector. The public gener-ally think of public services as being inferior to private services, but they continue to hold the view that profit-maximizers should not dominate areas where service is very important. Many informed people hold that certain services are best kept public because the staff are motivated by a sense of duty, but they simultaneously recognize public services are often poor because staff are badly paid and hence badly motivated. The public are quite able to recognize that the 'public service ethos' can exist beyond the not-for-profit sector in ordinary profit-maximizing firms – the milkman who cheerily says hello on his round and looks in on his elderly customers for example, or more controversially nurses in private health services (who behave rather like nurses in public health services).

Lest you should think this sounds like an attack on the romantic nostalgia of post-war socialism, let us not forget that these views are not confined to the left – the conservative middle class holds them; and forget not the hard right wing's own romanticism when it comes to those public services it likes to cherish – defence, the police and strike-breaking coal-mines.

Now it is not impossible for good administration to emerge from this kind of mish-mash of confused views; the inconsistent instincts of the public can be solidly founded, and richer in common sense than the intellectually-crafted judgements of the experts. But the instincts of the public do not offer an easy practical guide to public policy, and in the case of these values, a careless interpretation of the public's well-founded instincts has been allowed to justify a state apparatus far larger and far less efficient than is truly necessary to serve the public's taste. In this chapter we shall take a look at each of the eight values listed. The goal is to demonstrate that a careful and consistent formulation of commonly held attitudes towards public service values does not – in most cases – justify the state that we have got.

Redistribution

The goal of redistribution cannot be separated from the choice to have extended the state, and it is the change in distribution that would occur by dismantling the state that primarily deters large portions of the population from supporting such a policy. But what kind of redistribution do people want? It could be equality as an end in itself: that we would like as equal a set of outcomes as we can achieve, subject to keeping a reasonable level of efficiency in the economy. Or it could be that we regard equality as a matter of indifference, but that we are concerned with protecting those at the bottom of the distribution, what we might call a 'safety net' view of redistribution.

It is hard to argue a case between these notions of redistribution – one's choice is obviously a matter of taste. Suffice it to say that we ought to be clear about the implications of each different view. You are clearly someone in favour of the egalitarian principle if you believe that it would be socially advantageous to take money from Paul McCartney and give it to George Michael, as George Michael is poorer than Paul McCartney. If, on the other hand, you are completely indifferent to the distribution of income between the quite rich, the very rich, and the mega rich, then you are probably more inclined to worry about the bottom of the distribution than you are about equality per se.

It is hard to get to grips with our fundamental values on the distribution of income and wealth. Perhaps the main reason for this is that we all have some vested interest: either we are rich, and might be rather well disposed towards no redistribution; or we are poor, and might find hundreds of good reasons for the state to act as Robin Hood. Ideally, if we wanted to test the public on their desire for redistribution, we would canvass everybody's views *prior to their knowing where they will sit in the distribution of incomes*. We would conduct opinion polls prior to our knowing who was going to conceive us, and certainly before birth. That alone would allow the polls to extract an honest view of our tastes, untainted by perceptions of narrow self-interest. Ask us what we want once we have drawn our ticket in the lottery of life, and we will simply say we believe in greater help going to people in our particular situation.

Unfortunately, this kind of polling is difficult and there is room for argument over what kind of redistribution we would support if we were ignorant of our own circumstances.[1] But people have attempted to test the idea. Norman Frohlich, Joe Oppenheimer and Cheryl Eavey performed an experiment on 145 North American students, who were put into small groups and told to reach agreement on a principle of

---

1. John Rawls – the American political philosopher and the great exponent of polling people before they know who they are – argues that all of us would select policies to maximize the welfare of the poor. We would do that *whatever the cost to the rich*. But, he argues, we wouldn't be punitive – we wouldn't take income from the rich, unless it really could be used to help the poor.

justice, and who were then paid for their effort in terms of the principle they chose. Now, it's not like they staked their lives on the outcome, and it is hardly a real test of our virgin views of social justice, but it was instructive that 25 out of 29 groups chose the principle based on the safety net view of distribution, that said we should maximize the average income, subject to ensuring no one fell below a certain floor (a constraint of $11,000 a year at 1980s prices). Not one group chose a principle that was in favour of equality as an end in itself.

In truth, observation of the press at least would suggest most people probably hold a casual adherence to some level of equality; but that they modify this support with a sense of personal responsibility for each making the best of their circumstances; they modify it too with a sense that equality is not worth imposing at unlimited economic cost; and apart from that, most of us do not think about things carefully enough to draw a distinction between the moderated equality view, or the more limited 'safety net' view. For most of us, these amount to roughly the same thing.

So much for what views we have. To what extent does the old public sector deliver that redistribution? Table 1 gives the answer, drawn from the Office of National Statistics' *Economic Trends*. Although the figures are based on a number of rough assumptions, the table provides the nearest thing to official estimates of the benefits that accrue to households of different incomes from government spending. It excludes all the really public goods, like defence. But it looks at the value of benefits-in-kind (notably health and education), cash benefits and taxes for households on different incomes.

The most interesting conclusion to be drawn from the table is that the state is as much egalitarian as it is safety net. There is a small net distribution to people in the third quintile, and a distinct suppression of the differential between the fourth and fifth quintiles.

Perhaps more significant in the table is the use of the traditional public sector as a vehicle for redistribution. We do not just hand out cash to make sure the poor are better off, we have also built a large public sector to deliver benefits-in-kind to the poor and the rich together. From the table, you can see the value of the health system is roughly equivalent to a flat-rate uniform subsidy for the bottom half of the population; it then tapers for the richer half of the population.

Table 1: The Redistribution of Income

pounds per year, 1995–6

	Original income	Cash benefits	Taxation		Benefits in kind			Total	Total net income
			Direct	Indirect	Health	Education	Other		
Poorest 20%	2,430	4,910	1,130	1,930	1,893	1,813	241	3,950	8,230
Second quintile	6,090	4,660	1,520	2,340	1,833	1,300	176	3,310	10,200
Third quintile	13,790	3,360	3,130	3,290	1,730	1,425	105	3,260	13,990
Fourth quintile	22,450	2,130	5,180	4,090	1,519	1,070	85	2,670	17,980
Richest 20%	41,260	1,190	10,470	5,090	1,335	829	147	2,310	29,200
Average	17,200	3,250	4,290	3,350	1,662	1,287	151	3,100	15,920

Notes: Incomes have been converted into so-called *equivalent incomes* to reflect the needs of households – a couple with two children are not as well off as a single person on the same income, so in this table, for example, the income of couples with two children are deflated to put them on a par with single people: the result is a little arbitrary, but essentially allows us to translate incomes into a measure of living standards.

Numbers may not add up on account of rounding.

The benefits of universal services are allocated on a formula basis, depending on the number, age and other characteristics of the members of the household. The method does not purport to be sophisticated, so while there is some evidence the rich use the NHS more than the poor – because they tend to be more demanding and more health-conscious – this is not taken into account here. Nor is the fact that the rich are more likely to have private health care. The cost of social housing built into the 'other benefits-in-kind' column is just the direct cash cost, not the real economic cost as it was discussed in the last chapter.

Source: *Economic Trends*, March 1997.

Education varies a little more across the groups, reflecting the preponderance of children in different income categories. Other benefits-in-kind are housing and transport subsidies (the richest 10 per cent gain over £3 a week from transport subsidies) and school meals or milk.

The point to note is that for the poorest 20 per cent of the population, benefits-in-kind are worth substantially more than any original income – be it private pensions or earnings. Indeed, benefits-in-kind are worth four-fifths as much as cash benefits handed out by the state. The redistributive power of taxation combined with collective finance of more or less uniformly delivered services is clear:

> The richest 20 per cent pay £15,600 a year in tax, get £1,200 per year back in cash benefits, and get a mere £2,300 out of benefits-in-kind delivered. Benefits-in-kind represent just 8 per cent of their net final income.

> The poorest 20 per cent pay £3,100 a year in tax, get £4,900 per year back in cash benefits, and get £4,000 out of benefits-in-kind delivered. Benefits-in-kind represent almost half of their net final income.

> On top of the taxes they pay for public goods and social security, on a conservative estimate, the richest 20 per cent pay £3 in tax for every £1 of benefit-in-kind they get back.[1]

> The poorest 20 per cent in effect pay nothing for their benefits-in-kind.

So it is clear the old public sector model does achieve redistribution. But is it clear we need the whole panoply of the state to get that redistribution? Could we not just achieve the same objective by remov-

---

1. This is a simple calculation as follows: the richest fifth of the population make a tax payment to the state of £15,560, This covers government spending on cash transfer, on public goods and on private goods (benefits-in-kind). On a very rough calculation, the proportions of government spending in these three categories are 30 per cent, 25 per cent and 45 per cent. On a *proportional* allocation, therefore, we might say that the tax of the rich is divided as follows: £4,700 on social security; £3,900 on public goods; and £7,000 on private goods. That £7,000 is more than three times the estimated benefits-in-kind of £2,310 enjoyed by the richest 20 per cent. This calculation is merely a rough-and-ready indicator of the redistributive effect of benefits. It could be performed in a number of different ways, but rarely comes up with a figure that tells a very different story.

ing benefits-in-kind, and giving people cash instead? That way, we would get the same redistribution, but allow people far more freedom to spend money as they want.

In fact, one reason for engaging in redistribution-in-kind as we do is not that it is such an efficient means of achieving 'social justice'; it is that it represents a politic way of ensuring social justice is achieved. Those who want redistribution think it is easier to *sell* when it is delivered in uniformly supplied services, than it is when it is delivered at the post office in a girocheque.

Here is the logic of the argument that benefits-in-kind preserve social justice: the poor pay almost nothing for services, and will tend therefore to vote for more of them at election time. That is the easy bit. What about the rich? They will be in two minds. On the one hand, being rich, they will want better schools and better health care – after all they can afford it. On the other hand, because the system is redistributive, they find themselves paying more to everybody else when the levels of service improve. Now, assuming the rich are basically selfish, on balance it is not clear how they will vote given this ambiguity – they may end up voting for more service to satisfy their demand, or they may end up voting for less in order to minimize their subsidy to everyone else. But what is clear is that because redistribution is tied to consumption of services the rich want, they will end up voting for more redistribution than if they were voting on redistribution on its own.

That by and large appears to be the argument against targeting cash to only those who need it – as soon as redistribution is explicit, and isolated as a decision from other decisions, then it is assumed the rich will vote for less of it. Or, to put it another way, the state has chosen to exploit its monopoly power in the market for certain services to advance the cause of helping the poor. You cannot buy education (other than through the rather expensive private option which involves losing your subscription to state education) without also donating some extra money to the poor.

Of course, in this scheme, if the rich are allowed to opt out of state services, by getting health and education privately, then the promotional power of the device breaks down. They can have their education cake, without donating to the general pool of government revenues at all.

Hence, the instinctive opposition to independent provision among those to whom redistribution is so important.

The probable conclusion is therefore that we adopted the structure of the traditional public sector because we felt it was more likely to prove acceptable to those being asked to pay in more than they were getting out. The idea appeared to work – the rich by and large did not opt out of the state, and by and large were supportive of large elements of expansion in the level of service delivered.

But as time passes, obfuscating the truth becomes a less and less powerful tool in the pursuit of social objectives. In fact it appears the persuasive power of redistribution-in-kind has weakened, and that may not be altogether surprising. If the rich were going to object to explicit redistribution, they were bound to eventually work out what was going on with implicit redistribution. It might take a few years for them to spot how they were being treated, but once they did, the gains of this structure would disappear and the rich would opt out of public services to private ones, and would then vote for less public service and lower taxes. Moreover, because so much inefficiency is built into the structure of delivery-in-kind, it might have been inevitable the rich would become disenchanted more generally with the whole welfare state.

Overall then, our conclusion should be that whatever level of redistribution the public want, whatever level of public spending redistribution justifies, it does not justify the traditional public sector model very convincingly. Can any of the other values do better?

Equality of Access to Services

For many, the public service ethic means one simple thing: not selecting who to supply on the basis of income. The health system is the one in which this is the most emotive topic – the picture of the ambulance that drives away from the accident victim who isn't carrying his credit card provides the most powerful turn-off for public support of private health care systems. Even though you do not have to go as far as creating a whole National Health Service to avoid this rather extreme scenario, even the idea that a routine transfer in an ambulance might involve the use of a credit card seems somewhat undesirable.

There is something about the contingent nature of the relationship with a private health provider that we instinctively dislike. We dislike it, even though we think and subscribe to the service on offer from such providers. We dislike it, even though most of us, for good reason, accept the legitimacy of private pharmaceutical providers. There is something objectionable about it.

As far as emergency health cover goes, the old public sector values are easy to justify and explain. We all wish to feel secure, and we feel more secure if more emergency cover is available. We know that should an emergency arise, we do not want to be involved in a negotiation over the cost of service (we would be in a weak bargaining position to negotiate or shop around for an ambulance, lying with a broken leg on the roadside, for example). Thus, a general policy that says 'offer help now, ask questions later' is a perfectly sensible one to impose. It seems equally sensible to say that as far as urgent cover is concerned, every citizen should be covered by every provider.

What about non-urgent cover however? Or, what about schools? Or public libraries? What are our values here? Do we believe that everyone should have *equal access* to service at a uniform level of quality? Or is it that everybody should have access to a *reasonable service* by some provider? How far does our belief in equality of access go?[1] This matters of course, because the more extreme our belief in equality, the more justifiable the old public sector model of delivery looks.

In health, most people pay lip service at least to a true belief in equality. The debate over fundholding GPs, apparently offering better hospital access than other GPs, revealed a deeply-held suspicion of 'two-tier' services, even when the gains of the better served were not achieved at the expense of the worse served. There is more evidence in the fact that Tessa Jowell, the first ever minister in Britain for public health, has made much of inequalities in life expectancy between different social groups with little public questioning of her concern.

But to measure our real adherence to equality, we really need to know what price the public are willing to pay for it. How far would we accept a decline in the average quality of health care, or the average

---

1. This is a discussion entirely analogous to that of whether the state might foster egalitarianism, or a safety net.

life expectancy, in order to achieve perfect equality in health care, or life expectancy? Would most of us prefer a uniform 10 per cent improvement in health care, or perfect equality around the existing average, for example? Would Tessa Jowell prefer to add one day to the life expectancy of everybody, or equalize life expectancy around the current average?

Personally, I suspect that most of us would *not* be willing to pay a very high price for universal equal access to non-urgent health services. The prevalent feeling would surely be that for health – and education, housing and food – everybody should have access to a reasonable level. One might deduce these values from the fact that the public tolerate inequalities in housing and food, and make not even a token effort to eradicate them. And anyway, we do not by and large believe private medical care should be forbidden, and we do not find it deeply offensive that the jurisdiction in which you live should sometimes arbitrarily affect your permitted choice of school (as opposed to the choice being affected by distance from the establishment). Variation in service levels is thus currently widely accepted in important areas of basic service; indeed these areas include health itself.

If we cannot really justify much of the old public sector model on the grounds of universal equal access, are there grounds for justifying it in terms of ensuring that there is at least some access for everybody, and that nobody is left out altogether? The argument may run like this: if market forces fail to provide leisure activities for the poor, so be it. If Woolworth's disappears from the high street, leaving those without much money nowhere to buy cheap gifts, so be it. But if the market forces fail to provide health, housing or education, that is simply unacceptable. The state has to be the provider of last resort.

How plausible is it that if we abolished state education and health, replacing them with cash hand-outs, the market would fail to deliver services that appeal to, say, the poorest 10 per cent of the population? In fact, it is quite plausible. In a large number of industries – essential or not – there are large economies of scale in production, and as a result it is difficult to offer services to the poor that are not in some sense tied to the services of the rich. Airlines, telecoms, health – in all these cases it makes sense to have providers offering a service to a wide variety of different customers. (Even PPP and BUPA offer health packages of varying costs and levels of luxuriousness.) We observe that in some industries – such as package holidays – a very large range of tastes can be catered for. But without a guarantee that *every single* taste is catered for, there may be individuals who are unable to obtain cover in a market system.

Another reason for expecting the poor to be left out of certain markets is that the poor are often less desirable customers. In education, for example, would schools not prefer middle-class students to poor ones? Markets do, left to themselves, appear to under-provide low-income housing for example (for reasons taken up in Chapter 11); and it is not always easy for the poor to open bank accounts.

And the poor may be left out of a market if the middle classes – who can afford high-quality provision – appeal for high-quality regulation that drives out the cheap providers, who tend to be frequented by the poor. If contracts for rented accommodation have to meet gratuitously high standards, there will be less rented accommodation especially at the bottom of the market; if lawyers have to be over-trained, the market may not provide the equivalent of a Woolworth's lawyer; government will have to provide one instead.

So for all these reasons, market may not serve the poor to the minimum level we believe desirable. As a result, the state *may* choose to give some of its benefits in the form of directly provided services, as it does at the moment, and it may be sensible to do that even if the public are unconcerned about equality of service.

But when we ask whether the traditional public sector model is justified by this discussion, the answer is still that it is not. It is a solution to the problem of ensuring equal access; it is a sledgehammer to the problem of ensuring some reasonable access. Reasonable cover for all can be provided by compulsion, cash handouts, vouchers, subsidies to private operators, or by private companies on contract to the state. We do not need direct state provision for everybody, to obtain some cover for the poorest 20 per cent of the population.

Merit Goods

It is an important premise of the welfare state and state intervention that certain types of activity are inherently more desirable than others. One justification for public spending has been that it can subsidize and encourage those activities. Getting your teeth checked is a meritorious activity; eating sweets is not. Going to the public library, or watching the BBC are meritorious; watching ITV or Sky are not.

So one textbook explanation – for example available in the best textbook on the market in this area, *The Welfare State*, by Nicholas Barr of the London School of Economics – justifies in-kind benefits as so-called *merit goods*: public libraries, houses, health and education. These are things we want people to consume.

This surely, can explain why we don't just hand out cash to people, to spend as they please. The state is not just redistributing, it is steering us as well. Part of that may be paternalistic – many of us would not choose to spend our money on top-class health services if we had any say in the matter, but as it is better for us to have a top-class health service, we had better not have any say in the matter. Or, as long as there is some benefit to the rest of us from other people consuming these things (if it minimizes the spread of disease or fosters lower crime rates), then it may be better to redistribute income in this form.

Or, maybe it is an argument about altruism. If the rich want to redistribute to the poor out of pleasure, to feel good about themselves, say, and if the rich only feel good when the poor live in nice houses, and have access to nice hospitals, and if the rich do not feel happy about the poor drinking whiskey and buying lottery tickets, then the rich will sensibly tie their altruism to the condition that it is directed towards houses and hospitals, and not whiskey and lottery tickets. In essence, the poor get given the health service or nothing – they can't have the cash.

Recognition of merit goods can justify public provision, free at point of use. Indeed, an acceptance of this argument probably provides the strongest case yet for the state to deliver services rather than cash. However, one's attitude to this argument probably depends upon one's general political philosophy, and the extent to which one believes in government guidance at all.

And whatever our view of paternalistic government, there are plenty of ways for government to provide in-kind benefits without producing them for us itself. It could guide us without providing quite the state operation that it does: subsidizing private producers, offering vouchers to people, or even merely informing us of the benefits of certain activities ('get your gums looked at for longer-lasting teeth') are perfectly plausible alternatives.

Non-profit-maximizing Goals

The next two components of the public service ethos derive from restraint: a restraint that is inextricably linked to the fact that the organizations involved are unconcerned with whether they make money or not. The public service ethos in these cases is a value system – a sense of right or wrong on the part of suppliers; and a willingness to respond to that sense; to do the right thing, even though it may be hard in advance to define the right thing very clearly or flexibly.

The most general manifestation of this 'doing the right thing' is in the strategic decisions of the company – the services it provides and the way it provides them; public sector ethics would tell an airport management that comfort mattered, even if it didn't generate extra revenue. Similarly, the provision of rural telephone boxes, for example, may be a socially desirable offering, but it may be one for which the benefits cannot easily be translated into revenue; hence a non-profit supplier is more likely to offer this kind of service than a profit-oriented one.

But it would be quite wrong to believe that selfish decision-making is directly correlated with profit-maximization. In the BAA case, the vital ingredient that allows the selfish strategy to be sustained is that the market in airports is not sufficiently competitive to ensure passengers boycott uncomfortable airports. It is the lack of competition, as much as the profit-maximization, that creates the wrong strategy. This explains why some authors – for example, Sir Kenneth Cousins – have sought to defend the public service ethos in sectors where an economic function cannot for some reason be governed by competition. He argues, for example, that in the government of colonial India, a restrained ethic was appropriate. He is of course quite right. A similar suggestion has been made more recently by economist John Kay, for a new public sector model for the monopoly utilities, a model he calls the 'customer corporation'.

But the argument that a lack of competition is a necessary condition for the appropriate adoption of a public service ethic should not be interpreted as making an argument that it is a sufficient condition. Even if competition seems impossible, it may not be appropriate to eschew the services of profit-maximizing producers.

For one thing, the adoption of the public service ethos tends to diminish our incentive and interest in fostering competition where competition is desirable. In the past, the existence of the public sector with its attendant values led to an insufficient exploration of the competitive potential of different industries. The utilities in most cases can be competitive, for example, and within a few years they will be as long as we don't saddle them with guilt about having a commercial outlook on their behaviour.

Secondly, there should be a more profound concern that the traditional public sector model could ever lead to an effective assertion of public interests. Is not the public sector itself prone to exactly the selfish strategizing that one sees in the private sector? It is not difficult to draw examples from everyday experience: just to focus on a close personal example, why does London Transport allow the persistence of fifteen-minute queues for the ticket office at Earl's Court station each morning during busy tourist months? (A conservative estimate of the customer time wasted between 8 a.m. and 10 a.m. in these queues is about forty hours per day; however, the number of minutes in which the in-flow of traffic exceeds the rate at which the station can cope with it is probably about twenty minutes – if only extra facilities could be provided for that duration then a huge difference would be made for a much longer period.)

The ideal answer to these kinds of problems – public or private – is to promote competition and consumer choice in order that the private incentives of the suppliers are better matched with the social incentives. In this way, there would be revenue loss to BAA or London Transport from offering a terrible service. It is notable that few competitive operations allow such a poor service to persist.

But where competition is truly not viable or desirable, then there is an obvious alternative to the adoption of restrained behaviour by producers: it is the separation of delivery of the service from the setting of objectives; or to put it another way, the use of some kind of regulation. We allow people to make a profit, but we prohibit them from, say, polluting. Similarly, we can use regulation as a device for restraining monopoly firms like BAA or London Transport.

Regulation does raise problems – the regulator may have his or her own agenda, and may not have very good information. Regulators may find it hard to strike a balance between excessive day-to-day interference and hands-off rule-setting. But despite these problems, arm's-length regulation may be a superior route to that of the old public sector model, with public ownership and a public interest duty on the part of executives. Our experience with the previously nationalized utilities seems to demonstrate exactly the problem of asking suppliers to meet a loosely defined public service objective: it appears to be almost beyond the achievement of humankind for suppliers in that context to detach themselves from the interests of the organization within which they operate. Indeed, as Anthony Downs has noted, public organizations will develop a culture of their own, a culture which will differ from organization to organization, which will not be a profit-maximizing culture, but which may be no more related to the general public interest than a profit-maximizing culture would be. In the absence of measurable criteria of corporate success – like profits – the culture may tend to place a very heavy stress on straight loyalty to the organization itself.

Overall then, it is understandable that there should be a prejudice in favour of commercial restraint in those sectors of the economy where competition is necessarily lacking. But the old public sector model is probably best left to those areas both where competition is impossible, *and* where regulation is for some reason impossible as a means of imposing the consequent necessary restraint.

Responsible Advice to Customers

The second manifestation of restraint relates to behaviour by staff each day, rather than on the basis of larger strategic policies: dealings with individual members of the public, and whether these dealings are conducted to the best advantage of the member of the public, or to the best advantage of the supplier.

In the case of the Gatwick ticket-seller example above, the public service ethos has a clear answer: the customer's interest should prevail. If the customer's wishes are difficult to ascertain, the ticket-seller should make a best guess at what the customer *would* want, were he able to communicate his preferences.

This kind of case is surprisingly ubiquitous in our economy, arising almost whenever the supplier is better informed about the product on offer than the customer. In essence, it is a conflict-of-interest problem, in that the supplier of a service often advises the customer on how much to demand, even though the supplier typically has an interest in the customer demanding a lot. Everything from medical services, to professional advice, to mechanics and heating repairmen. In all these areas, one requires mechanisms of restraint to ensure the supplier does not exploit the potential conflict of interest with the customer by offering false expert testimony to generate extra business. The mis-selling of personal pensions in the late 1980s offers a large and dramatic lesson in the breakdown of the kind of restraint required.

This is a problem that occurs whenever buyers cannot detect the quality or desirability of purchase in advance of committing themselves to it. In many sectors, markets work badly, and providers with integrity find it hard to compete with those who have none: people take the advice of mechanics and builders with a pinch of salt. Litigation against those who misadvise is more costly to pursue than it is worth, and anyway a certain number of mistakes are legitimate, so proving a lack of integrity in the advice given is tough.

It is clear that in many public services – health, education, even the claiming of state benefits – we do not want there to be conflicts of interest between public agents and the public they deal with. So the public are justified in a faith that the public service ethos in these sectors is desirable, an ethos that says we do not, for example, charge people for things that an unbiased observer would say they do not need.

There are special applications of this kind of restraint in the public sector. In the civil service, there is the issue of integrity of conduct with ministers – civil servants are not supposed to offer bad advice, hide options ministers will find attractive, or lie about the costs of pursuing different paths. Then there are also the protective services. It would surely be unfortunate for the police, for example, to make judgements about likelihood of guilt, priority of investigation, and treatment in custody on the basis of their own convenience, or potential commercial gain. Most countries have found that opening law and order to full-blown markets is not conducive to the support of property rights. The Clint Eastwood movie *Unforgiven* offers a dramatic and not entirely appealing representation of life in a world where money governs law enforcement.

So much for the problem, how effective has the traditional public sector been – with all its caution and its rigour – in offering best advice to customers? It clearly works rather well in the civil service and protective services – in the UK at least. But what about more generally? Did the old British Rail ticket-seller lie about which ticket to buy? In fact, the old British Rail did go to some trouble to disguise from travellers the existence of cheap commuter services that were slower substitutes for the British Rail Gatwick Express. Indeed, the company used to go so far as lying about the destination of trains (pretending on indicator boards they terminated at Clapham Junction when in fact they were destined for Victoria) in order to herd people on to the service the company desired. In as far as the ticket-seller offered best advice, it was normally in contravention of his employer's desire.

Would a civil servant sell a dud pension? Not directly to an individual, but on ministerial instruction a civil servant might well sell a dud pension to a generation of taxpayers; or might withhold information about food safety in order not to engender a panic among consumers. There just happen to be government-type ways of doing things, and *most* of these habits are cautious and considered, and most of them avoid the crass commercialism that one might see as a problem in certain sectors. But not all.

And even if one could obtain integrity from an old-style British Rail Gatwick ticket-seller, it comes at a price: the old public sector model's means of getting him to be genuinely indifferent about which ticket he sells is to make him indifferent about selling a ticket at all. The mediocrity of the service that follows from that indifference is familiar to us all. So the traditional public sector can deliver a degree of integrity into a sector, but only at some cost to the verve with which life in that sector is conducted.

In any event, the old public sector model is again not necessary to create a 'clean industry' where the public are potential victims of sharp practices. The better solution is to separate the advice-giving service from any follow-up delivery of substantive service. Surveyors are typically used purely to offer advice, upon which a builder then acts. Pensions advisers are increasingly available on a per-hour basis to advise without there being any chance of a commission. The Gatwick ticket-seller could be someone (indeed, probably should be someone) who is not employed by anyone running trains from Gatwick.

It is true that in many cases this option is very expensive. Getting a diagnosis of your car, and then taking it elsewhere for repair is tricky, as it is much easier to repair it while dismantling it for diagnosis. And in certain professions, it would be impossible to expect one agent to simply carry out the orders of another: many surgeons would be reluctant to carry out an operation if they thought it was unsuitable, and if they did, and things went wrong, there would be no clear line of responsibility for the consumer to pursue in seeking redress.

Another possibility adopted by many of the professions is to formulate self-regulating solutions to these problems: professional ethics, as opposed to public service ethics. Codes of practice that impose a modest amount of restraint are drawn up, with a fair amount of nonsensical ritual attached to ensure a culture of compliance. These codes have the advantage of being flexible, and also of being policed by those in an informed enough position to judge reasonable from unreasonable practice. These industries are by and large more successful at achieving high standards of conduct than those without any such codes, although there is obviously some potential for the codes to be abused and used as a form of entry barrier to the industry.[1]

---

1. This argument can be exaggerated – one could hardly argue that we have too few lawyers or accountants.

Overall, though, it seems that the old public sector model is a relatively effective way of coping with the problems of sharp commercial practice relative to the alternatives – but it may have offsetting disadvantages and is not demonstrably the only solution. For the vast majority of the time, alternative solutions are more than adequate to the task. They may require the adoption of codes of conduct, supported by punishment for infringements; they may imply non-commission pay structures for staff who deal with the public; they may imply regulation of standards and rules and prohibitions. They surely do not imply the entire abandonment of commercial criteria in all aspects of company behaviour. We have experience of private services – educational, medical and financial – that do not appear to suffer conflict-of-interest problems hugely greater than their public counterparts. We should learn from those.

Stakeholderism

One might describe 'stakeholder personnel policies' as those that we associate with firms which enjoy a strong culture, a caring management, and a consequently loyal and effective staff. Marks & Spencer, for example, is a company one might associate with such an approach. Their employment style contrasts with that of the hire-and-fire culture; the treatment of labour as a commodity.

Stakeholder employment is not – as some appear to believe – mere soft-hearted and soft-headed management. Two areas of economic theory have been used to demonstrate that caring management can yield hard benefits. One area of theory is that of so-called *efficiency wages*: pay your workers above the market rate, and they will be better motivated because they really have something to lose if they are sacked. It sounds arcane, but the argument has been used to explain wage rigidities and the persistence of unemployment in apparently flexible labour markets (even Karl Marx espoused it, believing that hard-headed capitalists would engage in a policy of keeping a reserve army of the unemployed to act as a spur to hard work by those who have jobs). Henry Ford built a motorcar empire on the basis of wages that were publicly known to be above the going rate, and others have followed.

The second area of economic theory to justify such policies derives from game theory, a very fashionable area of economics that at its most useful allows a large variety of complicated situations to be characterized by reference to a small number of simple fables.[1] In particular there is a well-known fable of the prisoners' dilemma which caricatures a situation in which two prisoners are best off co-operating with each other and refusing to confess their crime; but in which they each end up behaving selfishly and confessing in order to minimize the long prison sentence they would get if shopped by the other. In the story as told, their selfishness is self-defeating – giving them a longer prison sentence than they would have got had they both shut up. The prisoners' dilemma has been used to characterize the situation in arms races, price wars and office in-fighting. In general, it demonstrates the possibility that in a wide range of plausible situations, 'co-operation' can pay but may be hard to achieve given private incentives towards selfishness. Crucially, however, economists can show (without recourse to naive exhortation to the better side of human nature) that the solution to these kinds of co-operation problems tends to lie in the development of long-term, flexible relationships – the 'you scratch my back and I'll scratch yours' culture. And this is often only possible in the context of an expectation of both parties being in the same relationship for some time, and of both parties taking the rough with the smooth over time.

The most effective organizations may be the ones who have established, and locked themselves into, a culture of co-operation; with long-serving staff who habitually act for the company, rather than themselves, and as a result are happy to exert some extra effort in order to help satisfy customers. A positive attitude towards those customers is harder to maintain for employees who hate the employer who stands to gain from the customers' satisfaction.[2]

1. At its *least* useful, game theory allows a small number of simple situations to be characterized by reference to a large array of complicated mathematical models.
2. Although the economics of stakeholderism is well-established and does a lot to justify any vague public prejudice in favour of stakeholder-type providers, it actually offers little in the way of specific policy advice because the models in practice are by and large uncalibrated. They tell us that co-operation can be good – but we all know that already. What we do not know is exactly *how much* co-operation is good, and on this rather important score, they offer us nothing. We should be sceptical of those who purport to use these models to do anything more than demonstrate the possibility of stakeholderism's commercial value.

Most of us probably hold some prejudice in favour of stakeholder-type management policies, if only because we prefer to be employed under them. There has been dismay at the apparent lack of motivation and involvement of private staff employed in, for example, hospital cleaning.

But do we need stakeholder-type management everywhere in the economy? Does the traditional public sector ensure it? In principle, stakeholder management is useful in those sectors where staff motivation is important to determining the quality of staff output. We do not need stakeholder companies for everything – in fact, cleaning may be one case where the cost of fostering motivation and involvement is simply higher than the benefit. The service is relatively easy to manage, and often the cheap service is better value (even if lower quality) than the one weighed down by the costs of generous personnel training and relationship-building. However, it is also clear that stakeholder management is highly desirable in other industries. So desirable, indeed, one despairs of the management inertia which appears to obstruct its intro- duction. The building industry, for example, where quality is hard to monitor but important to achieve, and in which Britain has half the labour productivity and twice the cost of supervision of its Dutch and German counterparts.[1]

But how important is the public service ethos in delivering stake- holder-type personnel policies? We should again be rather sceptical. Government in the UK (unusually for the developed world) tends to pay slightly less than the private sector. Casual experience of public services suggests workers in them are often poorly motivated. Richard Branson represents stakeholderism; not the NHS. This should be no surprise – the stakeholder principle is easily transferred to profit- maximizing, shareholder-oriented firms, in all but the most ineptly managed cases. Management that says, 'Hello everybody, work hard so the shareholders get more money' is unlikely to get anybody to work hard or give the shareholders any more money. That is about as attractive a way of presenting an offer as a marriage proposal based on the potential

1. This has been documented by a study published by the Joseph Rowntree Foundation in York and The Policy Press in Bristol: Linda Clarke and Christine Wall, *Skills and the Construction Process: A Comparative Study of Vocational Training and Quality in Social Housebuilding* (May 1996).

to engage in a mutually beneficial economic arrangement. In both cases, marriage and employment, the offer may be underpinned by a mutually advantageous economic arrangement, but will be understood as being a shared stake, and an expectation of care.

Moreover, there is plenty about a very large organization – which the public sector will remain – that makes it hard to cultivate a personal sense of belonging on the part of employees.

Again, it should be no surprise that the public sector might not be a leader in enlightened employment, given that one might view it as a form of investment, and government's record at investing and thinking long term is rather poor. Any opportunity to exploit a short-term saving is taken, whatever the apparent long-term cost, in relationship-building as elsewhere.

One might take the public sector's policy with regard to the teaching profession as an example. Governments may have started out after the war with a stakeholder approach, valuing teachers, motivating them, paying them. But the temptation to exploit its short-term market power was too much to resist. So economies were made in the relative salary paid to teachers. For a while, highly trained and motivated teachers carried on offering the service they were habituated to delivering, even though in pay they had fallen behind equivalent staff elsewhere. But the saving government made on that basis could only last one generation. Thereafter, young people of high quality avoided the profession, which looked rather unattractive. The net result is a far less motivated and far less satisfied profession.

In general, therefore, however desirable progressive personnel policies are, we should be suspicious of the idea that there is some one-to-one correlation between them and operations within the traditional public sector.

Non-profit-making Suppliers

The seventh component of the public service ethic on our list above is that profits should not be paid in order that costs can remain low. The public have a deep sense that paying out profits is a waste of money. For example, there is Christian Wolmar's book, *True Stories from the*

Great British Railway Disaster, taken from the column of the same name in the *Independent on Sunday*. It catalogues the supposed nonsenses that have occurred since the railways were privatized. Mr Wolmar says 'The railways will remain dependent on government subsidy. The notion of large amounts of taxpayers' money going into the pockets of private shareholders is a nonsense.'

In fact, we should be very suspicious of this argument. If profits diminished value for money, it would be odd that we choose to pay them out in sectors governing about three-quarters of the economy. We need to understand whether Mr Wolmar's profit aversion has any sensible basis to it at all.

As with each of the other values discussed, the answer is yes, but only in rather limited circumstances. The following example makes the point: suppose Glaxo-Wellcome plc was more likely to discover a cure for cancer than the Imperial Cancer Research Fund, and suppose that this was generally recognized to be the case. Would you rather donate money to Glaxo-Wellcome, or to the Imperial Cancer Research Fund? In fact, few of us do donate to Glaxo-Wellcome, despite its sterling efforts on the part of the world's sick, and plenty of us donate to cancer-research charities. There is a reason for this. Glaxo-Wellcome, as a profit-maximizing company, has probably set its research budget already, and thus any *extra* single pound of donation will probably go not to extra research, but to the shareholders. So, there is little point in any one of us making a marginal donation, however effective the organization.

The reason for this is that some proportion of Glaxo-Wellcome's profit is simply what is left over after all the company's costs have been met; it is a residual reflecting the difference between exact plans and outcomes. It can be large or small, positive or negative. But whatever it is, in private companies it is the shareholders who suffer and enjoy the burden and privilege of either side of that residual. Thus, at the margin, when things go well or badly, it is the shareholders who benefit or who lose. This means that the shareholders themselves enjoy a disproportionate return from any marginal pound paid into a share-holder-type organization.

The existence of shareholders who bear the benefit or loss of good news or bad news for the company is hugely important *when charitable donation is an important part of the basis of funding of a sector*. If we hope to collect resources on the basis of voluntarism, you cannot hope to have profit-maximizing shareholders as equity holders in the collecting organization. This is because, as we have established, it is the shareholders who enjoy the residual claims to a for-profit company's fortune. So, any marginal pound paid to a company effectively primarily benefits the shareholders. Knowing this, very few of us will voluntarily choose to donate to profit-maximizing firms.[1]

The argument is therefore that voluntary donation and the existence of equity holders who stand to gain or lose from that donation are simply incompatible. In as far as we wish to rely on private donation to causes, we need non-profit organizations. Profits drive out voluntarism, even where we all individually recognize that the profit-maximizer is an efficient and helpful firm.[2]

This argument can justify a non-profit basis for, say, the blood transfusion service, where donated blood is less likely to be tainted with problems than purchased blood. Few of us would donate blood if the company collecting it stood to make money out of our donation.

But does this justify the eradication of profit-makers in health, education, or the running of rail services? If you believe government subsidy is rather like a private donation, then you might be suspicious of profit-makers in these sectors. In fact, though, government subsidy is not like a private donation. It tends to be far larger, and hence less marginal; it tends to be conditional on the delivery of certain outputs and hence more like a purchase of services rendered; it can be set according to the expected level of profits made and hence avoid inflating profits to a level far higher than seems reasonable.

As for private donation in these areas, there may be some element

1. But, ideally, we might donate to the non-profit organization, and it can then buy its research from the most effective firm around, profit-maximizer or not. That way we get the effectiveness of profit-maximizers, and an increase in research from extra donations.
2. This account gives rise to an amazing paradox of political philosophy. Those who believe that welfare or socialized sectors of the economy should be based more fundamentally on donation, charity or voluntarism (i.e., the liberal right who detest taxation) should hope to promote a non-profit sector. They should see the disadvantages of shareholder-type organizations. Those who don't want charity to be based on voluntary donation (i.e., the left, which detests the idea that private donation should determine the welfare of the less well-off) should be happier accepting that profits can be paid.

of that in schools (where parental involvement of time is helpful); but that is not generally the norm throughout the public services. And it is hard to believe there are any rail services (with the possible exception of odd branch lines run by and for enthusiasts) that are run on the basis of voluntary donation – of time or money. Indeed, in the provision of most non-profit activities there is remarkably little donation. (In America, for example, according to Lester Salamon, only 18 per cent of the non-profits' revenues are donated privately. A third come from government grant.)

This may or may not have convincingly dispensed with the argument that profits are a problem. There is a second important argument, though. The real defence of the existence of profits in the vast bulk of our economy is that profits are not primarily a residual piece of good luck or bad luck to shareholders, but are a straight payment for resources that are used. They are entirely analogous to wages as return for labour: they are a return to those who offer capital, or they reward those who provide imagination, innovation and organizational initiative – entrepreneurship. Governments have to pay for capital and entrepreneurship like they have to pay for anything else – they may be able to get them slightly cheaper, but they certainly do not get them free. And nor should they. These are scarce resources, and there is no reason for that scarcity not to be reflected in the prices (or costs) we bear when we procure services.

We know, incidentally, that government has to pay for capital, because it spends something like 4 per cent of total GDP simply paying out interest on the capital it has borrowed. Some of that capital (rather too little in the opinion of some of us) was borrowed to support British Rail – the beloved cause of Christian Wolmar. It is hard to see why anyone would be that much more joyful at taxpayers' money being paid into the hands of private lenders, than they are at it being paid into the hands of private shareholders.[1] As for entrepreneurship, one cannot help but worry that as government has been loath to pay for it, it has simply not taken delivery of any.

1. Of course, government could pay less interest by taxing us more, and not borrowing as much. But that would still impose a cost on the rest of us. As long as money has a time value, then no amount of re-engineering of finances can eradicate that cost.

Profits may sometimes need to be quite large to compensate those providing capital and entrepreneurship to an economic activity. Often the activity is risky – naturally, if a company takes a 50 per cent chance on a project that will either succeed or fail, it needs to expect quite a substantial success if it does succeed, in order to compensate for the possibility it could have failed. In other words, what are in fact quite reasonable profits on an individual project may look excessive in hindsight, because it is only in hindsight that the risks of failure can be disregarded. A second reason that what are actually reasonable profits may look high, is that companies invest in intangible as well as tangible assets – they may forgo normal profits for several years while accumulating market share, honing their production skills, and developing market intelligence. It should not be a shock that they reap a return on those intangible investments later on.

Finally, notice that profits paid out by government to private companies are not a net cost to society; for every pound lost to some taxpayers, they are a net income for others. The fact the money goes into 'the pockets of private shareholders' is at least a sign it is not going down the drain. This may not sound too heartening, but as the vast bulk of the population are profit-earners, albeit in varying degrees, profits are not quite the problem they might appear. Pensioners, for example, rely on profits for their income. A message that cannot be hammered home too hard is that we should always be more worried about real economic costs that provide benefit to no one, than we are about transfers from one person to another. So if profits are enhancing efficiency, rather than detracting from it, then there is little reason to worry. As long as we think profits are taxed satisfactorily, and especially earned in a competitive or well-regulated market, there is little to fear from taxpayers paying money into anyone's pockets.

In conclusion, it is clear that the traditional public sector was a good way of eradicating profits, but it was not a good way of discriminating between good profits and bad profits. And most profits are good. Eradicating profits was unnecessary, however, as in most cases public services have not been based on voluntary donation where the profit principle is genuinely problematic. We should be as worried about paying profits to rail companies as we are about paying profits to food companies, or for that matter, drugs companies.

Intra-industry Co-operation

The last notion of the public service ethic is that suppliers within a sector co-operate with each other, rather than engaging in costly duplication and rivalry. The calls for an integrated transport policy often appeal to this kind of value, as do suggestions that it is wrong for doctors, hospitals or schools to compete against each other. Mr Wolmar's rail privatization book makes extensive fun of the problems arising out of unco-ordinated rail services. And it is not just a sixties-style soft-headed commitment to peace and love among humankind that justifies co-ordination – one can see a substantive value in it in all sorts of public industries. University admission procedures, hospital specialization, intra-library lending, interchangeability of railway tickets. In none of these cases would one throw away the co-operative elements lightly.

There is another reason why we might support co-operation rather than rivalry in certain sectors. It appears to stem from the desire for equality of access. Somehow, it appears that competition opens up the explicit idea that some suppliers are better than others. Competing suppliers will tend to suggest they are superior to rivals anyway; and the whole premise on which competition is based is that suppliers may differ. If people want more equality, or at least more pretence of equality, then the competition we value in most areas of the economy may be worth sacrificing in public services. (This should not be underestimated: the pain to a family of knowing a relative is not receiving the best available medical care is extreme, and considerably adds to the pain of a given level of disablement.) There is some value in a pretence of equality, and co-operation within an industry fosters that pretence.

Another reason for supporting non-competitive suppliers in some sectors is that competition can occasionally worsen service quality. Cream-skimming of profitable services, for example, can be a problem (although not very often, as it is usually best dealt with by explicit subsidy of uneconomic services); new entry in an industry, at the expense of those who have already sunk costs into it; and an excessive clustering of services around a market median (buses all running at the same time, the pop chart rundown occurring on competing radio stations simultaneously), with a consequent loss of minority provision. All these can result from deregulation in different markets.

Indeed, in all these cases there are solid economic arguments which can demonstrate that social welfare is potentially diminished by untrammelled *laissez-faire* economics. Such a conclusion should not be dismissed.

Now if we really want to arrange multiple suppliers, operating in an entirely co-ordinated form, then the old public sector model is an attractive way of doing so for one very good reason: it ensures the co-operation between suppliers is not exploited to create a cartel to distribute undeserved profits to shareholders at the expense of consumers. It is not hard to see how we get from the premise of co-ordinated activity, to the traditional public sector model.

If there are doubts in the traditions of the public sector, they must relate to whether you really do want to organize a co-ordinated industry, as opposed to unleashing competition at all. Take Mr Wolmar's view of the advantages of a co-ordinated railway system. Would you, if you could start again, take British Airways, the BAA, the Civil Aviation Authority, Virgin Atlantic and British Midland Airways, GPA (the aircraft leasing company) and pieces of British Aerospace and put them all into one large co-ordinated air services company? That, for example, was precisely the structure of railways under British Rail, and in the airline industry it would have exactly the same co-ordination benefits that the old British Rail had. It is hard to believe anyone would want to construct a company like that.

Similarly, would competition between schools be such a bad thing? Is there not some tendency for the co-ordination between them to act as a form of cartel delivering a quiet life to the staff, and a mediocre service to the customer? Why do we not believe in co-ordination when it comes to so many other sectors of the economy? Cinemas, supermarkets, pet food manufacturers – or even telephone companies. In all these cases, it is now broadly accepted that while there are some advantages to co-ordination, the best possible strategy is to allow a strong degree of competition. The traditional public sector was, again, too clumsy a model to deliver exactly the components of competition and co-ordination in the right proportions.

Do We Need a Public Sector?

Each of these eight preceding sections has been designed to explore our instincts and prejudices towards competitive commercial activity. When taken at their most simplistic, these instincts have tended to support the existence of direct state provision of essential services. In each case, there is a sound basis to our instincts in terms of a taste for just distribution or efficiency. Yet in each case, there is an enormous 'but'. In each case, our instincts really only justify a far more limited abandonment of commercial conduct than there has been.

This is not to say that the traditional public sector approach to public services is wrong – merely to argue that the premises that have been used to uphold its existence are not sufficient to do so. In particular, most of the broad goals of social distribution could be met with public spending on its own, without the state actually producing 15 per cent of GDP. The direct provision of public services by a public sector operating under a public service ethos can only be justified if in practice its results appear superior to those of the private, commercial sector.

It is not impossible to make a case that public sector provision is more efficient than commercial alternatives. The main such argument is that unlike private companies, government has a unique purchasing muscle, which it can use to limit spending on services, so costs do not escalate. It can buy things cheaply; and it can also borrow money at low interest rates, thus saving on some of the generous profits it would otherwise have to dish out to shareholders. To quote Anatole Kaletsky of *The Times*,[1] these factors 'are likely to outweigh by far the possible efficiencies that might be achieved by introducing better systems of management accounting, tighter financial control and more competition'. In fact, he says, 'commercializing public services will drive up costs'. This is a modern argument for the old public sector model.

Notice that this defence is *not* based on any conception of social justice. Far from it. In fact, it is quite literally based on the fact that

---

1. He was giving his interpretation of an article by John Flemming and Peter Oppenheimer in the *National Institute Economic Review*, 'Are Government Spending and Taxes Too High (or Too Low)?' (issue 157, July 1996).

government can exploit nurses by paying them too little – to the advantage of the taxpayer.

If the argument was right, the fact that it was offensive to traditional supporters of public sector ethics and values would not really matter. But is it? Big government *can* make economies, essentially by treating public suppliers badly, but it pays a price in the long term. Not only does it end up with a state structure characterized by poorly motivated staff and organizations that have no in-built incentives to reward entrepreneurial or innovative behaviour; but more to the point it ends up with personnel who merit the low wages government pays. In the long term, even though government may employ 15 per cent of the nation's workers, it does not have much market power. Eighty-five per cent of the nation's workers can go elsewhere. So, in the course of a pay-round or two government can extract economies from suppliers and staff. But in the course of a generation or two, it cannot.

Conclusion

Some people seem unable to think about issues of public spending other than through the soft-focus lens of values and altruism. Up to a point, they are correct. But in most cases, that thinking is a long way from the realities of public services. A far more refined approach to the organization of public services, based upon a heavy dose of economic logic, may well improve services considerably.

Many seem to think that an economic argument for something somehow debases it, and anyway that economic arguments frequently come up with the wrong answer to questions. Economists would never be able to justify the existence of public parks, for example, and would inevitably end up arguing for them to be sold and developed.

But the purpose of this chapter has been to argue against this point of view. The values which we think are so special are often best justified and explained in terms of good old-fashioned economic logic, just as many ancient religious taboos had sound practical foundations. At the same time, economic logic can tell you how to deliver social objectives in the most cost-effective way. (You want public parks, you can have public parks – there is nothing in economics to suggest you cannot, other than that the real costs and benefits should be taken into account.) And even if there is a conflict between economic objectives – the growth of GDP, for example – and the requirements of 'social justice' – a more equal distribution of income, for example – there is no need for conflict between those who are trained to think economically and those who are simply highly morally strung, as economic logic can help tell you how best to deliver any set of objectives you want. Indeed, breaches of sound economic logic in the model of the old public sector today mean that in many cases we are not serving social or economic objectives very well.

This chapter has been about the ways in which society can attempt to combine social values with practical industrial organization. This is not a problem for most people: either they are on the left, and so concerned with social values they are blind to whether they have designed practical means of delivering those values. Or, on the right, they are sceptical of the relevance of the values. The result has been a polarization around a model of public service delivery whose worth has never really been established. The monolithic nature of that model has done much to promote public disenchantment with government services. And the gusto with which the traditional model was adopted appears to have accentuated many of the natural problems that accompany public spending and public delivery.

Additional Reading

Barr, Nicholas (1993), *The Economics of the Welfare State* (second edition), Oxford University Press.

Cousins, Sir Kenneth (1985), 'The Principle of Public Service' in *Politics, Ethics and the Public Service*, Royal Institute of Public Administration, London.

Downs, Anthony (1966), *Inside Bureaucracy*, Little, Brown & Co.

Frohlich, Norman, Joe A. Oppenheimer, and Cheryl Eavey (1987), 'Laboratory Results on Rawl's Distributive Justice', *British Journal of Political Science*, Vol. 17, No. 1.

Kay, John (1996), 'The Future of UK Utility Regulation' in *Regulating Utilities: A Time for Change*, IEA Readings 44, Institute for Economic Affairs, London.

Martin, William T. (1988), *Motivation and Productivity in Public Sector Organisations*, Quorum.

Rawls, John (1971), *A Theory of Justice*, Harvard University Press, Cambridge, Massachusetts.

Salamon, Lester M. (1992), *America's Non-Profit Sector: A Primer*, The Foundation Center, New York.

Samuelson, P.A. (1958), 'Aspects of Public Expenditure Theories', *Review of Economics and Statistics*, 40.

Sefton, Tom (1997), *The Changing Distribution of the Social Wage*, STICERD Occasional Paper 21, London School of Economics.

Wolmar, Christian (ed.) (1996), *The Great British Railway Disaster*, Ian Allan Publishing, Shepperton, Surrey.

3 Do We Need Public Spending?

Economic principles in support of taxation

Recent discussion in Britain, by no means confined to Socialists,
stresses the need for State-sponsored social expenditure to provide in
the twentieth century what the pyramids, the cathedrals and the
railways provided in the past.

HAROLD WILSON, *The Relevance of British Socialism*, 1964.

Chapter 2 was about the values that have been used to justify public
sector provision of services; and it found that, however sensible they
were, they were largely insufficient to justify the state's large provider
role. Now we can turn our attention to public spending, and six
arguments that can be used to defend collective finance for services:
this allows us to be rather more positive about the role of the state.

The challenge is to delineate principles that allow government to
give us the right amount, and the right sort of items in our proverbial
weekly shopping basket. The world divides into those who believe that
government is up to this challenge, and those who do not. There are
those who think government is rational, or at least that it is close enough
to being rational that rationality is salvageable from current practices.
Under this view, the trade-off between baked beans and public transport
is one which can be discussed sensibly and calmly. The correct answer
as to how many beans we have, or how many buses, depends on public
preferences. And government is about responding to those preferences,
just as Marks & Spencer's must.

But on the other side, there are those who think government is not
rational and never will be. That in practice government does not aim
to optimize the trade-off between beans and buses; and as a matter of
prescription, it would be a mistake to try and get government to do that.

These two camps correspond to what one might call the optimistic view of government, and the pessimistic view. Optimists see government as a kind of 'direct debit arrangement'. Government is our agent; it purchases various items on our behalf, and conveniently extracts payment from our payslips with a minimum of fuss. Of course optimists would concede that in practice government is not perfect, but it can reasonably strive to be: the goal of civilization for an optimist is to promote enlightened decision-making. Pessimists on the other hand see government as a 'leviathan' – a monster, out of control, terrorizing us with an insatiable appetite for our money. Its only purpose: to consume and to grow. It has a life of its own, interests of its own, and those interests are quite different from ours. The goal of civilization for pessimists is to tame the beast, or at least confine it.[1]

Needless to say, dividing the world into optimists and pessimists is not an exact science. One is entitled to be optimistic about certain forms of government, or certain people in government, but not others. The crucial distinction is the one between those who see government as a threat, and those who see it as an opportunity.

Crucially, this is not the same as dividing the world into left and right, or into those in favour of big government and those in favour of small government. Optimists may more frequently be found on the left of politics – although by no means exclusively – and pessimists tend to be on the right. It is also true that pessimists tend to favour smaller government, because they think that most of what government does is a waste of time. But optimism about the potential of government is not the same as having the view that government must be large.

This chapter takes a view of government that is by and large optimistic – and it offers arguments that rely on the premise that it is not futile

---

1. History has delivered optimists and pessimists in about equal number, according to my analysis of quotations on the subject of government in the *Oxford Dictionary of Quotations*. Admittedly, of the sixty-one entries, almost exactly half have no bearing on the optimist/pessimist divide (Dickens' 'Your sister is given to government' for example, said by Joe Gargery in *Great Expectations*). But the rest divide almost equally between those who think the construction of good government is, by and large, a salvageable mission, and those who do not. In fact, the scorecard on my subjective reckoning is 17:15 just in favour of the optimists.

to attempt to arrange government on rational principles, and that government can act as a benevolent agent for the people. Government should aim to be an effective direct debit arrangement. Its central justification for taking our money is to provide those needs that cannot be satisfied through individual market transactions. We all know that defence and law and order can be justified on these grounds, primarily because they are not consumed individually. But there are plenty of other material wants for which decentralized markets are inappropriate. Indeed, the list of spending headings justified by economic principles runs at least as long as the traditional core of services we associate with government at the moment. So where and why do we need public spending?

The Impossibility of Charging for Everything

A good reason for using taxation to pay for a variety of things is that it is a great deal more practical than charging for them directly. If charges are not possible for a service, then nobody will be able to make money out of it, and it will not exist in a market-driven allocation of resources.

The BBC provides the most obvious actual case of tax finance substituting for market charges. It was not – when the corporation was created – possible to levy a fee for watching television, or for listening to radio. The only private source of finance for such services would have been advertising. Yet that would have not only spoiled the programmes, it would have been fortuitous if the desires of consumer-goods manufacturers to publicize their products had yielded the right level of finance for the broadcast media. It is quite likely that if people could have been charged for TV, they would have paid the charge. In the meantime, the tax was a reasonable substitute.

But the BBC is not the only case. We have hitherto taken the view that use of the roads, and consumption of water – both pieces of private consumption – are impractical to levy explicit fees for. In both cases, as with the BBC, we have attempted to levy certain specific taxes on the beneficiaries of the services in question – taxes that more or less mimic the degree to which the service is used – but the principle that taxation and public expenditure have been necessary in these areas was not really much disputed until relatively recently. Certainly not by taxpayers.

In fact, in principle, we could extend the argument further than we do. The cost of making a building look attractive is borne by the owner of the building; yet the benefit is widely enjoyed, and it is certainly not possible to charge passers-by for that benefit. What about keeping the environment clean and attractive? It is rather a hassle to charge people rambling up a country path for the privilege of enjoying a view. Or to charge anglers for the cost of keeping rivers clean and well-stocked with fish. Or to charge royalty-lovers for the civil list. Even research into pure science falls into this category – it is not easy to levy a fee to people for the particular use they derive from such research.

The impossibility of levying fees for services, or the possibility of levying them only at a cost quite disproportionate to the benefit of the service being provided, can justify tax finance. But it should not be seen as absolving us of a responsibility to attempt to find means of charging market prices for products to users. It will, for example, soon be fairly easy to charge directly for television. We should require fairly compelling new arguments for the maintenance of a licence-fee system that was introduced in a completely different age.

But it is not only the BBC that might face its reckoning. It is not difficult to charge for water directly – and indeed, compared to building large amounts of extra capacity in the distribution system, installing meters in most homes might be the simplest option. And thanks to new technology, the areas of our lives in which direct user fees are impossible to levy are disappearing apace. Technology in these cases is providing a good reason for collective finance through taxation to diminish.

The Problem of Price Discrimination

There is another category of markets in which taxation can be usefully deployed as a means of finance. It is those where charging is physically quite practical, but where levying a viable tariff is not. The best way to understand this argument is to focus on the one service to which it most closely applies: public transport.

Now for most people, we subsidize public transport – especially commuter transport from suburbia into city centres. This is not because we want to help suburban-dwellers (who tend to be middle class); nor because we want to help their employers recruit them. It is mainly because it is an essential service: for most commuters there is no practical alternative to it.

For the economist, these are not good reasons to subsidize public transport at all, but pretty good reasons for letting decentralized markets finance it. After all, if people really need a service, they will surely pay for it? If it is expensive, well that's all the more reason to make them pay for it themselves, so they understand the true costs of public transport when they make a choice about where to live. If for some peculiar reason we want to disburse cash to people living in suburbia, we can give them better schools and hospitals, and cleaner streets than those enjoyed by their inner-city counterparts. Why subsidize the one service for which direct charges are so easily levied?

The best answer to this, and the best justification for collective support of public transport, is actually rarely articulated, and is usually lost among some other far less persuasive arguments (such as that it is a bribe for keeping people off the roads when in fact it would be much better just to charge people for using the roads). It hinges on the fact that the total value that all users of public transport place on the service justifies the service, and that if you could charge all people the value they individually place on the service, it would be viable without subsidy. The difficulty is how you capture that value in the price you charge, given that different users apply different values to the service, and certainly have a different willingness to pay for it.

The rich probably have a greater willingness to pay than the poor, for example. People going to work probably have a greater willingness to pay than leisure travellers. The dilemma in applying market prices to public transport arises from the fact that at any time of day, you inevitably end up charging one price to all types of user. And that means you fail to capture some of the value consumers apply to the service, and you may as a result render it unviable.[1]

For example, if you charge a price that obtains from the workers the

1. In practice, there is quite a large variation in prices on public transport; but on commuter services at peak times there is very little, and certainly less than you would need to capture the customers' true varying valuations of the service.

necessary revenues, you have probably priced the poor leisure user out of the market. But modest as they may be, you often need the marginal revenues of the leisure users to tip the service into viability. If on the other hand, you charge a price that keeps the day-tripper on the trains, you are clearly allowing well-to-do commuters to get on board at a price far lower than that which they are willing to pay. And your overall revenues may not be sufficient.

So taxation has a big advantage over charging. It can finance a service that market prices will not finance, and incidentally it discriminates between the rich and the poor, which in a large number of cases is exactly the price discrimination that you would want to apply if you were charging for the service directly.

Of course, it is possible for the market prices to discriminate between different types of user, and the public transport services do achieve that in a number of ways: the plethora of savers, super-savers, blue-ticket savers, and greens and reds that confuse us when we buy InterCity rail tickets are examples, and they barely come close to the devices the airlines use to obtain more cash from some types of traveller than others. (In the US, simply persisting in asking whether there isn't a cheaper fare sometimes obtains you a substantial discount, because pushy, price-conscious customers are worth giving a discount to, as long as you don't have to share it with all passengers.) Many companies give student or pensioner discounts. None, however, actually succeeds in extracting the full value out of all users. To do that would require putting us all in a reliable lie-detector machine when we buy our ticket, and asking us how much it's worth to us.[1]

The impossibility of comprehensively applying price discrimination is a problem wherever the cost of the incremental consumer is lower than the average cost of all consumers − where the train or plane is running anyway, so all extra passenger revenues are welcome. It is a problem that applies beyond transport, though. This argument *possibly*

---

1. For some reason, competition policy authorities have tended to be deeply suspicious of price discrimination by private companies, mainly because it is not possible in a very competitive market where prices are driven down to cost for all users, so it is a symptom of market power. It is, however, usually a benign symptom. The average price rather than the variation in prices seems the more important variable.

justifies some degree of arts subsidy: if a play has empty seats, it would be nice to sell them very cheaply. But doing that undermines the theatre's ability to extract the necessary cash from the keen theatregoer. Pharmaceuticals are another obvious case in point. The cost of giving people drugs is not in the manufacture of them, it is in the development. Once developed, the drug company needs plenty of cash from the high-value customer to cover the development cost incurred; yet the company also wants to sell the drug to anyone who is truly willing to pay more than the modest cost of manufacturing the pill in which the drug is dispensed. As the potential for price discrimination is limited, overall profits will be lower than the consumers' valuation of the drug might justify, and the drug might never get developed.

There is one major problem with this justification for state action, however. Difficulty in price discriminating is a ubiquitous problem for suppliers: Perrier would undoubtedly like to be able to charge different amounts for its bottles of water as much as London Transport would for different users of its tickets. (The problem for Perrier is worse: not only can it not tell which type of consumer is buying each bottle, but it would be possible for low-cost buyers to sell their bottles to high-cost ones, undermining the discriminatory price structure.) Indeed, so ubiquitous is the problem, we need to find some basis on which we can prevent the lack of potential price discrimination justifying public subsidies for everything, Perrier included.

And the unfortunate truth is that we cannot. We just have to apply the argument judiciously to those sectors which are particularly important, or upon which many other sectors apparently rely – like public transport. This is one of those cases where there is a general argument that individual, decentralized market transactions may not yield a perfect allocation of resources – but where the only appropriate response in most sectors is still to say and do nothing about it.

The Failure of Private Capital Markets

There is a third advantage to taxation as a means of financing activity. The government has the power to levy it with methods far more intrusive than those we would ever allow private companies to adopt in levying charges or fees. Government has the power to send us to jail for not paying tax; it has the power to snoop into details of our income and to levy withholding taxes on our paycheques. Moreover, because government is the purveyor of such a large proportion of our weekly consumption, its costs of doing business are low. It is far easier for government to search us out and extract a lot of cash from us, than it is for the phone company to do so, for example. Finally, where a dispute arises – concerning the interpretation of a tax law, for example – unlike the private company, government has the power to change the law to its own preferred effect.

This might all sound a very dubious set of reasons for giving government the power to slice money out of our income. But there is one area where government's entitlements can facilitate economic activity: that is in lending. The market for credit often fails simply because lenders cannot be sure of getting their money back very reliably. Plenty of individuals – some of whom at least undoubtedly would be able to repay their loans – are simply unable to get credit because it is too expensive for banks to ascertain they are worthy of a loan.

The ability of government to extract money from us through taxation thus creates an unusual opportunity for government to be the one who gives money to us. And this power of government to act as a credit bank justifies one major piece of public spending: education.

The vast majority of parents want their children to be educated; and would be willing to pay for the service were it not provided free to the user. But a lot of parents would have difficulty in affording the cost of education, even if taxes were far lower than they are today. This in itself does not justify state finance: the market solution is for people to borrow the money they want to spend on education, and pay it back over the years in which the education benefits their young. Is that kind of market solution likely or possible? Unfortunately banks are a bit loath to lend large amounts of money (about £2,500 per child per year) long term, without some form of security. They are not generally satisfied that securing a loan against someone's future income is satisfactory, deprived as they are of the apparatus of government to help them claim back the money. It is far better for us all to use the government as a savings bank: we get the schooling when young, and pay back the loan in the form of tax when we go to work afterwards.

The same argument has been used to justify child benefit. However, this argument should not be taken too far: it works in school-level education because essentially that is something we all need. It is not much of a problem to give everybody an education, as everybody would be wanting one anyway. When it comes to university level education however, similar capital market failings arise but it is a bit unfair to charge everybody the tax that graduate education necessitates, given that people's consumption of graduate education varies hugely. A far more direct link between the amount drawn out of government, and the amount given back seems justified. Hence, it is not unreasonable for the government to act explicitly as a student lending bank (or the guarantor of a private student lending bank), rather than using taxation as a general means of finance.

The Value of Shared Institutions

There are certain commodities which are inherently valuable to individuals. A glass of water, for example. A glass, for example. My enjoyment of either is really a function of my own tastes, and the qualities of the glass, or the water. These are items in which individual purchases are likely to lead to sensible decision-making.

But there is another class of commodities whose value derives primarily *not* from the inherent features of the product, or the inherent tastes of the consumer, but primarily from the context in which the consumer enjoys the product. In particular, from the collective, or social, enjoyment of the product.

Consider an example: I may enjoy watching a video; but suppose I enjoy watching it more when I am with friends, or family. And suppose that I enjoy watching the video with friends and family more than just spending time with friends and family without watching a video. Clearly there is some interaction between my utility of watching the video and my utility of enjoying company, and it is hard to apply a unique value to the video without the context being taken into account.

Now consider the same phenomenon at the national, or near national, level. Do we not as a nation derive pleasure from sharing certain experiences – a pleasure quite beyond that which most of us would derive from those experiences in the absence of a national excitement at them? The FA Cup final is more interesting, and more worthy of attention, than the same game played by the same teams in a friendly pre-season match. The National Lottery is (marginally) more interesting as a game that is widely played, and discussed in offices around the country, than it would be as an equivalent odds contest that we played in our own time. The Royal Family is, in a sense, a shared national experience too. My only interest in them derives from everyone else's, and theirs each derives from everyone else's too.

The interesting thing about experiences whose value derives from their being shared is that they can appear arbitrary in their selection, and yet once they have been selected are highly valuable, and indeed not arbitrary at all.

There is a fashionable area of economics that concerns arbitrary but valuable shared social phenomena: it is the economics of 'standards'. It is largely arbitrary that I use a keyboard with 'qwerty' as the arrangement of keys; but as long as everyone else does, I will, and as long as lots of people adopt the same logic, the qwerty keyboard will persist. Similarly with VHS video cassettes, PC-standard computers, etc. These are all products whose most important characteristic is general acceptance, rather than innate technical superiority. We can view 'shared-pleasure commodities' as standards in themselves: as a society, we more or less arbitrarily choose as a standard certain events or products which we will enjoy collectively, to satiate our taste for collective as opposed to individual pleasure.

Now there are some people who support the notion of the minimal state and who deny the existence of these kinds of shared experiences. It is quite possible they do not themselves enjoy sharing experiences. But it would be impoverishing to denude society of these kinds of experiences if the vast bulk of us actually do have a taste for some shared pleasures.

Accepting then that we want some shared pleasures, does the state need to finance them? Clearly, not usually. The FA Cup final hardly requires state subsidy. Nor do Wimbledon, the Olympic Games, perhaps not even the Royal Family. In most of these cases, the joy deriving from the shared nature of the consumption involved is no obstacle to a charge being levied to cover the cost of the event. Indeed, in many of these examples the challenge for policy-makers is not to find cash for the shared event, but to prevent the promoters – people with an implicit national licence to organize a shared-pleasure event – from reaping too much profit from their asset.

Nevertheless, it is possible that there are some items of shared enjoyment which do require subsidy. Markets do not always work well when it comes to setting standards. Markets can fail to lead us towards certain items, or do so more slowly and clumsily than the public would desire. People may be split as to whether to buy VHS or Betamax, and much money is wasted in the process of VHS coming to predominance. In these markets, government can exploit its important and central buying role in the nation, to commit all of us to an item of shared consumption, in case individual transactions would find us fumbling. In other words, markets can and do establish standards. But there is more of a potential role for government in helping them do so, than there is for government in the provision of most commodities.

What examples does this argument justify? Sometimes, one can hear people argue a case rather like this for great national institutions like the NHS. That is a problem. Much as the NHS is a great shared national institution, its value must stand or fall on its ability to provide health care.

Instead, this argument can really only apply to some of the luxuries of public spending: sport, arts, national celebrations and festivals, areas of national pride. Indeed, while there are many lessons to be learned from the experience of the National Lottery, one of them is that people almost anywhere on the political spectrum can take pleasure in public spending on these kinds of items to some degree. Again, the important judgement is to prevent the argument being overused, and any public asset being marketed as some kind of shared cultural experience that private provision could not possibly attempt to deliver.

The Problem of Missing Jurisdictions

Some of these arguments justify to some extent state finance for what might be termed private goods – such as education. Other arguments concern the genuinely national 'public goods' – defence and law and order. But many arguments over public spending concern those that fall somewhere in between. They arise over the goods or services which have a strong 'public good' element to them, but which are the concern of only a small section of the population. Consider the following examples of public spending, both controversial, and ask yourself whether these are 'collective' goods or not:

Research into treatments for HIV and Aids, or indeed the provision of any medical services predominantly aimed at the sexually promiscuous.

The Millennium Experience.

Both of these might be called 'minority tastes'. Yet each is substantially financed by the taxpayer at large. Why? Why should those who are not interested in the millennium party pay for it? Why should the vast bulk of monogamous, married couples finance research into medical conditions from which they are not going to suffer?

The answer to these questions is 'because there is no other way of paying for them'. *Each of these services has the nature of a public good for the community which uses it, but there is no relevant tax-raising authority to finance those public goods by taxing the relevant community.* In essence, one reason it might be argued that we should all pay for HIV research, even if we are never likely to benefit from it, is that there is really no clear jurisdiction of HIV-vulnerable people who can be taxed directly to pay for the research directly.

We might call these goods 'minority public goods' – they are public goods for the selective club of users, but they are not genuinely public, as most – or at least a large proportion – of the public have no interest in using them.[1] When it comes to these, we have a difficult choice. Either we deny the interest group of users the good which they want. Or we make the community at large pay for things which the community at large has no interest in consuming.

The dilemma is rarely articulated. In most cases of minority public

---

1. It is tempting to draw a phrase from public choice literature for these items, 'club goods'. However, this phrase has a slightly more specific connotation, referring to general public goods that groups of individuals can provide for themselves by clubbing together, and which they can exclude others from enjoying.

goods, the temptation for those who support state spending on them is to argue that there *is* some large, general interest in providing them. People argue that it is important we as a nation recognize the coming of the millennium, or that it is important we make the option of millennium parties available to everybody. Or, they argue that HIV threatens the population at large.

But equally, there is a temptation for those who want a much smaller state to argue that these are private goods and that private individuals should pay for them. The majority are not interested in the millennium party, so the taxpayer should not pay for the millennium party; or that we should make users pay for visiting the millennium party, or indeed the genito-urinary clinic.

Neither side quite seems to capture the problem. The communities most at risk from HIV may actually be willing to pay any costs over and above those they could normally expect to be financed by the NHS. But how can those communities finance that extra spending? There is no gay council or drug-users' council, with the power to levy a special tax. But without a legally imposed tax, each individual at risk has the incentive to let other individuals at risk pay. When it comes to the Millennium Experience, it may not be possible to charge a viable levy at the door, or one reflecting the necessary degree of price discrimination, and thus the event may not be possible without tax-financed support.

For 'minority public goods' that have a geographically well-defined user base, it is clear that local taxation is a solution. London Transport has public good qualities that are far from national. It would not seem unreasonable for Londoners to subsidize it (with national government throwing in a contribution to cover the benefits of the system to non-Londoners). Similarly with provincial theatre, for example. The difficulty is that many 'minority public goods' are not geographically well-defined.

There is no easy solution to the problem. Overall, it is clear that from the point of view of delivering an economy that reflects people's preferences, government *should* use its monopoly power to levy taxes to benefit minorities, however small or specialist their need is. That being said, however, tax finance of minority tastes gives rise to two important problems. For one thing, it encourages the minority to exaggerate their desire for the service; after all, the more they can get the public to subsidize them, the better. *They* have no reason to restrict their request for cash to cover the purely public good element of their taste. They would like more subsidy, regardless of whether it can be justified according to an arcane argument about the minority public good aspects of it. For those keen to celebrate the millennium, a really big and expensive festival would be nice, as a public or private item of consumption. As for the rest of us, we only want to subsidize the Millennium Experience in as far as it is sensible to provide those people with something they would themselves be willing to pay for, but have no means of financing.

The second, and perhaps more worrying, consequence of tax finance is that it removes any incentive for minorities to organize their own provision. Some communities – notably, religious groups – are capable of raising donations, obtaining voluntary labour and purchasing their own public goods (church roofs, for example). Other communities do not seem to be as well defined or as tightly organized. It would be far better if they were, and if they could provide for themselves the actual service they want at no cost to the taxpayer at all. Far be it from the state to come in with its fat chequebook and destroy the civil institutions that could arise spontaneously.

With this rider, it still seems sensible for the state to recognize minority public goods, but to do so judiciously and with caution. It is a policy with a number of capricious distributional effects, but we are all probably members of some minority or other, so we probably lose on some and gain on others.

There are those on the right who argue that we should finance the public good element of the two examples mentioned by voluntary donation. It cannot be stressed enough, however, that we could in theory finance anything by voluntary donation, but there is no reason at all to expect sufficient resources to be forthcoming. We could finance national defence by donation as well. Unfortunately if we attempted to do so, we would not have very much of it. The vast bulk of us would donate, but only a fraction of the £17 pounds a week we currently do. If evil monarchs had not invented taxes to finance their wars, benign governments would have done so anyway.

Redistribution and the Failure of Insurance Markets

So far we have not touched on any arguments that might justify public finance for the greatest areas of public spending: social security and health. Indeed, the last chapter argued against the idea that we necessarily need an NHS in order to help the poor meet their health bills, because we could give them cash and let them buy their own health care. Without jumping ahead into a discussion of how health and social security might be organized and delivered, this section on redistribution *is* the spot to articulate the arguments for spending money in these areas.

The common point about health and most social security (excluding pensions) is that they are there to support people who are in some way enduring bad luck, or at least a bad phase in their life. In this characteristic, health and social security are entirely analogous to insurance and are probably best viewed as a form of state insurance policy. The natural starting place for a discussion of why the state has a role in these areas, then, is to ask why we could not rely on private insurance markets to fulfil the function the state fulfils in these areas. Why will those on the right who wish to replace social security or the NHS with private insurance never get their way?

There are two answers to this question. The first is that no insurance market will ever be able to offer as much insurance to the unlucky as our taste for redistribution requires. The second reason is that insurance markets do not work at all well, and the state has a role to play in offering cover that the market will manifestly not be able to offer. Let us take a look at these arguments in turn.

Insurance Against Bad Luck at Birth

Why is private insurance unable to offer the redistribution merited by the tastes of the population? The answer relates to the types of bad luck that might be worthy of insurance. In particular, there is an important distinction to be made between the bad luck we are born with, and that which strikes us during our life. We may be born stupid, unhealthy, disabled, or even pre-disposed towards unemployment. Those are risks that face us at conception. Equally, there are risks we face here in our earthly life, risks such as a devastating accident, ill health, bad luck at work. Whatever our fundamental traits, we are still subject to all sorts of chance and random events that make us lucky or unlucky within our lives.

The interesting thing is, of course, that if insurance markets were reliable and if we had the right distribution of income, the state would not have to worry about 'within-life' risks, because we would all buy our own insurance for those. What insurance markets will never cover us for, however, are those risks we are born with. By the time you arrive out of your mother's womb, your first realistic opportunity to pay an insurance premium, it is too late to buy insurance for many of the most important catastrophes life will bring. Insurance companies will not insure people for bad luck that has already materialized, any more than they will provide cover for a burglary that has already occurred. Given this, and given that we probably have a taste for some redistribution to those who are born unlucky, the state will always have a redistributive role.

The redistributive role of the state can be summarized thus: it is to act as a kind of pre-conception insurance policy. To execute that role, in principle the state should brand our character at birth; give us each an endowment, or a bill, to reflect any bad luck or good luck we are born with; and then leave us be: insurance markets would sort out all the other good or bad luck that might swing our way during our lifetimes.

Your response to this argument may reasonably take one of a number of forms. You might have a distaste for redistribution, in which case you will simply say that the state should not insure us against misfortune at birth. That is fair enough. There is no argument for or against such a proposition. Most people just disagree with it, and blanch at the idea that, for example, those born severely disabled should be left to fend for themselves.

On the other hand, you might say that you think there should be redistribution to the unfortunate for a far simpler reason than the rather obtuse rationale outlined here: it is the decent thing to help our fellow citizens when they are down. Nevertheless, it is worth reiterating that either our fellow citizen is unlucky in life – in which case, in principle, insurance is probably available for them. Or, our fellow citizen is born unlucky, in which case insurance may not be available; and that is where government may appropriately step in. In as far as the problem with insurance for within-life risks is that the poor will not be able to afford their insurance premiums, then of course that is because they are not born sufficiently lucky to be able to earn enough to finance premiums. One way or other, all problems are either (in principle) insurable or they are there at birth.

That establishes a case for cash hand-outs to those born unlucky: those who are born with income support requirements, or health requirements, greater than the norm. However, how could a state make any kind of practical policy out of a desire to be a pre-conception insurance company? While it is possible to tell very roughly who is a lucky and who is an unlucky baby, it is not possible to do so with sufficient precision to endow the unlucky with a lump-sum, or even an income, that leaves them sorted for life. So a more practical system of redistribution has to be found.

And it is that practical attempt at redistribution that leads us towards the social security and health system that we have. Inevitably, the state learns something about how unlucky or lucky an individual was at birth by observing that person's life. Thus, one way of making the desired redistribution is to make it conditional on life's outcome. That means that the unlucky who get unemployed most often, or who fail to get a job paying enough to support a family, or who fall sick frequently, might expect to draw income from the state. That is a good reason for a broadly redistributive social security system, and it suggests any system of insurance for bad luck at birth will inevitably end up in practice insuring people against bad luck in life, in as far as that tells us about a person's general luck or bad luck at birth.

Now the idea that the state is the only possible authority to insure us against bad luck at birth ironically supports an argument for state intervention that is growing in importance very dramatically at the moment. Advances in genetics are making it easier and easier to identify the luck someone is born with, and hence they are making it harder and harder to insure against all sorts of risks that have been insurable in the past. Fewer and fewer of life's misfortunes are categorizable as within-life risks. More and more are categorizable as bad luck at birth.

As well as the physical traits we are born with, it is possible that we will discover a genetic base for all sorts of dangerous behaviour which involves health or life risks of one kind or another: love of speed, disposition towards addiction, or even longevity (requiring a durable cover). These are risks that will become less and less insurable in private markets. Either the state reacts to these developments by allowing good or bad luck at birth to impose a greater and greater burden upon us; or the state replaces the private insurance markets in those risks that are apparently moving from the 'within-life' to the 'at birth' category.

Insurance Market Failures

There is a second argument for a state role in health and social security that relates to the inadequate functioning of insurance markets. Even for those within-life risks that in principle we could leave people to insure themselves against, the state has a role simply because those private insurance markets do not work very well.

There are several problems with insurance markets. Well recognized is the problem that the keenest customers – the first in the queue for insurance – are the worst risks. And indeed, low-risk individuals might rationally avoid bundling themselves into an insurance policy with a lot of more 'expensive' people. Unfortunately, the insurance company is not as able to rate the riskiness of its customers as the customers themselves, and thus the fact that customers self-select, means they *adversely select*. This is a genuine and serious problem, and can only really be countered by ensuring that people insuring do not self-select. That may require a state role in compelling everybody to insure, or in providing insurance itself.

Another role for the state in a world of private insurance is to provide for people who choose not to cover themselves, but nevertheless need help. When those terrible events that do occur in life befall those who have opted out of the private insurance market, society has a choice: it leaves them to suffer, or to beg, steal or borrow. Or, more likely, it takes the view that something has to be done to prevent people dying in the streets. As long as society does have a taste for preventing death in the streets, then it will have to express that taste by either compelling people to insure themselves, or by offering effective back-up insurance to those who make no provision for themselves against extreme and socially distressing outcomes.

A final, perhaps the most important and least recognized, practical failure of insurance markets is that it is almost impossible to commit an insurance company to provide cover for as long a period as you would want them to. The experience of the people of Montserrat who insured against volcano damage is revealing. Once the Montserrat volcano actually exploded, some insurance companies removed the right of residents to renew their cover, even though the volcano was still upsetting livelihoods. Many would argue that there is little point in signing annual insurance contracts if the average misfortune persists beyond a year, giving the insurance company time to withdraw from its obligations before the costly misfortune has been fully dealt with.

This is a very general problem with all sorts of insurable risks. Someone with private medical insurance who discovers a chronic medical condition may find their policy impossible to renew. In practice, the companies sometimes do renew policies; sometimes they bump up the premium (which really represents a partial withdrawal of insurance), and sometimes they will withdraw cover altogether. To avoid the danger of having a policy withdrawn, the only possible precaution is to sign a very long-term contract with an insurance company – a lifetime insurance policy. That would in effect prevent the insurance company from gathering information about the insured individual and using that information to decide on the cost of premiums.

Yet lifetime insurance policies are far from ideal. Competition between companies does not work as well as when there are year-by-year contests. The ability of the insurance company to change the terms of the policy for quite legitimate reasons unrelated to individual risk is limited by long contracts, and the removal of flexibility for such a long period as would be necessary in a committed contract could be dangerous to the viability of the insurance industry. There is no very easy way out of this dilemma. But the fact that annual contracts persist, and are likely to render large numbers of people for whom chronic problems arise uninsured or uninsurable, emphasizes the need for some back-up state role.

To summarize this discussion, even from the perspective of relatively liberal market economics, we can at least understand why government spending on social security and health is likely to remain important. This is not to say, though, that there is nothing that can be done to reform particularly the social security system, or even that we cannot do so in very radical ways. In Chapter 11 we will take a further look at the subject, and ask whether the state shouldn't simply buy us insurance, rather than provide an insurance policy itself.

How Much Public Spending?

The Efficiency Principle

The principles delineated so far in support of public spending are largely uncalibrated, and rather broad. Some on the right will react by asserting that they open the door to too much spending. So there is one more important principle to add: the principle that governs *how much* we should spend on any particular item. This has been implicit in the discussion so far, but it is the most crucial principle of all.

If there is one thing that makes for a good economy, it is that we, the public, get what we are willing to pay for . . . and that we get no more. This is a principle of devastating simplicity but immense importance, as it is the principle that governs so-called *allocative efficiency*. It ensures the economy is deploying resources in the right way. Whether it's bread or missiles, the rule holds. If we value something more than the amount it costs to make the thing, then the public interest is served by buying it. The benefits of making and selling the item outweigh the costs. So, if we value the security provided to us by a new missile system at more than the cost to a manufacturer of making and servicing that system, then we should buy it.

Now, real life is rather complicated as there are a number of different ways of counting the cost even of a loaf of bread, let alone the cost of a missile system. It is difficult for *one* of us to decide how much we value a loaf of bread, let alone how much we all collectively value a missile system. And there are also important complications relating to who exactly it is who bears the costs and benefits of decisions, or gets the profit connected to any purchase.

But the principle is still key to the allocation of scarce resources. If society values a missile at only £200m, and nevertheless ends up buying it when it actually costs £300m, society has effectively thrown away £100m. That is a waste identical to the waste of *not* buying the missile when it costs only £100m. In either case – buying things that we don't really want, or not buying things we do really want – the missing millions are every bit as wasteful as vandals smashing up £100m's worth of bus shelters. They are so-called 'deadweight' costs – costs with no discernible corresponding benefits. Sensible management of public resources really does matter.

Unfortunately, the vandalism involved in getting these kinds of decisions wrong will not show up in any national statistics, as the public's valuation of different items is largely impossible to measure with the normal accuracy we have come to associate with the Office for National Statistics. Understanding the public's taste for public spending, however, is a vastly underperformed research topic.

Does Public Spending Make us Happy?

There is one final complication worth mentioning. It does not invalidate the efficiency principle, but suggests an important qualification in applying it.

The argument is that public spending gives society more happiness than the equivalent amount of individual spending. Why? The most recent enunciation of the answer has come from Robert Frank, an economist at Cornell University, writing in the *Economic Journal* in November 1997. Much of our individual spending is simply designed to 'keep up with the Joneses'. We are unhappy if they are ahead of us, and we are particularly happy if we are ahead of them. As long as this is true, the social impact of individual spending is more subtle than is generally appreciated. If the Joneses buy a bigger car, it will generate extra happiness for the Joneses, but will detract from the happiness of the Joneses' neighbours. The net extra happiness generated by an individual purchase is thus rather smaller than that which accrues to the buyer. This will tend to be true as long as our happiness derives not from how much we consume privately, but from how much we consume *relative to everyone else*.

If relative consumption matters, private consumption may well be driven to levels higher than anyone would actually want as we all strive to get ahead of everyone else. Of course, we can't all succeed in getting ahead of everyone else, so all that results is generalized misery as we spend too much of our money on pointless ostentatious consumption to keep up. Governments may help us all by imposing a truce, and taking some of our money to devote to items which are collectively consumed, and hence which do not arouse feelings of envy.

Of course, the degree to which private consumption decisions are collective by nature, rather than truly individual, is arguable. In so far as they are collective, they might mostly be expected to corrupt our personal savings decisions. They would not reduce our likelihood of voting for high government spending and taxation, so the relevant practical object of our research into how much government spending there should be is still the public's taste for public spending. That is the subject of Chapter 4.

Additional Reading

Frank, Robert (1997), 'The Frame of Reference as a Public Good', *Economic Journal*, November.

For conventional accounts of the arguments surrounding public goods:
Bator, F. (1958), 'The Anatomy of Market Failure', *Quarterly Journal of Economics*, 72.
Mueller, Dennis C. (1989), *Public Choice II*, Cambridge University Press.
Stiglitz, Joseph E. (1988), *Economics of the Public Sector*, W.W. Norton & Co., New York.

4 The Demand for Public Spending

The tastes of a tax-resistant public

> . . . suggestions included the offer of 'I'd go for 5p extra for everyone'.
> When pressed what that might mean, it became obvious that it did not
> mean raising the standard rate by 5p in the pound, since even that
> concept of taxation was not understood. A penny increase in the
> standard rate is taken to mean, literally, one extra penny paid in tax . . .
>
> Report on the outcome of a public focus group conducted by Opinion
> Leader Research for the Fabian Society (Radice and Pollard, 1993).

A Tax-resistant Public

If the public's tastes should provide the basis for decisions on public
spending, what do we, the population, actually want?

The public thinks that politicians lie about taxes and spending. But
while that may or may not be true, a bigger problem for the country
today is that we, the public, in fact don't tell the truth about tax and
spending ourselves. The politicians would love to know exactly what
we want, but when it comes to the balance between taxes and spending,
reading the country's mind is a tricky business.

Ask us what we want directly and we give pretty clear views: we
want more spending. Table 1 takes a question asked continuously since
1983 in the British Social Attitudes Survey. This is not a freak poll
result, it is a consistent pattern identified in virtually every survey
conducted since the mid-1980s: majority support for tax increases
among the electorate as a whole; and overwhelming opposition to tax
cuts from supporters of any party (twice as many of us think pornography
should be on sale anywhere – as opposed to special adult shops – than
think taxes should be cut).

Table 1: What the Public Says it Wants

percentages

If the government had to choose it should . . .	All voters, 1983	All voters, 1994	Tory supporters, 1994	Labour supporters, 1994	Lib Deb supporters, 1994
. . . reduce taxes and spend *less* on health, education and social benefits	9	4	4	4	2
. . . keep taxes and spending at the *same* level as now	54	33	47	24	30
. . . increase taxes and spend *more* on health, education and social benefits	32	58	46	69	65

Source: *British Social Attitudes: the 12th Report*, 1995.

Table 2: The Public's Spending Priorities

percentages giving first or second priority to each category

	1983	1994
Health	74	72
Education	49	57
Housing	20	20
Help for industry	29	11
Social security	12	12
Police and prisons	8	12

Source: *British Social Attitudes: the 12th Report*, 1995.

Other responses in the survey – in Table 2 – suggest self-interest is an important part of the public's motivation: people apply a high priority to the types of spending they consume, notably health and education. And at the time of the 1992 general election – generally held to have been fought on the issue of tax – polls also suggested that the level of

Table 3: Historical Opinions

percentages

If the government had a choice between reducing
taxes and spending more on the social services,

which should it do?	1963	1966	1969	1970
Tax cuts	52	55	69	65
Social services increase	41	36	21	27

Social services and benefits . . .	Feb 1974	Oct 1974	1979
. . . have gone too far and should be cut back [either 'a bit' or 'a lot']	33	38	49
. . . should stay much as they are	35	32	26
More social services and benefits are needed	32	27	20

Source: Taylor-Gooby (1985).

taxation was not an important issue in determining who we voted for.

Although the form of the poll questions changes somewhat, this appears to reflect a shift from the period before the Conservatives came to power in 1979. Then, there appeared to be majority support for tax cuts – growing through the 1960s and 1970s – at the expense of 'social services' (see Table 3). So it is not inevitable that we, the public, suggest we want more public spending; but recently we have been saying that we do.

But despite this plethora of poll evidence, the 1997 election was fought by two main political parties each promising to be tough on spending, and each attempting to outbid the other in implied promises of lower taxes. While it used to be the case that the parties promised everything – apparently making unaffordable spending pledges to a gullible electorate – that is not so any more. Today in Britain, winning parties tend to boast about how they have costed their spending proposals, how taxes need not rise, how they will be more careful – or at least as careful – as the other parties. Elections are fought in terms in which it is curiously difficult to tell the tax and spending plans of parties apart. The only party to stand out in Britain is the Liberal Democrats (with less than 20 per cent of the vote) who have, in the last two elections, boldly suggested tax increases.

So somewhere something funny has been happening. Either the

politicians are curiously out of line with public opinion – which would be odd as they have good professional reasons for making the right call – or the politicians' own judgements of what the public want are for some reason more accurate than the oft-stated opinions of the public themselves. Before going any further, therefore, we have to understand who is right, the polls or the politicians.

Are the Polls Wrong?

The first, and most popular view, is that the polls lie; that the public say 'yes' to higher taxes, when they mean 'no'. Why might this be? One strain of explanations relates to mechanical features of opinion polls and elections. In the Social Attitudes survey, for example, respondents are asked to prioritize different areas of public spending *before* they are asked whether they want more spending or not. That ordering of questions might focus their minds on the breadth of their shopping list, rather than the burden of extra taxes that spending might entail. We know that these small biases can make a big difference to poll results, particularly where the attitudes being tested are rather vague or weak.

We also know that on most surveys there are a large number of non-respondents. In Social Attitudes, for example, some 6,000 households were selected; over 10 per cent were vacant, derelict or otherwise out of scope, almost a quarter refused to answer, 218 were unable to be contacted and 179 had other reasons for not being included. So in fact interviews were conducted in only 3,469 households, fewer than two-thirds of the original addresses selected. Samples of this size are sufficiently large to overcome the problem of random statistical error – but there is always a problem that the non-respondents may not be random. They may disproportionately be one type of person. The Social Attitudes survey organizers do not juggle with the results to adjust for any non-response bias.

A third possible problem is that subjects might believe it is more socially acceptable to give certain types of answers than others. In polls, the failure to admit a disposition to vote Conservative, apparently lest that should be seen as a sign of selfishness and greed, has evidently caught pollsters out in the past. In the Social Attitudes survey, answers on taxes and spending were solicited early in a face-to-face interview, when shy respondents may not have felt able to admit to their tax-cutting instincts.

But these mechanical explanations appear far more important in hindsight than they did before the discrepancy arose. None really looks like it ought to be important, and our tendency is to believe them only when no other explanation is on hand. The response bias could easily err in favour of there being excessive support for tax cuts in polls, rather than apparently excessive support for spending. The size of pro-tax support among those who admit to supporting the Conservative Party argues against the idea that embarrassment is driving the result. And given the conformity of results among supporters of different parties, it is unlikely that non-respondents would be particularly peculiar on the specific issues of taxes and spending.

Whatever the mechanics, some suggest polls are an inappropriate means of soliciting information at all. One quite plausible explanation of the public opinion paradox is that we, the public, are simply inconsistent in our preferences. Ask us if we want more services, and we say 'yes'. Ask us if we want lower taxes, and we say 'yes'. Of course, if you ask us to make real decisions – at election time – we will. But if you ask us to hypothesize about decisions, we can't: we don't really know what constraints apply, our thoughts are uncalibrated. How can we give precise answers to questions?

Interestingly, those economists who make a career of understanding preferences are well acquainted with the problem. Time after time, the framing of the question makes a big difference to the answer elicited. In one American study, people were asked how much they would pay each week to preserve their clean New Mexico air from the pollutants of a new coal-fired power station. The answer averaged $4.75. When asked how much they would have to be paid to be compensated for a reduction in air quality from a new coal-fired power station – approximately the same question as before – the answer came back as $24.50.[1]

Do the polls reveal any reliable information at all? They probably

---

1. British academics have also faced this problem. The Economic and Social Research Council's *Economic Beliefs and Behaviour* programme, conducted by, among others, Professor Robert Sugden of East Anglia University, is investigating whether inconsistencies are simple errors of understanding, or whether they are deeper.

do: despite the usual problems, the results are too consistent, too enduring, too insensitive to day-to-day political events. The polls offer inconsistent and capricious results where the attitudes being tested are really non-attitudes. That does not appear to be the case on this issue. The public probably mean what they say – they would like their governments to deliver better public services.

Are the Public Willing to Pay?

Instead of belittling polls – an activity which became less popular after the 1997 election in any event – we need to explain the paradox of the polls and politicians' views of public opinion in more subtle ways.

One explanation, often proffered by the right, invites us to question what the poll results actually tell us. Certainly, at face value, the polls suggest that people would like to live in a society where taxes and public spending were higher. *What that does not tell us is whether the public would themselves be willing to pay more tax for better public services.* Yet it is this latter question, 'would *you* pay more tax for better public services?', which is truly the important one in determining what politicians ought to do. It is the sum of individuals' willingness to pay for more services that determines whether spending should rise or fall by the criterion of the efficiency principle, delineated in the last chapter.

Why might the questions generally asked by pollsters reveal more about general political philosophy than about personal willingness to pay more tax? The answer of course is that with progressive taxes, large numbers of people must be inclined to say they want more spending merely because they think someone else will be paying for it. If this is the case, actually *spending* more is a bad idea. All the public are telling you is that they want a more redistributive tax and spending system, preferably one under which they personally pay less. If people only want services when others pay for them, they are *really* saying they want more cash, rather than more services. Whether we actually give them more cash or not is a separate debate, but only an imperfect governmental system would deliver them services rather than cash.

There is some evidence that this interpretation explains the public's

Table 4: A Consensus on Extra Taxation

1994, percentage saying tax level is . . .

	too low	about right	too high
For those on high incomes	56	32	12
For those on medium incomes	8	66	26
For those on low incomes	3	21	76

Source: *British Social Attitudes: the 12th Report*, 1995.

enthusiasm for extra spending in opinion polls. When we are asked whether in principle we would like more spending, we say 'yes'. When we are asked how that should be paid for, we say 'the rich should pay extra tax'. As Table 4 shows, there is no consensus that anyone else should pay more.

And equally revealing on this issue are not polls as such, but more detailed interviews with small groups of people – groups with whom interviewers can interact, converse and draw qualitative assessments, as well as monosyllabic answers. One of the most extensive focus group exercises on the subject in Britain lately was conducted by Opinion Leader Research for the Fabian Society (written up by Stephen Pollard and Giles Radice in 1993). Although repeated over several years and covering a wide range of issues, in 1993 the groups focused on issues of taxes and benefits. Ten groups of C1/C2 social classes were interviewed, all the participants having voted Conservative at the 1992 election. Opinion Leader's report on the outcome of the focus groups documents results similar to those of the large-scale polls, but they add weight to the 'someone else should pay' theory of what these polls tell us:

'When forced to make the choice, most respondents (very reluctantly) claim to prefer tax increases to cuts in public spending (especially if someone else is paying).'

'Health and education are seen as the main priorities.'

'Respondents are reluctant to suggest areas for cuts. Overseas aid is the most common suggestion.'

'Most favour increases [in tax] on the rich (those earning over £40K) . . . a small minority would be willing to pay more themselves.'

Table 5: A Consensus on Extra Spending?

You think more should be spent on health . . .

Would you personally be willing to pay more in taxes so that more money could be spent on health?

     Yes   55%

There is in fact more than one way of doing this – looking at all three options, which option would you prefer?

Spend less on other services	49%
Make some charges to people as they use the services	26%
Pay more in tax	20%

Source: Harris and Seldon (1987).

These and other comments from those conducting the groups suggest the poll results are partly explained by the fact that people primarily want spending increases when they are financed by other people's tax increases.

Work by the Institute of Economic Affairs adds weight to this argument. For example, as we saw from Table 2, by far the most popular spending heading in polls is the health service. But Table 5, based on Institute of Economic Affairs market research from the 1980s (and the polls have not changed significantly since then), highlights how complicated it is to interpret that: of those wanting extra health spending, just over half (55 per cent) were willing to pay more tax for it. That however was less than half the sample: so in a simple referendum on a tax-financed increase in health spending (in which everybody paid some extra tax), on the basis of this poll, the proposition would fall. Even more interesting was the fact that half those wanting more health spending (49 per cent) thought cutting other spending was the best way to find the resources necessary.

But although important, this account does not allow us to dismiss entirely the fact that the public *would* be willing to pay for more public services. If people simply wanted others to pay for more public spending, why would they not vote for a party that promised that? Also, why do the rich support more spending and higher taxes *for themselves*? The polls suggest that literally half the richest third of the population believe that the rich pay too little tax. It is true that the public's willingness to pay for services is lower than their general desire that they should have better services; but there has to be another good reason for the politician's instinctive reticence about raising taxes.

The Disconnection Hypothesis

That other factor is that while the public may want more taxation and spending, they have a deep-seated scepticism about the claim that higher taxes would deliver better public services. One description of this view has come from one of Britain's most eminent analysts of public opinion, Peter Kellner, whose post-mortem of the 1992 election concluded, 'In truth, too many believed that Labour would make such a mess of the economy that taxes would rise but public services would *not* improve. It was not Labour's tax-and-spend values that cost the party votes, but its poor reputation for economic competence.'

We might take this view further, however, and question whether it was not simply Labour's general economic competence that was at issue, but its competence at delivering the services people would like taxes to buy. Or indeed, the competence of the Conservative Party at doing so. If we do not believe either party will deliver good services for our money, then it is not surprising we will vote on other issues, or for the one promising to take the least money from us.

Under this interpretation, what the polls do is invite us to offer our support for an ideal; it is a hypothetical question as to whether we would like more taxation and public spending. The answer in an ideal world might be 'yes'. When it comes to an election, however, we are not voting between different ideal states; we are voting for a particular real government, with all its flaws. We were never asked in the polls to comment on a particular programme of higher taxes and spending, but in elections it is particular programmes on offer, and these may be far less attractive than the ones we can conjure up in our heads, standing in front of a pollster. It is not surprising that the politicians might feel they do not want to dangle tax increases in front of us, even though in an ideal world, tax and spending increases might be popular.

Why might we ideally want more tax-and-spend in principle, but not in practice? This is where the notion of disconnection between the public and public spending is appropriately invoked, that in some way we feel detached from the services that in practice we get. Maybe we feel the delivery of public services themselves is unimpressive: they do not respond to public taste in, say, as effective a way as private, competitively delivered services.

There is some evidence for this proposition. Again, however, we have to turn to opinion polls to find it. Table 6 cites a 1995 poll from MORI, and another one with the same pattern of answers from the British Social Attitudes Survey. Both consist of a list of national institutions and the proportion of respondents rating the effectiveness of each. The first thing to notice is that public institutions can score well. The universities exhibit the lowest dissatisfaction rating in Social Attitudes. The police perform adequately in both, and the BBC performs fine in one, while TV programmes perform astonishingly badly in the other. But the top of both lists is perhaps more interesting, where the core government services fall. The NHS and local government far outperform anyone else in underperformance in one poll. Roads, buses, trains, schools and the NHS top the other.

One might be tempted to conclude that the NHS score was being taken as a referendum on the incumbent government's health service reforms, but for the fact that local government comes right behind, with far fewer associations with the governing party at the time. State schools – of which arguably more of the population have regular direct recent experience – rank just superior to trade unions, civil servants and the press. All are judged far less effective than industry, or even the unpopular banks.

This general result is largely supported by the National Consumer Council's *Consumer Concerns* survey, also conducted by MORI, which in 1995 focused on local government. It found that only 40 per cent of us believe local government is good value for money.

Things may have changed somewhat in the last few years: reforms in the public sector have had some impact, although other polls suggest the public are not in general enamoured of them, and successes have been sporadic rather than comprehensive.

That is one manifestation of disconnection – in the *delivery* of services. There is a second potential disconnection when it comes to the *choice*

Table 6: Well Run or Not?

Percentage believing institution is 'not very well run' or 'not at all well run'		Percentage of those 'impressed with regard to the quality of service' minus those 'disappointed'	
National Health Service	65.8	Roads	−29
Local government	58.2	TV programmes	−28
Press	50.7	Trains	−14
Civil service	49.0	Buses	−12
Trade unions	48.8	State education	−4
State schools	46.0	NHS	−3
Industry	37.6	Banking	−3
BBC	35.7	Water supply	−1
Banks	34.7	Public parks	3
Police	30.0	Police	3
Universities	22.6	Rubbish collection	5
		Electricity supply	6
		Restaurants	9
		Gas supply	9
		Telephone services	11
		Postal service	14
		Private education	16
		Package holidays	17
		Private health care	23

Source: *British Social Attitudes: the 12th Report*, 1995.

Source: MORI, *British Public Opinion*, August 1995.

of services delivered. Even though we may like to buy certain services through higher taxation, we may not believe that is what higher taxation will buy. It is the case of 'many a slip 'twixt cup and lip'. We may vote for a better NHS, but get more missiles and social security.

Disconnection has a certain introspective plausibility about it. You may believe that your child's school would benefit in a worthwhile way if every parent was to give it an extra hundred pounds a year. Asked whether you would like more money spent on your child's school, you may say 'yes'. You may be delighted to pay that hundred pounds. But would you really believe that you would see a benefit to your child's school from a £2-a-week tax increase? The tax revenue may not be devoted to education; if it is, it still may be lost to other schools or other forms of education. And even if it ends up at your own child's school, it will probably come with bureaucratic strings attached, and with some great national ideological baggage. It would be no wonder if you preferred to keep the hundred pounds. Paying it over in tax is very different to paying it over directly.

If we walked out of a store after a big weekly shop with a basket of goods most of which we had not meant to buy, and if we discovered that we had failed to purchase half the items we actually wanted, we would be pretty irritated with ourselves. Indeed, if we found week after week that we were leaving the shop with a trolley heaving with the wrong goods, we might become a little resistant to putting very much in our trolley at all in future. The public's preferences for public services do matter.

Some respond to this perception of disconnection with a view that the authorities ought to explain what they do with our money better. But, to be blunt, there is little point in them telling us what they are doing if telling us will make no difference to what they are doing. The ignorance most of us have about what government does is more than just a communications failure. The policy-makers – politicians and professional public servants – get on with policy-making and the rest of us leave them to it, at least until it comes to an election.

This disconnection bears on the general issue of the standing in which politicians are held. The pervasive distrust of politicians is another manifestation of the fact that we don't wish to hand over larger amounts of our money to them. It is an interesting phenomenon, for example, that even though the American population votes for the President, when a film like *Independence Day* depicts the White House being blown up by alien invaders, American audiences (outside Washington DC) are reported to have cheered gleefully. It would be a mistake to portray that kind of cynicism as a new facet of political life: in individualistic nations, we have always had a tendency to look upon authority with suspicion, even when we fully respect the legitimacy of that authority. But there is a deeper problem when public cynicism is fuelled by a belief that politicians lack common sense, common values, or effective management skills.

In summary, therefore, the disconnection thesis in its various manifestations provides a plausible general account of why the population may be resistant to paying taxes and allowing the government to spend more on public services, even while expressing a general desire for more public services. A large number of people may well support extra spending, and many may well be willing to pay for it, *but only in the ideal world where that extra spending is well directed*. In the far from ideal world where it is directed by central and local government, it is a much less attractive proposition. If people exhibit a schizophrenia on the issue of taxes and spending, it is because many do want more of the items that are currently provided by the public sector – they are just suspicious of their chances of getting good value, quality delivery of the specific items they individually want.

The Public Expectations Gap

In his enchanting description of public disenchantment, *The Moral Basis of Backward Society*, Edward Banfield described civic life in a small southern Italian town in the 1960s. He noticed that progress was stifled in the town, as the political culture was set in a mould of anti-social incentives. The voters assumed the politicians were corrupt, and regularly voted them out of office on that basis. Any self-interested politician knowing this, was induced to exploit his single term of office while he could – thus justifying and perpetuating the public's initial perception. Enterprise was stifled in this situation, and services were poor.

If the analysis of Britain in this chapter is correct, we are not far off a similar situation. Indeed, it is perhaps the problem of the Western world. Nations are locked into a downward cycle of self-reinforcing trends of poor perceptions, underfunded services, poor services and thus poorer perceptions. There is an 'expectations gap' on the part of the public – they are simply not happy with the value for money they get out of government.

Now this diagnosis has an important implication. A *gap* can only be closed by moving one side of the gap closer to the other. If expectations and actual performance are currently some way apart, then the problem of the expectations gap will never be solved by moving both expectations and actual performance in the same direction by the same amount. The gap can only be closed by moving expectations *or* performance. So suggesting governments deal with the problem of public perception by spending more, or by spending less, will achieve little, other than an alteration of the point at which the expectations gap manifests itself.

Thus if governments choose to spend more, public expectations will rise by as much as the extra spending – indeed, probably by more, as the public will hope the extra spending is more efficient than the current spending. As for cuts in spending and corresponding cuts in taxes, if the diagnosis is correct that won't work either: the public will become more dissatisfied with the new level of services and always be one step ahead in demanding tax cuts to reflect the new lower level of services being provided.

The argument so far suggests the fundamental reason for disenchantment is the high degree of disconnection between the public, the public sector and public spending. Reconnecting these together – and closing the expectations gap – can only be achieved by improving the public sector's performance. Under this diagnosis, the gap exists primarily because the public are used to the norms of the private sector and the choices allowed in private spending; we expect the public sector to live up to those norms. Under this diagnosis, the supply–side reform agenda seems the most appropriate – placing an emphasis on improving the delivery of public services.

There are however two alternative schools more inclined to the view that demand-side policies are more appropriate: that governments should spend more or that governments should spend less.

Articulating and trying to promote the idea of spending and taxing *more* is almost exclusively the preserve of the Liberal Democrats and a declining number of left-field political players. Those who support this option implicitly diagnose the problem not as being one of a gap between expectations of performance and actual delivery, but as a gap between the amount of public service people want to buy, and the amount they are being sold. We want more education – we don't like leaky school roofs for example – but we are deprived of that choice. In this account, it is governments that are cynical, the people who are not.

The group of supporters of this option is probably larger than it seems, if one adds in those who think more spending would be desirable in principle, but not realistic given the propensity of the population to vote in ways which encourage governments to limit tax rises. So, those who argue that the health service needs more money, or that those in poverty should be given another fifteen pounds a week (like the Joseph Rowntree Foundation report, *Life on a Low Income*), are people who really believe that value for money is not a problem as much as the amount of money being spent.

But this group has been losing the political argument. It is possible that the political argument has shifted perversely, and will shift back to greater support for public spending. But perhaps the most persuasive evidence that this is not so is that the left itself has given birth to new movements which by and large accept the diagnosis of the expectations gap.[1]

What about the second alternative approach, of trimming the state back? This has become fashionable among more conservative thinkers. But when people suggest that public spending needs to be cut, they can only mean one of two things: that people should have less of the things taxes buy – like health, education or pensions. Or that people should be made to pay for the things taxes buy through means other than taxation. The former seems to be in contravention of public opinion outlined here; the second may have merit, but whether taxation or private finance should be used to pay for things should be determined by whether taxation or private finance is the best means of financing spending. This topic is amazingly often absent from discussion on the right, which is more typically dominated by emotive attacks on the deadening hand of government. Like the diagnosis from the left, the diagnosis from the right fails to capture just what public preferences merit.

1. For example, in a book called *In the Public Interest*, written in 1993 and published by a trade union federation, Brendan Martin supports the view that public services need reforming. In his view, the argument does not so much concern the size of the state, as the correct route to changing it. Mr Martin is a former official of NALGO (the National and Local Government Officers' Association). His book comes with an endorsement from Rodney Bickerstaffe, and is far from offering old prescriptions to the public sector.

Conclusion

This takes us back to the starting point of the chapter. What is right in economic terms is what the public want. Public preferences are complicated, but they are far less volatile than the political cycle; they are determined by the fundamentals of an economy and our make-up as human beings: they are not likely to be tampered with by politicians.

The problem in most Western economies is that there appear to be a lot of things the public want and are willing to pay for, but the only store in town selling them is run by someone the public fundamentally doesn't trust. The loss in welfare to the nation from this problem could be considerable – it could represent an awfully large number of vandalized bus stops.

Additional Reading

Asher, Herbert (1988), *Polling and the Public*, C Q Press, Congressional Quarterly Inc., Washington D C.

Banfield, Edward (1967), *The Moral Basis of Backward Society*, First Free Press, New York.

Besley, Timothy, John Hall and Ian Preston (1996), *Private Health Insurance and the State of the NHS*, Institute for Fiscal Studies, Commentary No. 52, London.

Harris, Ralph and Arthur Seldon (1987), *Welfare Without the State*, Hobart Paperback 26, Institute of Economic Affairs, London.

Kellner, Peter (1996), 'What do the Public Think' in Dan Corry (ed.), *Public Expenditure: Effective Management and Control*, Dryden Press, London.

Kempson, Elaine (1996), *Life on a Low Income*, Joseph Rowntree Foundation, York.

Martin, Brendan (1993), *In the Public Interest: Privatisation and Public Sector Reform*, Zed Books, London, in association with Public Services International, France.

Radice, Giles and Stephen Pollard (1993), *More Southern Discomfort. A year on – taxing and spending*, Fabian Society Pamphlet 560, London.

Taylor-Gooby, Peter (1985), *Public Opinion, Ideology and State Welfare*, Routledge & Kegan Paul, London.

Taylor-Gooby, Peter (1995), 'Comfortable, Marginal and Excluded: Who Should Pay Higher Taxes for a Better Welfare State?' in Jowell, Roger et al. (eds), *British Social Attitudes: the 12th Report*, Social & Community Planning Research, Dartmouth Publishing, Aldershot.

Part Two
Problems

Problems, problems. We have seen that public spending is far removed from the public, and hence the ultimate beneficiaries of public spending do not appear to want to pay for it, even though they would probably like more of the services government is responsible for supplying. We have looked at the way the state has generally chosen to deliver public services to the public – through a monolithic model of public sector supply whose existence was justified on the basis of a number of rather exaggerated benefits.

Before we look at ways in which the traditional public sector is being, and can be, reformed, this section takes a more systematic look at the problems raised by public spending. In particular, it discusses the following arguments:

> That the choice of the public sector as the delivery vehicle for public services had a high cost: it led to a kind of stagnation; in contrast to activity under private governance, where change is imposed more or less automatically, and where incentives for innovation are large.

> That public spending raises special problems in decision-making; the process of deciding on public spending is often governed by irrationality. In the short term it is not very transparent, it is vulnerable to hijack by interest groups and bureaucrats. In the long term, it is hard to retrench from spending commitments even when they patently no longer have any use.

> That when government offers a collectively financed, uniform service, it dampens individual choice, and ends up buying things some people do not really want, or not buying things people do want; and at the same time it distorts all our choices by mixing up a policy of redistributing income with a policy of financing important pieces of spending.

Also, in Chapter 8 we look at the idea that big government spending can crowd out private investment in a country, by lowering the share of profits in an economy.

None of these problems is an argument against public spending per se. All of them augur in favour of a careful policy with regard to public spending: in favour of ensuring that the spending engaged in really reflects true public preferences; in favour of taking up the traditional public sector model on an 'à la carte' basis, rather than on a monolithic basis, and so limiting the 'public' nature of our spending and our economy to the pieces that need to be public.

5 Poor Value for Money?

Efficiency and effectiveness in the public sector

> Imagine a mouse that was subjected to a minuscule selection pressure
> for increased size – say, a one per cent reproductive advantage for
> offspring that were one per cent bigger. Some arithmetic shows that
> the mouse's descendants would evolve to the size of an elephant in a
> few thousand generations, an evolutionary eyeblink.
>
> STEVEN PINKER in *The Language Instinct*.

The Question

You may have heard of cases of apparently wasted public money: for
example, the headquarters of the European Bank for Reconstruction
and Development in London, with its notorious Carrara marble (costing
£750,000). Or, in the US, the case of the Pentagon buying standard
screws, available for 3 cents at any hardware shop, for $91 each.

Stories of public sector waste – which may or may not be true –
normally attract great attention, and the perception that public organizations waste money is widespread. But the abuse of public money is
bound to attract more attention than the abuse of private money: it is,
after all, public. The stories above make good dinner party conversation,
but the EBRD aside, one could hardly argue that British public
buildings in general represent a lavish waste of hard-earned taxpayers'
money. On the contrary, they are typically distinguished only by their
mediocrity. And one could hardly argue that public agents are careless
with our money – in general they are bureaucratically scrupulous to
an excessive degree. (In the Treasury, for example, phone calls are
monitored, and even staff who work beyond the call of duty are asked
to pay for personal calls, say, from London to Birmingham.)

So aside from silly anecdotes about it, can we make general and systematic judgements about the relative effectiveness of the traditional model of the public sector as a means of delivering services effectively? Is the public sector more effective – for any given system of paying for services – than the conventional corporate model of delivery that is so much more common in Western economies? In this chapter we compare the governance of economic activity through the traditional model of the public sector with the governance of activity through the commercial alternative.

In making this comparison, one is *not* simply comparing public versus private ownership. The public sector could be run almost identically to the private sector, were the government minded to commercialize it. So our real focus is not just on the public ownership of assets, but on the whole bundle of characteristics that go with it – the combination of public sector ownership and public service values.

How does public governance do? In fact, we are lucky in being able to import a lot of arguments from a well-rehearsed debate of the 1980s concerning nationalized industries and privatization. At that time, there was much discussion about whether public ownership of industries like telecoms, energy, steel and cars mattered or not. Although our concern is wider than with mere ownership per se, and although yesterday's nationalized industries are different from schools, hospitals and passport offices, they still provide an experiment in changed style of corporate governance. So what message can one draw from that experience?

An Answer from the Nationalized Industries

The Evidence

Privatized utilities may often be despised: they may make big profits; they may pay their chief executives more than they need to; they may have caused social dislocation and hardship in the process of improving their efficiency. But no one seriously believes there is any going back. Few think Britain would be better off if we put BT back into the old GPO and merged it with the new cable operations, with the only customer's choice being which of two plain old handsets to rent.

In general, evidence suggests both efficiency and service have

Table 1: Job-shedding in the Privatized Industries

Utility	Year privatized	Employees at privatization	1996	Percentage change
British Gas	1986	89,000	49,000	−45
British Steel	1988	52,000	44,000	−15
Electricity industry	1990	128,699	92,782 (1994/95)	−27
Water industry	1989	47,807	37,418 (1995)	−22
British Telecom	1984	240,000	130,000	−45
British Airways	1987	40,759	55,296	+35

1. This includes National Power and Power Gen, the National Grid Company, the Scottish electric companies, and the twelve regional electricity retailers.

2. The ten English and Welsh water companies.

Source: various companies themselves and the Centre for Regulated Industries.

improved since privatization. Table 1 catalogues the lay-offs that have occurred in different companies. The table understates the gains in efficiency achieved, because some of the companies included (like British Airways) have expanded their operations since privatization. While job losses are a negative for the economy in the short run – causing unemployment and distress – jobs that were ineffective are a burden on the economy in the long run. It serves little economic or social purpose artificially to prolong the existence of pointless employment, or to maintain a pretence that a job is worth doing when it is not. Keeping people in dead jobs numbs the ability of the economy to nurture live ones.

The experience of the old nationalized sector suggests there was simply a lot of slack in the pre-privatized organizations. On average, about 40 per cent of the staff employed were apparently unnecessary. The evidence of contracted-out services such as refuse collection and street cleaning offers another example of the magnitude of gains that can be achieved by dismantling traditional public governance from a sector. Simon Domberger, a British academic now working in Australia, has made something of a career measuring the costs and quality delivered in cleaning contracts. The headline fact to emerge from his studies is that costs fell by 20 per cent once contracting out started. Is this because quality is lower under such contracts? Not according to his most recent work. There were also concerns over whether the 20 per cent just reflected a cut in the wages paid to employees (in other words, the 20 per cent was not an overall benefit, just a redistribution from staff to customers), but these too appear to have been convincingly dispelled.

But it was not simply efficiency that was enhanced by the more commercialized operations. It was the whole thrust of management decision-making, which manifested itself in a variety of ways unimagined prior to the whole experience.

For example, the nuclear programme of the Central Electricity Generating Board – Britain's old integrated electricity monopoly – was never apparently costed properly until privatization occurred. It then became obvious that it was a white elephant and has been largely scrapped. The CEGB had a value system – and a chief executive – that supported large-scale, cutting-edge experimental projects. Nuclear fitted the bill. That would have been fine but for the fact that there were no adequate accounting or accountability mechanisms to ensure the true costs and benefits of such projects were properly considered. The cost to the nation of this project has been calculated at billions.

Procurement by public organizations was often determined by political rather than commercial criteria. So for example, the acquisition of System X – a digital telephone switching system – by the then Post Office was offered to a British consortium despite the fact that the consortium had yet to develop a digital switching system. The alternative – of buying a Swedish system off the shelf – could have been installed at lower cost and far more speedily, obviating the need to install a whole new vintage of old-style analogue exchanges to hold the system together while a British digital system was invented. The cost of the decision to go with the British system has been estimated at £3.2 billion in 1980 prices, or about £7.2 billion today.[1]

As a state airline, British Airways developed a reputation for being not just inefficient, but also uncaring of customers. Far from there being any 'public service ethos' in which staff placed a duty of customer care

1. Peter Grindley, *System X: The Failure of Procurement*, Centre for Business Strategy Working Paper 29, London Business School, 1987.

above the needs of short-term profits, the airline simply appeared to be run for the benefit of those lucky enough to have a job with it. The tough drive for profits appears to have enhanced a sense of urgency among staff in making the airline attractive to customers. The Spanish practices of the old-style British Airways persist in state-run airlines in other countries like Spain and Italy.

In the private sector, strategic management has been far more evident than it ever was in the public sector. For example, BAA – the owner of Britain's main airports – has seen that one of its most important activities is airport retailing. Having obtained substantial expertise in franchising and managing shopping centres in its airports, the company has attempted to extend its activities towards retail management more generally, opening a mall in a joint venture at Cheshire Oaks near Chester, with others near Paris and in Swindon. British Gas, on the other hand, which had always attempted to run a gas appliance retail business – without any apparent competitive advantage in that sector – has reduced its presence in the sector from about a thousand stores to close to 250. The incentive to maximize shareholder returns in each case has led to strategic, profit-maximizing decisions that have been to the general benefit of society.

The fact that private companies can be taken over has led to a vibrant market in utility companies. This has engendered two important developments. First is the impact of foreign management and ownership, which ensures that advanced practices from elsewhere in the world are more likely than before to drift into the UK. There is little incentive for foreign owners to install working practices and management styles that are inferior to those in operation already. Thus, at worst, foreign involvement suggests things will carry on as before; at best, it can support the dissemination of new and better practices. This is an important benefit if you believe the quality of management in the UK has been poor. But secondly, the takeover market has also generated the emergence of the mixed utility – companies like United Utilities which sells water and electricity in the North-west. It should be able to spread overheads and thus lower costs over the two – previously separate – businesses. It was a market-led development, rather than a government-initiated development, and because the market has driven the process in a slow, piecemeal fashion, it can be seen as a giant experiment, in which shareholders have borne the risks.

Companies in the old public sector were subject to the financial constraints of the Treasury. The mindset of the Treasury – particularly in the hands of a Tory government – is rather conservative and financially cautious. That may well be appropriate for a body that exists to control public spending. It is not appropriate for organizations that need to be nimble, flexible and imaginative. Many public sector organizations were effectively underinvested and starved of capital. Often, their needs were subverted to the Treasury's desires for macroeconomic management. Investment was held back even when there was a convincing return to be made on new capital. (Often, prices were held at inappropriate levels for other purposes.) In the private sector, investment has been selected on the usual private criteria. In the long run, that is a far better route to efficiency. In short, public sector management in practice was far more short term in its thinking than the private capital markets.

You might think that in privatized companies the staff have been maltreated. Yet in fact, even though private managers have tended to be far less tolerant of poor workplace practices, there are a number of cases where the new management have instilled a greater sense of spirit and motivation in their staff. One Labour minister who visited the private Tower Colliery, for example, was surprised at the change at what had been an uncommercial operation in the public sector, which had become a more effective operator in the private sector but with employees motivated to a degree rarely known in the latter days of the old British Coal. Similarly, National Freight has had better-motivated and harder-working staff since it was released from government control. In 1982, 84 per cent of NFC equity was held by staff, pensioners and their families. That appears to have aligned the perceived interests of employees, shareholders and customers. But much the same has occurred in other privatized cases, where the staff stake has been smaller. (Even in NFC, the staff stake has fallen as the value of the company has risen.)

This may all sound like a gushing tribute to Margaret Thatcher, but she was no closer to predicting the gains from privatization – or indeed articulating the reasons for privatization – than anyone else. The only question to answer – and it is a serious question – is why there has apparently been so much room for doubt and argument about it. Why did it never seem as clear-cut at the time? Why have academics been half-hearted about it all?

A Short History of the Debate

In general, the academic evidence on public sector performance did appear to be far less clear-cut than the account given here. It all seemed mightily complicated. For example, prior to the wave of privatizations in Britain and elsewhere, various studies provided an ambiguous tale. A study by D.W. Caves and L.R. Christensen of the two Canadian Railroads operators – both in a competitive environment – suggested the public one matched the private one. On the other hand, equivalent British studies made the public-owned part look *un*favourable: Richard Pryke took cross-Channel ferries, airlines and gas and electricity retailing and found vastly superior private performance. But then, in a monopoly industry – electricity supply – a study by Robert Millward of American electricity supply found lower costs pertaining to *public* operators.

Even though there was some evidence in favour of private delivery regardless of competition (Dennis Mueller's *Public Choice II* book cites no fewer than forty-nine studies comparing the two[1] – all prior to 1981 and not one from the United Kingdom – and these tended to support the idea that the private sector was more efficient), there was always just enough ambiguity therein to justify attempts to derive more complicated findings. And that was what economists in Britain tried to do.

So early in the privatization process – somewhere between British Telecom and British Gas – an academic consensus emerged around a simple message on where economic performance could be expected to be effective, and where it could be expected to be ineffective. The consensus asserted that the existence of competition in an industry mattered, and had a large effect on performance; and that ownership of a firm, whether it be public or private, mattered less.

Those at the helm – notably John Kay and colleagues at the Institute for Fiscal Studies – drew additional conclusions: that private ownership was preferable to public ownership *for firms in competitive industries*, but that transferring monopoly firms from the public to the private sector

1. Dennis Mueller, *Public Choice II*, pp. 262–5, Cambridge University Press, 1989.

was probably marginally damaging to the interests of the economy. Indeed, promoting the sale of shares in a company often conflicted with the demands of promoting competition, which typically lowered the value of the company being sold.

As UK privatization experiences accumulated, generally with large accompanying efficiency improvements, the picture became more confused, not less. Were the general changes of the 1980s accounting for the gains, or not? It was a decade of huge productivity growth throughout the industrial UK economy. As the power of organized labour to inhibit productivity growth was removed, large reorganization gains were possible everywhere. The privatized firms had anyway made very large productivity gains *while still in the public sector*. It also became clear that public sector organizations which were not privatized, nor billed for privatization, like the BBC and the Post Office, were able to make large productivity gains.

Anyway, as privatization proceeded, anecdotal evidence to support public provision emerged. For example, in the management of security and prisons, the private operators Group 4 became a national joke when a disturbingly large number of prisoners in their charge escaped. Then, in the cases of big infrastructure projects where the public sector had a lamentable record of cost overruns and delivery problems, the private equivalents – notably Canary Wharf and Eurotunnel – demonstrated the same. These stories all gave some plausibility to the impression that a verdict on privatization was a kind of 'pick your anecdote', and that either side could make a case. Academic studies flourished, as did academic ambivalence.

But as time has passed, the gains of privatization have become inescapable. Efficiencies continued to be discovered year after year, and more and more subtle advantages became apparent. At the same time, the criticisms of privatization became more and more trivial. Today, it should not be surprising that even the academic mainstream admits that the success of privatization has exceeded expectation – competition or no competition. For example, the most comprehensive recent UK volume of essays on privatization, *Privatization and Economic Performance* edited by John Kay and others, asserts:

Even where competition has been absent, there have been gains to privatization. Contrary to what was originally anticipated, privatized utilities have displayed significant improvements in efficiency even where there has been little or no competition. The incentive effects of share prices have been an important spur to efficiency.

Although the authors are a bit churlish in their admission, bundling it up with legitimate criticisms of the regulatory system and arguing the obvious point that privatization could have been handled better, this paragraph is actually an admission that in one of the truly great microeconomic debates of recent times, economists came up with the wrong answer, and politicians came up with the right one. Privatization, even in cases where no competition was occurring, was the right thing to have done.

Why did economists get it wrong? There was one point that the academic debate might have missed. Many factors improving the performance of companies were difficult to incorporate into controlled tests. Comparisons tend to look at the performance of operators *in doing what they are doing*. It is much harder for them to assess whether they could more appropriately be doing completely different things. Yet the anecdotal evidence suggests it is this which provides one of the great advantages of private operations.

This may be important. For example, when express coaches were deregulated, private operators – like Trathens of south-west England – were the first to introduce luxury vehicles with toilets and hostesses on board. Prior to that, coach had been an even more homogenous and uncomfortable means of travel than it is today. If introducing luxury is a substantial benefit in the industry, it is one which can only be measured after it has occurred. If the dominance of a public operator prevented it happening, then it would not have been measured as a weakness of the public operator that it had not occurred; no study can value the cost of a non-existent phenomenon. Or imagine that a private firm *did* innovate in that kind of way and the public firm copied the innovation: a naive comparative study will simply find that the two operators are running similar services. This would be despite the fact that the innovation represented an advantage of a competitive market.

In short, academic study should probably have focused less on comparing the performance of public and private operators, and more on the comparative performance of whole sectors predominantly ruled either by public sector monopolies, or by privately competing firms.

Privatization versus Commercialization

But this is not the end of the story. There was another crucial reason why the academic debate came up with what looks to have been the wrong answer. The economists who were sceptical of the benefits of the privatization programme focused their doubts on ownership *per se*, and they asked whether it was ownership that mattered very much. They were interested in the effect of being in the public sector alone, once you have removed all the baggage that goes with it. Their view that ownership – once all the relevant baggage has been dispensed with – does not matter much remains quite possibly correct. Maybe if you remove the whole value structure, the lack of competition, the public service ethic, and the capital structure, you can run an efficient public sector organization.

But one has to ask, who cares? If public organizations didn't have to carry the baggage of public ownership, then they would not usually be publicly owned. The publicly owned organizations carrying relatively little public service baggage – for example, BP – were privatized without controversy, and have attracted nothing like as much academic attention as the big cases where the baggage was key.

So does ownership matter? Yes and no. 'No' in the sense that when all other things are equal – like the degree of industry competition, the capital and management structure of the company – ownership turns out to be unimportant. But the answer is 'yes' in the sense that public ownership tends to stop other things being equal. Probably in retrospect we can settle the argument once and for all by arguing that the great benefit of privatization was not in changing ownership, but in fostering the application of more commercial pressures in the companies involved.

This is all of undoubted importance in any argument about whether the conclusions we have drawn about privatized energy and transport providers could extend to health and education. The question of whether reform of the traditional public sector involves privatization itself or not is probably secondary to the question of whether any kind of commercialization is desirable.

Explaining the Failures of the Traditional Public Sector

There is a remaining question that has not been so readily settled. That is *why* the application of styles of management common in the private sector have tended to deliver more efficient services than those common in the public sector. That is an issue on which there is plenty of work still to be done, but on which some speculation is possible.

It is not easy to explain the weaknesses of the old public sector for one simple reason: that organizations consist of individuals, and that the kinds of individual behaviour that you see in large organizations appear much the same in public or private. Sure, it is believable that a small proprietor who owns his own firm, whose staff all know each other by name and who keep an informal eye on each other, could run a more motivated and driven organization than a civil-service-type bureaucracy. But once you are in the domain of large organizations, does an individual worker or manager in British Aerospace care whether the company's shareholders are in the Department of Trade and Industry or in the City? Or whether the organization lives by the principles of public services, or by the goal of shareholder-value maximization? At a very down-to-earth level, it just seems impossible that a change in corporate structure could make that much difference to corporate performance.

In fact, there is an overwhelming reason to think that the traditional public sector has failed compared to its commercial counterparts. All investment and capacity is allocated by administrators, rather than by decentralized markets responding to observations about which services customers choose. We have various reasons to expect that sectors subject to capital market disciplines would tend to progress far quicker than the traditional public sector. In the world of decentralized capital markets, there is a potential for reward for initiative, effort or innovation, thus giving an incentive to people (or perhaps companies) who are motivated by such rewards to supply initiative, effort or innovation. In the world of decentralized capital markets, the performance of an operator today feeds back into its market presence tomorrow. Or, to put it more simply, the good guys tend to grow, and the bad guys tend to shrink.

These processes of natural selection are built upon the broader raft of capitalist ideas abandoned in the traditional public sector: competition is the most obvious, with consumers choosing between different suppliers and hence affecting their profit levels. Profit itself is another, with the existence of returns on capital at least sometimes at levels higher than the bare minimum necessary to finance investment. Clear objectives set in terms of profits feed a profit-hungry capital market determining the capacity of each market player. And the potential for new market entry to be relatively unimpeded helps as well. These mechanisms are lubricated by corporate exchanges, takeovers and bankruptcies, which tend to accelerate and ease change. Whereas change under private governance is decentralized and automatic, under public governance there often is no change, and where it does occur it is politicized and centralized.

The very fact that it is an ability to adapt and progress which one gets from private-sector-type governance tells us not to expect immediate miracles from it – the long-term effects of private governance vastly exceed the short-term ones. In a one-off project, like organizing an Olympic games, you have little reason for thinking that private companies will do much better than municipal appointees. But over time, and putting it at its strongest, the general problem with the traditional public sector appears to have been a kind of stagnation. That stagnation does not imply that every organization in the public sector is bad – some effective organizations can stagnate around a high standard. And there are bound to be poor private sector organizations – at any one time, there will be a good number. *The advantage of the private capital market is, however, that they will not stick around for ever.* Good practice is more likely to develop under private governance, and best practice is more likely to spread under private governance.

Let us look at the core mechanisms of change in the world of private-sector-type governance in more detail.

Private Entrepreneurship

The first mechanism derives from the fact that entrepreneurship – simply used here as a general word for initiative, organizational effort and innovation – can be rewarded. This is particularly obvious in the case of individual citizens who start their own enterprises. Someone who spots a good market opportunity and succeeds in building a company to serve it is far more likely to make big money than someone who tries to earn their way to riches. There is a good reason for this: if the entrepreneur's judgement is good, the company will be profitable; if the company is profitable, it can be sold. But when a company is sold, it fetches a price close to the value today of all its future profits. It is the lifetime value of the company that the entrepreneur gets, not the value of profits for the duration of his involvement. That means entrepreneurs really can capture a large portion of the value of their ideas, even if they are not around to run the company for the duration of the exploitation of the idea.

This is not an entirely fanciful picture of the workings of capitalism. Peter Wood, the businessman who founded Direct Line Insurance in 1984, personally initiated a change in the insurance market from broker-based transactions towards telephone-based transactions. Other companies soon followed. The shift had consequent effects on costs in the whole industry worth billions of pounds. Mr Wood himself appropriated millions. He operated the venture with the Royal Bank of Scotland, and enjoyed healthy performance-related bonuses. In November 1993, the Royal Bank bought him out of his contract for £20m. He had already made more than an additional £20m in bonus for the fifteen months to January 1994. That remuneration still probably represents a small proportion of his contribution to the industry, but doubtless it was adequate to the purpose. It is a material question whether we could imagine any such revolution occurring in the public sector. Mr Wood probably did not need to make as much as he did to entice him into entrepreneurship; but if he worked for a large salary – with or without a bonus – he is unlikely to have striven as far as he did, or risked his career or personal assets. Letting him – and others like him – win a very big jackpot if they are very lucky with their entrepreneurial venture is as important in promoting entrepreneurs as allowing mega-prizes is important in selling lottery tickets.

There were three different components to the entrepreneurship mechanism in this description: the potential for the sale of companies in their corporate form; private equity stakes in firms; and of course profits. It is possible that even without these, the glory and self-promotion that accrue from translating good ideas into practice might act as a spur to change. But in the public sector, there is an absence of any significant incentives of any kind for entrepreneurship.

In practice, however, the case of the individual entrepreneur in the profit-making private sector is a rather special one. Had Mr Wood worked in the back office of Royal Insurance, would Direct Line ever have materialized? This is a much harder question to answer. It is unlikely that junior employees have much more chance of influencing policy in a large corporation than they do in a large public bureaucracy. In neither situation is it impossible, but in neither is it easy – and the incentives will probably not be very different in the two cases.

But what about the ideas and initiatives of senior employees in large companies, where personal equity stakes are modest? Is there any reason to think that their ideas may translate into action faster or more effectively in the private sector than in the public? The answer is probably yes, although one should not overstate the case. It is not that in the brains of private sector managers neurons spark more frequently or more quickly than in their public sector counterparts. Instead, even in big organizations, private managers have more incentives to apply them-selves towards developing ideas, and more resources to exploit those ideas, than in public ones.

Those incentives derive from the market in corporate control – the takeover market in which companies are bought and sold, and the managers changed with the owners. It is a market replete with problems and faults, yet the constraints and opportunities upon managers within that market do appear to extract a good degree of corporate vision. At the same time, finance for companies is more flexibly available than it is for government departments. A good idea can be financed by bank loans, bonds or rights issues. None has to await the end of the annual budgeting period, or be fought over in a hierarchy of committees. Cash is not rationed other than by the potential profitability of the venture. That has not generally been so in centralized public sectors.

Corporate Turnover

A second mechanism for change within sectors dominated by private companies is the existence of a feedback between performance and future market presence. In a competitive industry, it is pretty obvious that the good can expand and the bad can contract as a result of consumers voting with their purses for the suppliers they favour. This induces good performance by concentrating the minds of producers on delivering a service consumers want. But were there no incentive effects at all, just as long as there are good producers and bad producers – perhaps even randomly scattered – the feedback mechanism is important. The simple mechanics of changing control can have spectacular effects over a long time period.

Take some illustrative arithmetic to demonstrate the point. Every year, in each sector of the economy, some old operators close down and go bankrupt, some new operators open up, and some existing operators expand or contract. This is natural corporate turnover and it is this which allows change to occur. Imagine – modestly – that about 5 per cent of the capacity of an industry turns over in this way annually. And also suppose that the profit-hungry capital market has to finance that new capacity or arrange the new management of old capacity; suppose too that the capital market offers finance to the best operators in a sector, rather than to the average operators; and finally, for illustration only, suppose that the best operators are 10 per cent better than the average. They produce the same output at 10 per cent lower cost, or they produce outputs which are 10 per cent more valuable at the same cost.

That would mean that the reallocation of capacity from the average suppliers towards the best suppliers would yield benefits of 10 per cent in 5 per cent of the industry. That is a purely mechanical switch from the mediocre to the superior, and on its own in this illustrative case it would be achieving gains in the industry worth half of 1 per cent of the total turnover each year.

That may not sound like very much, but it cumulates to a very great deal. Over the course of two full parliaments, improvement like that would amount to a gain in value equivalent to a little more than 5 per cent. Such a gain would, for example, be equivalent to getting one or two billion pounds on the current education budget every decade. It may not be as large as governments would like, but if we had enjoyed that kind of gain from such an approach pursued since 1960, it would be equivalent to extra spending on education of about £5bn or so. Certainly more than any prospective budget increase today could remotely hope to provide.

Now these illustrative calculations are probably extremely conservative. It is worth looking at each of the steps in the argument more carefully.

First, consider corporate turnover: there is plenty of turnover in most private markets each year. As a start, consider the percentage of active, registered private companies that enter insolvency each year. As a fair approximation, it is reasonable to think of the private sector attrition rate being a little under 2 per cent annually. What would that mean if it applied to, say, schools? It would mean some 500 going under, or being subject to a complete management overhaul each year. Contrast that with what has actually happened in the schools sector, where special attention under this government and the last has been given to the problem of failing schools. By early 1996, the cumulative number of schools identified as failing was 120. Three had been closed, with proposals to close 'a number of other schools'. Management had been changed at one.

But capacity also gets allocated as a result of market growth: on average the economy grows at about 2 per cent a year, and new capacity has to follow that growth. And each year some old capacity wears out and some new capacity has to replace it. A conservative depreciation rate would be 5 per cent. On top of that, some capacity merely changes hands as a result of takeovers or mergers. Corporate turnover of 5 per cent would be a low estimate therefore. The more turnover there is, the more opportunity for a refreshment of the standards and styles of delivery.

The second component of the argument was that corporate turnover can only be important if the standards of suppliers tend to differ. If everybody is the same, then turning companies over achieves nothing. But the 10 per cent figure used in the illustrative calculation is a modest estimate of the variation between the value of different outputs from different suppliers. The difference between Sainsbury and Tesco in sales per square foot is 22 per cent (in favour of Sainsbury); in net operating margin it has been 40 per cent.[1] There are many factors behind these differences, but they do illustrate the fact that company performance can vary very substantially.

Finally, to accept that industry standards are inexorably driven upwards from the gusty winds of corporate turnover, we have to believe that private markets allocate capacity efficiently – to the better suppliers rather than the worse. Will profit-hungry capital markets, decentralized as they are and uncoordinated, finance and arrange for good shops, good factories and good service-providers to expand faster or slower than the bad? Without dwelling on this argument here, it is probably uncontroversial that the private capital market will finance the capacity which on average is expected to be most profitable. So a crucial step in the argument relates to the transmission between profits and public interest. If you take the view that profits reflect success in general, and correlate with good service, then you can take the view that the best operators are the winning operators in the private capital market. If you take the view that in a competitive struggle for capital, the most profitable operators are not likely to be the best from a wider perspective, then the argument that corporate turnover is a force for improvement has yet to be established.

We are not concerned here with the practicality of imposing the winds of market change on schools and hospitals, that is the concern of Chapters 9 and 10. The point of this discussion is to show that, whether or not it is *possible* to let schools rise and fall like supermarkets, the fact that they do not inevitably means that an important force for change is deactivated. If no alternatives can be found, then one should not be surprised if the service given by schools appears mediocre.

These back-of-the-envelope musings are merely suggestive. But to illustrate the fact that in the private sector turnover is high, one might reflect on the fact that between 1984, when the FTSE 100 share index was created, and 1996, no fewer than 45 companies left it.

And remember the process of change referred to is simply mechanical – changes that you get from replacing mediocre performers with more

1. These figures relate to 1994–5, and were kindly provided by Verdict Research, London.

effective ones. In the illustrative calculation, no one had to work harder or longer to generate the benefits: they derive from simply putting people or organizations into the right jobs. Of course, the source of any variation does not matter: whether the good are good because they are lucky or skilful, and the bad are bad because they are unlucky or wilful is of no relevance at all.

In general, though, many of the changes that derive from this kind of progression do not occur smoothly or continuously: instead, progress probably jumps and stalls its way forward. The introduction of direct insurance and banking services has transformed the financial services sector, but the changes appeared to be almost non-existent for decades, then revolutionary for a few years. That does not undermine the argument. Indeed, it is possible to assert that the capitalist economy is the most effective at stirring up the storms which cause such change.

The Overall Impact

This account of why the traditional public sector may progress more slowly than a commercial operation open to the private capital market was perhaps best described by Joseph Schumpeter, an Austrian who failed as a politician and a businessman, but who settled into an idiosyncratic academic life at Harvard University. His book *Capitalism, Socialism and Democracy* was first published in 1942, and much of its substance was concerned with the nature of democracy, the durability of capitalism and the potential for a socialist alternative. For economics today, though, his sharpest relevant insight concerned the nature of competition. He was very critical of economists who viewed competition as a sort of price-cutting game between almost identical suppliers; he felt competition was closer to a process of 'creative destruction':

> 'The problem that is usually being visualized is how capitalism administers existing structures, whereas the relevant problem is how it creates or destroys them.'

> 'Economists are at long last emerging from the stage in which price competition was all they saw. As soon as quality competition and sales effort are admitted into the sacred precincts of theory, the price variable is ousted from its dominant position. However it is still competition within a rigid pattern

of invariant conditions, methods of production and forms of industrial organization in particular that practically monopolizes attention. But in capitalist reality, as distinguished from its textbook picture, it is not that kind of competition which counts but the competition from the new commodity, the new technology, the new source of supply, the new type of organization.'

'In the case of the retail trade the competition that matters arises not from additional shops of the same type, but from the department store, the chain store, the mail-order house and the supermarket . . . Now a theoretical construction which neglects this essential element of the case neglects all that is most typically capitalist about it; even if correct in logic as well as in fact, it is like *Hamlet* without the Danish Prince.'

In the discussion here, it is entrepreneurship and creative destruction that are cited as the advantages of private governance. It is not the competition between Tesco's and Sainsbury's that occasionally drives the price of baked beans down to 3p; it is the competition between Tesco's and Sainsbury's for new ideas, new product lines, store locations and choices, and above all, capital to invest in new capacity. It is the competition between both Tesco's and Sainsbury's, and home delivery services. And most of all, it is competition for capital as well as competition for customers.

Change in the Public Sector

So far, the discussion has focused on the potentially favourable impact of change in the private sector. But are there not incentives for improvements in the public sector? Do not the politicians and civil servants want the best to flourish and the worst to shrink? Are they averse to good ideas? Are they less able to judge good and bad providers than young analysts in the City offices of investment banks?

In practice, the individuals in traditional public organizations are surely not that different to their private counterparts, but it is possible to argue that they operate under the burden of significantly more restrictive structures.

After all, there is the lack of any substantial reward for entrepreneurship. In the absence of profits (sometimes at 'jackpot' levels), one of the most important mechanisms of improvement has no incentive to operate. The other potential incentive, personal promotion and advancement, is also far harder to achieve in the large, formal management structures that necessarily characterize traditional public organizations.

Entrepreneurs in the public sector also face a one-shot game in attempting to promote their ideas. In a public organization, there is a chain of command that decides upon a policy. A suggestion made by an employee may be considered up the chain of command, with some chance of success or failure. But it only faces that one shot. Once the chain of command has rejected the idea of adopting a policy or resourcing a new activity, that is it. There is no second go, no appeal. Contrast that with the decentralized private capital market, and you can see that if one potential sponsor rejects an idea, there are more opportunities to see others. Only one needs to be persuaded of the merits of an idea for it to come to the market.

There is a related problem with regard to resources. In a decentralized capital market, any particular entrepreneurial idea – a scheme for a new shop for example – is not competing for capital against any other particular shop or any other particular idea. Each project application stands or falls on its own merits. The bank manager, the City institutions, the venture funds, all judge it against the prevailing market standard for marginal projects. It is a highly depersonalized contest. That is not so in the public sector. Formal budgeting requires funds to be allocated to departments in advance. That means a new idea for money in one department requires another idea to have less money. It is not easy in the context of government spending to match each project up against the most marginal project in government across all departments. Budgeting does not work as well as a decentralized banking and financial system that sets hurdle rates which projects have to beat, rather than rationing capital out in a number of confined contests.

Then a third problem is the existence of monopoly across large sections of public services. When politicians or civil servants make a decision that Lambeth needs a new school, there has really been only one provider to select to organize it: Lambeth Education Authority. In taking the decision to employ Lambeth, irrespective of its record, a lot of the potential for introducing alternative management styles has been thrown away.

Of course, there is still a residual process of change and improvement. Lambeth will still select the founding governors and managers for a new school, and thus some kind of selection process still occurs. Moreover, Lambeth Council faces election by the voters of Lambeth, so the authority has every incentive to set up the best new school it can. But the driver of that change – the political process – just doesn't seem as powerful as a more liberal competitive environment.

And that is the fourth and most overwhelming problem: the weakness of political incentives when it comes to making tough decisions about who should expand and contract in the public sector. Even with huge political effort expended in a desire to close or reform failing schools, we are unlikely to come close to the number of failures typical of a similarly sized sector of the economy governed by the private capital market.

It could be that under public governance change does occur, but it occurs under different guises. We do not observe schools going bankrupt or being taken over, for example; instead, we observe headmasters being sacked. This would be a fair argument but for the fact that change in this form is more common – and more brutal – in the private sector. Moreover, the kind of change that is often most conducive to progress is the kind that thoroughly overhauls organizations, with whole new cultures introduced and working practices imposed. It is unlikely that the sorts of change in management we observe in the public sector – or at least that we have observed in the past – would be nearly as refreshing as the changes we witness in the private sector.

A plausible reason for suggesting the political process is weak as a spur to change is perhaps best captured by the comment of a former Chancellor of the Exchequer who spoke approvingly of the policy of letting failing institutions go to the wall, saying 'I think we would have let Cardiff University go, but it's in Wales so we couldn't.' In short, elected politicians face odd incentives and a short time horizon. In particular, they will rarely be around in twenty-five years to take their reward from tough decisions made today that improve the quality of schools or hospitals.

In addition, on any particular issue politicians have some incentive to identify with the narrow group to whom that issue really matters – the group which is most affected is most likely to let the issue determine its vote. The bulk of the population, only marginally affected by an issue, will probably take too little interest in it to allow a sensible decision on it to affect their support one way or the other. For many services, it is the people who provide them who turn out to be the narrow interest group attracting political attention. As a result, it is not surprising that producers – management and labour – rather than the much larger number of their clients, occupy a disproportionately large space in political decision-making.

The idea that politicians come to identify their own interests, society's interests, and the interests of the public sector all as one is not new. It is one special form of what is known in the literature on regulation as 'regulatory capture'. The result is that objective decision-making is often lacking. If capture is a problem, the solution is for there to be a very clear separation of roles between producers and purchasers. That separation is exactly what a decentralized, anonymous capital market produces, and it is the objectivity fostered by the capital market in its assessment of different suppliers that gives it its effectiveness.

Conclusion

The presentation here may sound one-sided. If you have difficulty in accepting the idea that a constant process of improvement is the painful but desirable feature of market-driven economies, consider the differences between East and West Germany after the war, a forty-year experiment on the impact of corporate change. Bankruptcy and the related mechanisms of change were absent from the East German economy. But this was not because East German companies were so strong they had achieved high rates of survivability; in fact they were merely stagnating. East Germany was – being generous – about 40 per cent as productive as the West at the end of the experiment, a difference that averages out at a growth performance in the West about 2 to 2½ per cent a year better than in the East. Some of the difference can be explained by the different treatment the two sides endured at the hands of their war-time conquerors, but not much. Nor was it short-term errors in policy that hurt East Germany: it did not suffer a catastrophe on day one, from which it never recovered. No, East Germany's problems accumulated during its existence because it was devoid of any mechanism for generating improvement.

But the strength of this whole account of why private governance tends to achieve better results than public is its modesty. It does not purport to show that institutions magically transform themselves by operating privately; nor does it say that by taking a public organization and making it private you will suddenly improve it. It does not assert that private companies cannot fail, or that there will not be Eurotunnels and EuroDisneys in the private sector, or in the public sector.

It merely says that as change occurs in a firm, industry or market, private governance will tend to steer that change more speedily and in the right direction. The experience with privatization in the UK offers some evidence for this, despite being very young in terms of the time scale on which industrial change occurs. The politicization of decisions (like those on procurement), the stagnation of decision-making, and the dominant role of those who worked in the industry as opposed to the wider interest, all served to hold back the nationalized sector.

But the message here is not one that says everything must be private; it simply says that some way of emulating the mechanisms of change in the private sector needs to be found. The requirements of an adaptable public sector − or at least one set of requirements − are outlined in Chapter 10.

Additional Reading

Bishop, M., John Kay and Colin Mayer (1994), *Privatization and Economic Performance*, Oxford University Press.

Caves, D.W. and L.R. Christensen (1980), 'The Relative Efficiency of Public and Private Firms in a Competitive Environment: The Case of Canadian Railroads', *Journal of Political Economy* 88, 958−76.

Domberger, S., C. Hall and E.A.L. Li (1995), 'The Determinants of Price and Quality in Competitively Tendered Contracts', *Economic Journal*, Vol. 105, No. 433, November.

Kay, J.A. and David Thompson (1986), 'Privatization: A Policy in Search of a Rationale', *Economic Journal*, March.

Kerr, Allan and Mike Radford (1995), 'CCT Challenged', *New Economy*, spring. Institute for Public Policy Research, London.

Millward, Robert (1982), 'The Comparative Performance of Public and Private Ownership' in Lord Roll (ed.), *The Mixed Economy*, Macmillan, London; Holmes and Meier, New York.

National Economic Research Associates (1997), *The Performance of Privatised Industries: A Report* by NERA for the *Centre for Policy Studies*, CPS, London.

Pryke, Richard (1982), 'The Comparative Performance of Public and Private Enterprise', *Fiscal Studies*, Vol. 3, No. 2.

Schumpeter, Joseph (1943), *Capitalism, Socialism and Democracy* (reprinted 1992), Routledge, London.

Szymanski, Stefan and Sean Wilkins (1993), 'Cheap Rubbish? Competitive tendering and contracting out in refuse collection, 1981–1988', *Fiscal Studies*, Vol. 14, No. 3.

Szymanski, Stefan (1994), 'CCT: A Clean Solution', *New Economy*, summer. Institute for Public Policy Research, London.

6 Irrational Spending Decisions?

Public spending and public choice

CHANNEL 4

7.50 Comment Sarah Zebaida
runs a fruit juice bar and says
the government should provide
business incentives to encourage
people to eat more fruit and
vegetables.

Financial Times, TV listings,
24 Nov 1992.

If the traditional public sector is not great at delivering services, is government generally any better at paying for them? Is public spending likely to be good spending? The answer to these questions is the determining factor in whether people are optimists or pessimists about government, whether they view it as a direct debit arrangement or a leviathan. The distinction between the two is built upon whether they think the political and administrative processes that govern public spending are reliable processes. Some worry that there is something peculiarly bad about the way we take decisions on public money: that the forces which dominate are bound to be unhealthy; are bound to lead to the wrong kind of spending or, more commonly, to too much spending, especially on items which are bad value for money. They worry that the Sarah Zebaidas will get too much TV airtime, with their worthy schemes for spending our cash on making us eat fruit and veg, and that somehow there is no one around to protect the taxpayer.

Short-term Pressures for Spending

It is not uncommon for people to point out the apparently infinite list
of requests that pressure groups are apt to make for 'more resources' to
be made available to different things. The Social Market Foundation
obtained some attention in 1995 for 'costing' a week of the *Today*
programme on Radio 4. Andrew Cooper, the author of the piece,
listened to the programme for a week and added up the cost of the
suggestions made on the programme. He concluded that to meet the
demands would cost 'more than £14bn in additional public expenditure
or extra costs on the private sector . . . if each week produced a similar
ledger of undeclared costs, it would take just over three weeks
to double the basic rate of income tax and nine-and-a-half weeks
for the consequential basic rate of income tax to exceed 100p in the
pound.'

In fact, Cooper's central finding – albeit not intended to be taken
very literally – was dodgy, and it was so for a very telling reason. Several
of the fourteen billion are actually accounted for by a proposal for a
tax cut. So it appears that the SMF simply added the demands for tax
cuts to the demands for extra spending – as though all these demands
cumulate into one big demand. In fact, demands are not cumulative;
they are in conflict with each other. Cooper betrayed his 'Leviathan'
view of government, portraying the £14bn as reflecting some community of politicians, charities, interest groups, international organizations and think-tanks who conspire to rob middle Britain of its income.
In fact it is not quite like that: you have different groups arguing for
different measures, with differential impacts on different constituencies.
Clearly not all their demands are compatible with each other. As all
change involves losses to some groups and benefits to others, you cannot
just tot up the negative impacts of all changes without also totting up
some positive impacts too.

Anyway, there is nothing wrong with the fact that the demands for
public spending vastly exceed the level of acceptable spending. That is
bound to be the case in a society where wants are not satiated. The
same is true of our private spending. It is also appropriate that desires
are expressed publicly, in order that an intelligent choice can be made

about what to spend money on. So it is not really fair to describe the *Today* programme as 'The BBC way to bankrupt Britain' as the *Daily Express* did at the time (although it might be right to blame the *Today* programme for having been unimaginative in its agenda). It is not right to blame pressure groups for making demands, any more than it is right to blame shopkeepers for trying to sell us things.

If there is a mistake in the coverage of public spending on programmes like *Today*, it is in the implication made by pressure groups that the lack of spending on the heading with which they are concerned is somehow indicative of a general government meanness. It is not. Policy and spending choices are more often than not simply a form of arbitration between different groups, who stand to gain and lose. It is meaningless to use the word 'mean' to describe any decisions in this kind of situation.

This may sound a modest or even pedantic conclusion, but it is one of profound importance. However 'generous' the government is in spending terms, the queue for more will always be there and there is no reason to believe the length of that queue is in any way affected by the overall level of spending, any more than an arbitration in a rich couple's divorce is any easier than an arbitration in a poor couple's one. One of the biggest casual mistakes that one can make in characterizing public debate is to believe that there is an objectively determined list of demands on the public purse, and that therefore the more the government spends, the closer it comes to meeting them in full. It is not like that. The day politicians find they are spending as much as anybody wants, and there are no extra demands being put on them, they can be sure they have failed.

For all its faults, the SMF study struck a resonance in one or two tabloid newspapers that cannot be lightly dismissed. It highlights three main strands of argument about the control of public spending which raise serious concerns:

> That because small, concentrated interest groups can most easily form pressure groups and lobbies, small concentrated groups exert a disproportionate influence on the policy scene and influence government to give more money than they should get (to put it another way, there is an *asymmetry of pressures*).

That public agents, politicians and their agencies are keen to engage in expansion to serve their own personal ambitions rather than the public interest (the technical term for this idea is *the principal-agent problem*).

That the public are lethargic in the face of such demands, having little idea of the true costs of public spending (the key concept here is *fiscal illusion*).

The three arguments interact: public servants share an interest with the lobby groups who argue for their department to have a bigger budget; while the public, unable to connect costs and benefits, fail to punish the authorities which indulge in the process of budget inflation. There is an extensive literature on the motivation of pressure groups and bureaucracies, and their interaction with democratic systems. Justice will not be done to this thinking in this chapter. Those who thirst for more should read any of a number of books on the topic, mostly by the 1986 economics Nobel prizewinner, James Buchanan, who has undoubtedly been the most famous proponent of this strand of thinking, a strand that comes from what is called the 'public-choice school'. He is, by and large, pessimistic about the prospects for democracy, and supports the introduction of constitutional restrictions on the discretion of politicians to spend.

In addition to these three conventional public-choice arguments, let me offer two more that in practice probably have as much significance, but which have not been as publicly renowned:

That, quite apart from fiscal illusion, the public suffer certain forms of irrationality when it comes to assessing the magnitudes involved in certain types of spending decision.

That governments take decisions they know are wrong, for fear that the right decision would be misinterpreted; their actions, in other words, are motivated by a desire to say something about themselves, or to demonstrate their good intentions (this draws on a body of economic theory about *signalling*).

So there are five arguments in all. How much weight might we attach to each?

The Pressure of Interest Groups

First is the argument that there is an *asymmetry of pressure in demands for spending, as opposed to cuts in taxes*. There is, it is suggested, an in-built pressure to yield to higher demands, as the benefits to politicians of serving a narrow interest group outweigh the cost of hurting everyone in the general population by a small amount.

There is perhaps no better example of this principle in action than the distribution of spending across the nations of the United Kingdom. It would not be an outrageous characterization of the facts to suggest that the best way to enjoy good public services in the UK is to move to Scotland.[1] It has 1,506 patients per doctor, compared with 1,887 in England; it has 15.4 schoolchildren per teacher, compared with 17.7 in England; it has 354 people per policeman, compared with 408 in England and Wales. The reason is that the government spends about 23 per cent more per head in Scotland than it does in England.[2]

There is little justification for the differential. Scotland's needs were once assessed as greater than England's, and it was always accepted that it would require some extra spending to deliver equivalent services – the figure of 16 per cent per capita was the accepted premium. But the actual premium has been far higher, and it has been an objective of governments since James Callaghan was Prime Minister to narrow the difference over time. That narrowing was designed to occur by ensuring that any *growth* in spending was distributed proportionally to the population.[3] Even with a formula in place to narrow the gap, Scotland's

1. It is easiest to focus on Scotland as it is more generously funded than Wales, and this is less easy to explain with reference to special circumstances, as in Northern Ireland.
2. This is *identifiable* spending. Much of the total government budget – on real public goods – is not attributable to particular geographical areas. Scottish nationalists have suggested that the distribution of this non-identifiable spending, on things like defence and the civil service, is disproportionately spent in England; but this betrays a fundamental confusion. The *output* of the civil servants and defence forces based around London is administration and defence for the whole UK, not just for the London metropolitan area. One might argue that government should build military bases in Scotland, but one cannot argue that such a move would improve public services in Scotland.
3. This is under the so-called Barnet formula, named after the former Chief Secretary to the Treasury, Joel (now Lord) Barnet.

spending premium has persisted. For one thing, governments bypassed the formula to deliver extra funds to the country. For another, for no particular reason at all, the government used out-of-date population figures in allocating funds, with the effect that even Scotland's share of new spending was disproportionate to its size (although regular updating of population allocations was announced in December 1997).

There is a simple reason why nothing is done about the discrepancy though: the amounts of money are small as far as England is concerned, but very large as far as Scotland is concerned. It would be a brave government that confronted the situation.

The Pressure of Bureaucrats

A second fundamental problem of government highlighted by the public-choice school is that the public servants responsible for spending money themselves become an influential lobby in favour of their own spending heading. There is a whole area of economics called *principal-agent theory*, usually filling several chapters of any credible micro-economic textbook. The subject tells of the problems of getting an agent – be it a travel agent, a financial adviser or even an employee – to act in the best interest of the person employing him. Agents will always have their own ideas about what they want – the travel agent may get a bigger commission by selling you a more expensive product than you need. At the same time, agents are difficult to control. They are better informed than their employers, who cannot really monitor or measure what they are up to very closely.

Public servants are themselves agents for the public, and as long as they know more about what they do than we do, and as long as they are not entirely motivated by the same desires as us, then we are susceptible to the principal-agent problem. The argument has been most forcefully articulated by William Niskanen, whose 1973 work, *Bureaucracy: Servant or Master?* was apparently placed on a reading list for civil servants by the Conservative minister, Sir Keith Joseph. Niskanen was in fact once a Vice President of the Ford Motor Company, and became a member of the Council of Economic Advisors in the Ronald Reagan Presidency in the US.

He postulated that bureaucrats have a natural tendency to look after themselves rather than the public interest: in particular, in his 1971 work, *Bureaucracy and Representative Government*, he said they seek to maximize 'salary, perquisites of the office, public reputation, power, patronage, output of the bureau, ease of making changes and ease in managing the bureau'. This list, if right, probably gives them a general interest in increasing the size of their empire, rather than the good which they do. And perversely, in this account, bureaucrats benefit from inefficiency – which means bigger than necessary budgets and an easier life. As most bureaucracies are in some sense monopoly providers of services (there is only one driving licence dispensing organization in the UK), it is difficult for voters to determine whether the service is efficient or not – there's nothing to compare it to.

In addition (on top of the principal-agent problem), the monopoly power of bureaucrats can allow them to behave very strategically, in presenting a limited range of policy choices for example. So bureaucrats in this world are able to foster ignorance by holding back information about alternative policies to those they support. They can stack a list of policy options with policies that they support and hopeless policies that no one will support: viable and sensible alternatives to their favoured choice will be excluded.

It would be impossible to argue that politicians and public servants have no personal interest in the fate of their department. Take this quotation from the *Financial Times* in reporting the discovery of apparent evidence of life once having existed on Mars:

> The mood at NASA was one of barely disguised excitement that the media excitement at the possibility of life on Mars would lead to a bigger budget. It said that it relied on 'the public writing to their congresspeople' to push through budget increases. That could happen quickly: the agency has submitted its 1997 budget but it has not yet been passed by Congress and could still be amended, said NASA.[1]

Apart from the fact one has to take a slightly sceptical view of research findings released in the context of such apparent institutional desperation, one can hardly view NASA as a kind of objective agent of the public, simply reporting the scientific evidence the public has paid the

1. *Financial Times*, 8 August 1996.

organization to investigate. It is far more involved than that. In the UK, why is it that public bodies like the BBC employ large teams of people effectively to lobby government? It would be quite absurd to argue that the BBC identifies no interest with itself, and simply wishes to serve the public.

For many, this would be evidence for the Leviathan view of government – that the BBC and other government bodies are more than mere agents, seeing their job as spending the money allocated to them. They are, if you like, organisms with a life of their own – in particular, with their own desires, quite separate from those of the principal they are employed to serve.

This caricature undoubtedly has some validity, although the truth is always a little more complicated. The BBC has more information than most of the population about the needs of the broadcasting industry. Indeed, that is at least one reason why we employ the BBC to broadcast, and do not assign the task randomly. (And according to the economic theory of principals and agents, if the BBC had no more information than the rest of us, then it would be hard-pressed to advance its own interest at our expense.) Now if the BBC knows more about broadcasting than the rest of us, it is justified in informing us of policy changes that can help the broadcasting industry. Ignoring the BBC, or any other agent, involves losing the benefit of the agent's wisdom. Yet yielding to the agent's opinion involves subverting the national interest to that of the agent's interest.

To complicate the matter even further, agents themselves are not typically deliberately cynical or manipulative; their power to persuade *themselves* that what they advocate is in some sense in the wider interest is impossible to overstate. And this is an understandable and pervasive characteristic of mankind. It is reminiscent, for example, of the advice in the *Financial Times* staff style guide under the word 'dramatic': 'What is dramatic to an economist is not necessarily so to anybody else. Beware.' Quite simply, you cannot trust those deeply involved in something – be they advocates of the broadcasting industry, or economics correspondents making news judgements – to be the final arbiter of policy.

The Hidden Costs of Taxation

Thirdly, it is worth looking at the argument that we the public are too lenient on those who ask us for money; that we fail to punish those politicians who give in to political pressure to spend money unwisely. Why might this be so? The conventional argument has it that we are duped by the fact that the cost of spending is hidden in the small print: the price we pay for it in taxation can be disguised from us.

The central concept here is called *fiscal illusion* – the simple idea that politicians can conjure up revenues without us realizing. If the population doesn't read the newspaper, if it doesn't know how much VAT is included in the price of things, if it never checks its payslips to see how much income tax is paid, if it doesn't realize that National Insurance is a tax, and if it doesn't understand that debt has to be serviced, it may get an exaggerated view of government's ability to deliver services at a given cost.

Another way of disguising costs is to forgo revenue that would otherwise be available to taxpayers. This is an argument beloved of this book: if government owns assets and chooses to make them available at below market rates, then in effect it is spending taxpayers' money, because if it rented the assets out at the best available rate, it would be able to cut taxes. As we saw in Chapter 1, the government has done this extensively, particularly with its stock of residential housing, and as a result, true government spending has, for years, been understated.

There is another, related way of hiding spending: that is to finance it by reference to what one might call the capital account: to sell the family silver to pay for current consumption, and as long as no one is keeping much of a check on how much silver there is, then few will spot the cost of government's behaviour. How do you sell the family silver? For one thing, selling government debt – i.e., borrowing money – is a form of selling silver. Another is to sell government assets – the effect of privatization in helping maintain the appearance of healthy accounts has been significant in the last fifteen years.

Or yet another possible form of illusion, highlighted by W.E. Oates in 1975, is the idea that the public focus on the *rate* of tax they pay, rather than the amount of tax they pay. For example, if economy-wide wages rise faster than tax exemptions, allowances and thresholds, then more and more people will find themselves paying more tax – through higher rate bands, or relatively lower allowances – and as a result the government enjoys buoyant revenues without ever having to face the population and tell them that tax rates are rising.

It is quite true that the distinction is insufficiently understood. In Britain, we have always tended to rate the tax-cutting machismo of politicians by their approach to the basic rate of income tax – even though income tax only collects a quarter of total revenue, so that a dramatic cut of 5p in the basic rate actually cuts revenue by 4 per cent or so. The adoption of so-called fiscal accelerators – automatic, year-on-year increases in the real level of petrol and tobacco taxes – has allowed British governments to enjoy extra revenues over the course of a parliament without having to do more than make one single announcement of a tax increase.[1]

Oates himself looked at the growth of spending by US city and state governments, and the natural buoyancy of the tax revenues there (so-called 'tax elasticity'), and he found that there was a positive relationship – governments with naturally rising taxes tended to spend more. Others have sought to uphold or knock down the idea. In any event it is a hard proposition to establish, because it may be that governments who have already chosen to spend a lot choose to design their tax system to be buoyant. Correlation does not imply causality.

Anecdotally, all these forms of irrationality do plausibly suggest that the public in the short term are not very aware of the true costs and benefits of different types of government spending. This idea has encouraged some to recommend PAYE income tax should be abolished and be replaced by direct taxpayer levies, in the hope that the greater transparency would lead to a general downward pressure on taxes.[2] Unfortunately, the reform would more likely lead to a generalized diminution in the payment of taxes, and like the poll tax (itself motivated

1. The escalators are currently 6 per cent on petrol duty and 5 per cent on cigarettes; these raise about an extra £1.5bn a year, but that cumulates. In the final year of a parliament, a government would be about £7.5bn better off than at the start.

2. The person who has come closest to that view in public is Andrew Tyrie, now a Conservative MP, in his 1996 Social Market Foundation monograph, *The Prospects for Public Spending*.

by a similar line of reasoning) would simply involve government in spending a great deal of money in the otherwise unproductive enforcement of simple rules.

We should be careful anyway about ascribing too much weight to the idea that fiscal illusion leads to big government. Remember that when politicians raise money by devious means, they do not have to spend that money. They can – and in fact do – use that cash to lower the more visible forms of tax. At the margin, to a politician, the power to obscure tax raising does nothing to change the trade-off between spending and visible taxes.

Moreover, if fiscal illusion pure and simple was our only problem, then we could disabuse ourselves of the illusion by pointing out to everybody the true costs of public spending. So the fact that we are duped does not entirely capture the apparent lethargy of the public in terms of spending. In fact, there appear to be some other forms of irrationality in our judgement, regardless of whether the politicians attempt to disguise the costs.

Public Irrationality

In his book *Irrationality*, Stuart Sutherland documents some systematic biases in the way we judge issues. For example, people make serious misjudgements about the likelihood of small probability events (when they choose to buy a lottery ticket). In particular, we have a systematic tendency to make judgements on the basis of first impressions or on the most available mental image (the so-called availability error); as a result, we apply a disproportionately high weight to vivid outcomes (like winning the lottery) as opposed to more probable plain outcomes (like losing it).

That tendency affects our judgements of public spending and taxation: we apply a far higher weight to the visible than we do to the invisible or the imperceptibly small. The cost of the Queen and the civil list, which represents a taxpayer burden of £7.9m a year, or a little under a penny a week to each household in the country, tends to be hugely overstated in the public mind, for example.

But this same tendency also makes it easy for us to say 'yes' to spending on specific projects, with clear benefits that are easily imagined.

That is precisely because the benefits are more vivid in our minds than the corresponding costs. If the project is small, say under £100,000, mere public debate on the spending almost inevitably results in it occurring.

An example might be expensive surgery on a specific child suffering from leukaemia. The tax burden on the population is not going to change as a result of going ahead, while the child's life may be saved – a tangible benefit once the child's predicament has come into public view. Indeed, that spending may ignite another irrational strain in human thought – the so-called 'representativeness error'. Because, in our thoughts, one specific child represents a whole category of people – sick children – we tend to see a solution to the one case as a solution to the problem of the whole category. So, for example, if the cost of a course of treatment quoted in public is the cost of treating one child, public debate can be quite skewed by implicitly assessing the benefits in terms of a whole cluster of children.

All this argument is saying is that the public themselves in effect find it hard to say 'no' to certain types of spending demand. It is as though we are constantly bombarded with requests of the following kind: 'If you will all just give me one penny each, you won't notice any loss, but I will notice a large benefit,' and we are unable to articulate any logical counter to that proposition.

This form of irrationality is highly understandable, and highly undesirable. It again has a systematic effect – to put unwarranted burdens on large populations, to the benefit of small ones. As the extra tax needed to finance any one particular project is invariably rather small, it puts upward pressure on government spending.

There are other types of public irrationality too – there appears to be a phenomenon of public hysteria in which concern about an issue appears to reinforce and thus magnify concern, to a point at which public judgement becomes quite removed from all reality. In the Social Market Foundation paper, *Pressure Group Politics in Modern Britain*, Peter Bazalgette (a member of the government's Health of the Nation task force) provides a witty account of American hysteria over Daminozide spray on apples. After a TV documentary claiming it was potentially carcinogenic and could affect children, there was widespread outrage – Meryl Streep headed a pressure group dedicated to banning it. 'One mother even called out the police to chase and stop the school bus her daughter was on to reclaim the killer apple from her lunch box.' In fact, apples sprayed with Daminozide only contained one-thousandth of the amount of the dangerous substance that natural mushrooms do. Meryl Streep eventually changed her mind on the issue.

One does not have to look to the US for examples of panic feeding on panic to generate more panic – a process fuelled by competing media outlets that quite reasonably want to concern themselves with the public's worries. Policy-makers are driven to demonstrate their concern with issues like children's health, or safety, by committing expenditure or passing regulations that save lives, but at a hugely inefficient cost. David Willetts, in another Social Market Foundation pamphlet, *Deregulation*, lists ten areas where policy is plainly irrational: 'How can you spend £200m a year on safety and increase transport deaths? The answer is clear. You require one of the safest forms of transport – rail – to spend that much every year on safety measures after some comparatively rare accidents; accept that it will have to raise fares to cover the costs of the expensive safety investment programme; and thus drive people on to the roads as a result.'

In light of the pressure that naturally builds up as the media and the public mould their own view of a topic in light of their observation of everyone else's, it is hard for politicians to follow the guiding prescription, 'Don't just do something, stand there' – even though in many cases it is the best motto to follow. This leads, then, to the final short-term force towards irrationality – that policy is made with a view to saying something about the policy-maker, as much as it is about effecting a change in policy.

Signalling as an Explanation of Poor Decision-making

Without any recourse to irrationality on the part of either governments or the electorate, the idea that politicians need to be seen in a particular way quite clearly skews their decision on an issue. They sometimes *know* what is right, but they *do* what is wrong in order to send a signal out about themselves, to say something, as a token or gesture.

Here is an example: a government may sensibly believe that a particular missile system would cost a great deal and add little to the effectiveness of the nation's defence. On a rational basis, it should not opt to purchase the missile system. However, look at how the public may interpret this decision. The public – *with no irrationality at all* – has not studied the decision closely and cannot tell whether the government is a sensible and prudent government, or whether the government is in fact an unpatriotic government, careless with the nation's defence. There is no systematic illusion in the public's mind about the value of the missile system, or the cost of the missile system. It is simply that the public cannot tell which motivation accounts for the government's action in not purchasing the system. It is no good the government merely saying that it is patriotic – any government, patriotic or not, would say that. So the public can only guess at the intentions of government from its actions.

Inevitably in this kind of situation, especially where there is some reasonable doubt over what the right decision is, the government is motivated by the need to demonstrate its good intent. It may end up buying the missile system. Only by putting the public's money where its mouth is, can the government truly signal that it is a patriotic government.

We can generalize this argument a little. The population cannot tell the difference, if you like, between a Type A government (a good government) and a Type B government (a bad government). The government naturally has to incur some cost to demonstrate its true, Type A, nature.

The idea that someone may do something costly purely as a device for helping people distinguish whether they are Type A or Type B has become a ubiquitous tool in economics: it is used to explain all sorts of behaviour that had previously looked irrational – advertising, going to college, paying out corporate dividends – have all been analysed in this way. In each case, you have to show there is a Type A and a Type B that someone would like to tell apart (the high-quality product and the low-quality product; the clever job applicant and the stupid job applicant; the manager who believes his company is going somewhere and the manager who knows the company is going nowhere). Then you have to show that it is hard to simply ask who is Type A and who is Type B (the Type Bs can lie and say they are Type As). Then you have to identify a device that discriminates between the two: it must be a device that is more costly for the Type Bs to pursue, than for the Type As. If it is the right kind of device, then only the Type As will engage in it, and so the device acts as a successful screen. Higher education is insufferable for stupid people, so you can tell that someone who has endured it must be clever. It would be worth the clever going to college, even if it added nothing to their ability to do a job. High-quality products benefit more from advertising than low-quality products because the initial flurry of sales will endure longer for high-quality products; so they can afford to advertise more than low-quality products, so advertising screens the two apart.

There are many cases where governments act to demonstrate a desirable intention. The desire to demonstrate compassion – however futile the spending resulting – is a common one for governments, leading them to spend money on the vulnerable, on war widows, on the overseas poor. In many cases the spending can be justified, but in many cases, whether or not the spending can be justified is irrelevant to the decision to spend.

Under this account, populations do not, by and large, react negatively to difficult decisions that are clearly good; we do not vote against good government; there are few sensible measures that are 'politically impossible'. We just appear to sometimes vote against such measures because it is not clear to us that the decision is good, and we suspect the motives of the politicians imposing them.

This reasoning is powerful, and the kind of explanation it provides does appear to play a part in all sorts of actions. It also plays a part in persuading governments to spend public money on items that attempt merely to show the public what kind of government we have. It is an inevitable feature of the imperfect information under which the political process operates. And the economics of screening and signalling imply that despite the apparently high deadweight costs of sending signals about yourself, it is still better to have the information sent than not sent. Or put it this way – if signalling costs a few billion pounds, but results in the election of better governments, it can be a price worth paying. The only solution is to find other – cheaper – ways of furnishing the same information if that is possible. It may be possible, but it is certainly not easy.

The Long-term Limits to Irrationality

Often the arguments of the public-choice school are presented in economics textbooks in a theoretical form, replete with diagrams and equations. It is possible to portray the arguments as arcane pieces of theory. In reality, they are far from it. They are perhaps embedded in a more sassy reading of how people really behave than most other public economics, which typically describes the behaviour of a type of altruistic, informed and rational dictator rarely found in a senior political role. The public-choice school has a point that many of us can probably recognize from daily experience.

But there is a difference between daily experience and long-term performance. As a rule in lots of areas of economics it is fair to assume that in the short term, illusion, irrationality, tactical ploys and effective campaigning can make or break decisions – and here the public-choice school wins the point. *In the long term*, however, it is much harder to believe such things can work: in the long term, the truth will out. The assumptions of rational economics begin to look more plausible. The fundamental preferences of the population will assert themselves. Good political tactics are likely to be exposed as such the longer they are used to influence a piece of policy. Bureaucrats are more likely to be exposed as performing well or not over long periods of time. There are, in short, some reasons to think that the irrationalities of short-term decision-making are unlikely to last.

As it happens, it does appear that the worries of the public-choice school have – by the 1990s – turned out to be of diminishing concern. There was a limit to how far the socially irrational processes could go. To put it in the language of author Edward Tenner, there are 'revenge effects' that counter those the public-choice school has noted.

For one thing, there turned out to be such a thing as political entrepreneurs, who saw a political opportunity when it arose. They set up new political forces to lead an anti-tax rebellion when the gravy train of special interests and lobbying bureaucrats, fuelled by hidden taxes, became overladen.

In America, for example, one revolution against high taxes occurred in 1776; another occurred 202 years later in 1978. It was the Jarvis–

Gann Property Tax Initiative in California, subsequently labelled Proposition 13. It limited property taxes to 1 per cent of the cash value of the property (based on valuations made three years before) and it required all future tax increases to have two-thirds support in the state legislature. It was passed in a state referendum with 65 per cent support (in suburban areas it was passed by three-to-one margins).

It was not the first time such a measure had been attempted – in 1968 a similar scheme had been defeated by a two-to-one margin. But voters had witnessed big increases in taxes over the following decade and were persuaded enough was enough. Between 1978 and 1981, state and local spending in California declined by 0.73 per cent a year in real terms. With a series of similar initiatives in other states, a series of attempts at pre-emptive action by policy-makers in others, and with the election of Ronald Reagan in 1980, 'The proclaimed goals of Howard Jarvis, the sponsor of Proposition 13 who until 1978 had been a neglected, though shrill, voice in the California political wilderness, became enshrined as national policy.'[1]

In Britain, the form of tax revolt was different, but the effect not dissimilar: Margaret Thatcher's election saw the end of the days in which making promises of new spending won votes. It cannot be overstated that the broad political pressure in the Anglo-Saxon countries today is for spending to be held roughly constant, not for it to rise. In as far as irrationality governs decisions, it as much appears to obstruct sensible projects as it does to promote stupid ones. When it comes to the making of large, strategic decisions – in national elections – the public has made its reticence about paying taxes sufficiently clear for politicians and other public agents to strive to make do without much in the way of extra resources.

Another long-term phenomenon has been the absence of so-called fiscal illusion. Somehow, the public have just turned out to be cleverer than the public-choice theorists imagined. Governments who used inflation to finance spending unearthed a revenge effect in that inflation became as unpopular as tax increases. Little was to be gained from printing money. It is even possible that governments who use borrowing

---

1. The quotation is from Jack Citrin, in *California and the American Tax Revolt*, edited by Terry Schwadron, published by University of California Press, Berkeley, 1984, p. 4.

to finance tax cuts gain little. We, the public can broadly tell whether the tax cut is affordable and sustainable or not, and we reward it appropriately. As for the idea that we do not notice tax rises if the tax rates do not change, that appears to have been undermined by the Proposition 13 story, where it was *automatic* increases in property taxes that had generated huge increases in state revenues, and prompted taxpayer revolt.

In addition politicians themselves know there are gains to being seen as long-term responsible, and for that reason in many jurisdictions they have forgone the power to exert full fiscal discretion. The Maastricht Treaty limits on deficits and debt are a form of constitutional limit on the degree of fiscal illusion politicians are allowed to exploit – a limit set by politicians themselves.

Even among those on the right, who tend towards the leviathan model of government, there is support for the idea that the public cannot be fooled by manipulative politicians. The concept of *rational expectations* – popular as a modelling tool by economists in the *laissez-faire* tradition – is a creed based on the idea that the public will spot what politicians are doing and offset political choices with their own private choices. If politicians choose to finance spending by printing money, the public will immediately anticipate inflation, and take it into account in all wage negotiations, for example. These are not the assumptions of soft-hearted liberal economists, defending government, but of the core right-wing economists who seek to demonstrate its powerlessness to do good.

Another dampener on the endless power of government to grow is that the very forces that can lead to too much spending can turn against spending. The signalling argument, for example, which explained why governments may have wanted to pursue unwanted projects merely to demonstrate their compassion, patriotism or toughness on crime, can be used against spending by governments keen to demonstrate their prudence, loyalty to the taxpayer, and toughness against lobbies. The signal governments want to send will be the signal that responds to the latest political concern. It is quite possible for signalling to result in sensible projects being rejected simply so governments can demonstrate their tax-cutting credentials.

All in all then, while it is worth keeping watch on government, and while the crude Leviathan view has some merit, it does not fundamentally explain what is driving government. The marketing guys simply can't con us for ever.

Inertia in Public Spending Decisions

There is one final set of considerations to be outlined in assessing the government's ability to spend the right amount. Even if there is a limit to the validity of the idea that the state endlessly spends too much, there are still grounds for worry. Even if tax revolts and sassy voters manage to prevent spending from increasing uncontrollably, it seems irrational choices made in the past have a tendency to persist into the present.

The reason for this is that once spending on an item has been committed, it is very hard not to commit it again. Even when an item is well beyond its sell-by date, government finds it extremely hard to retrench. There appears to be an inertia, a bias in favour of the status quo, or a 'ratchet effect' that ensures that once spending has started, it continues.

It is interesting to ask why this is. Why do we persist in spending money on items when it clearly makes no sense? Why does Britain pay overseas aid to Hong Kong and Singapore – albeit only half a million pounds between them – when both are considered to enjoy a higher per capita income than the UK? Or, more strikingly, why do we persist – through the EU – in paying such large subsidies to farmers through the Common Agricultural Policy (CAP)? However good an idea it might have seemed at the time we started, surely no one could seriously argue that paying out grants of thousands of pounds a year to people in one particular profession (it is not even a very low-paid profession) is socially equitable. Why is it easier to refrain from raising the pay of public servants than it is to cut the pay of public servants? Or to take a less invidious example, would we really finance motorways and university education through taxation if we were starting again, or might we not resort to tolls and loans? Or would we give out so many tax concessions if we were starting again? Can you really imagine that the duty-free privilege of those travelling abroad is a sensible way of forgoing revenue?

To answer these questions, it is worth first looking at our own personal spending. A modicum of introspection reveals that when we decide what to buy, the history of our spending decisions is important; each purchase is influenced in a host of ways by purchases we have already made. Often, the effect is to inhibit change in our spending:

> We develop habits and addictions (once we start smoking, we continue smoking) or we acquire tastes (once we have discovered the joys of Post-it notes, we find ourselves using them more and more).

> We find that different purchasing decisions are self-reinforcing (we have a car, and we choose to buy a caravan, but that of course means we then need to maintain a reasonably decent car).

> We find that what we buy tells others what kind of people we are (the signalling argument again), and therefore we are sometimes reluctant to change our spending, lest others should think we have changed more generally ('I'm darned if we aren't going to have our regular Christmas party this year just because we can't afford it').

> And most of us are probably also prone to the habit of repeating purchases in order to justify our earlier spending decisions to ourselves (we stick to our subscription to the *London Review of Books* because, even though we never actually read it, we don't wish to admit that to ourselves).

All these kinds of phenomena lead to behaviour that we might describe as 'habit-forming' when it comes to our shopping. We cannot – as economists typically do – view each purchase that we make as a fresh transaction, made on the basis of a fresh calculation of its merits.[1]

The striking thing is that government-provided goods and services are often prone to the very same inertia that our private purchases are. We exhibit a certain conservatism as individuals in our tastes and preferences that affects our judgement of policy.

Let us itemize some of the ways in which inertia might arise. First, there may be no direct public spending equivalent of addiction, habit or acquired tastes – these are very individual psychological traits – but

---

1. There is a technical phrase for the phenomenon being described: 'endogeneity of preferences'.

it *is* quite possible that as individuals we acquire tastes for publicly provided goods, and if enough individuals do acquire such tastes, then of course the state may find itself under pressure to carry on providing what it once started providing. You could not explain the national taste for schools or hospitals this way, but some analogy to the addiction argument is offered as an explanation of social security spending. If you believe people who endure some temporary need can become stuck in dependency, you recognize the power of this argument. On this view, once the recipients have fallen into this situation, it is a cruel and difficult decision to break off the benefit on which they are now genuinely dependent.

Again, as in the case of personal spending, different public purchasing decisions tend to reinforce each other. The most obvious example concerns capital expenditure. Once you have built that hospital or library, you are inclined to service it – so by building it, you have in fact committed yourself to future spending. This is probably even more true of new projects financed under the Private Finance Initiative, where government is signing contracts committing itself to future spending.[1]

Another source of inertia derives from the fact that changes in policy are taken to signal something about the decision-maker more often than merely sticking to a policy is, so whatever merit the signalling argument has, it is magnified with respect to policy changes. Change attracts more attention than it deserves on its own merits. Signalling can also lead to a status quo bias in budgeting because those who lose under a change will tend to have in mind the idea that it sets a precedent, and that if they do not act now, they will set in train another shift against them. Of course, often they are right – small shifts in policy do have a value in signalling larger changes in priority. But that means even those small shifts in policy that do not signal any grand intent tend to arouse more opposition than they inherently justify.

A fourth source of inertia is the attempt to justify past decisions by repeating them. This is very clearly evident in public spending. The decision to carry on with programmes, even though they are evidently

---

1. This was a concern expressed by Nick Bosanquet in his *Public Spending into the Millennium* monograph for the Social Market Foundation.

not worthwhile, has been noted with regard to nuclear power stations and Concorde, both of which it would have been sensible to abandon a long way into their development. Even at quite a late stage in the life of some of these projects it would have been better to write off the costs so far incurred, and to have avoided incurring any more. But even though good sense may tell you that because you have sunk money into something in the past, that does not mean you should sink more money into it, good politics may prevent administrators from being willing to reveal that things did not turn out as they had expected.

In addition to these factors that might create inertia in both private and public spending, there are several more worth outlining in the public sphere alone. Inertia can be explained – and indeed justified – by two quite convincing equity arguments. For one thing, people take account of the status quo in public spending in their actions and as a result it can genuinely be unfair to remove the spending on which they might have based expensive decisions. Removing transport subsidies, for example, can lower the value of people's homes. If the impression had been given that subsidies were permanent, it is obviously an unanticipated windfall loss to those who bought their homes in the expectation of a subsidy. And remember that as these people might have bought their homes once the subsidy was already operating, they themselves would not have benefited from it: the day-to-day gain they might enjoy from the subsidy was paid for by a higher price for the house they live in. It was the person who owned the home at the time the original subsidy was introduced who benefited from it, enjoying a windfall gain in the value of their property. In these circumstances, it is not surprising that removal of the subsidy would attract substantial opposition. Farmers who pay a lot for land on the basis that agriculture is subsidized will quite reasonably object to a policy that removes the subsidy. Ferry companies which buy ships and establish operations on the basis of a duty-free concession will be worse off without it than they would have been had it never existed. This is a serious issue that makes it very difficult to eradicate subsidies, even if it is done quite slowly.

Another equity argument is that the state might legitimately refrain from withdrawing support from one group of people if it has already given support to another similar group. So, the government paid for university education, or pensions, for one generation – would it not now be unreasonable for it not to pay the same for the next?

The penultimate item in this list of factors explaining inertia in public decision-making is the strength of the status quo in providing an important psychological focal point in determining the power of interest groups to battle for resources. When it comes to deciding whether to fight for a cause, it is easier to muster a posse, and the posse will be better motivated, if you are seeing off a raid on your budget, than if you are leading a raid to get a bigger budget. Your cause will have more credibility among waverers. You are less likely to look opportunistic or greedy, and more credibly able to argue that suffering will occur if people have to respond to a cut in budgets, rather than not respond to an increase in them. For example, on pay, it is more acceptable to people not to have an increase than it is to accept a cut. It is more likely that workers will be motivated to strike or fight against a pay cut than fight for a pay increase; and they are more likely to enjoy public support if they do.

And last but far from least in this catalogue of reasons for inertia is the potential for political paralysis when the politicians have to agree on an alternative course of action. The status quo is typically the default policy option; majorities have to be found not just for changing the status quo, but for advancing a particular change from the status quo. Even when the broad direction of change is agreed, obtaining consensus on the specifics is not easy.

This tendency to political paralysis might be written off as some feature of weak-willed politicians, a failure of leadership, or a reflection of stubbornness. It may or may not be one or more of these, but calling it by a derogatory name is unhelpful. The key is to understand the pathology of a situation that makes paralysis likely. In fact, it can be described using the tool of game theory. Political paralysis can be likened to the game known as 'Battle of the Sexes'. The fable runs thus: husband and wife would like to spend their evening together; *he* wants to go to the ballet; *she* wants to go to the boxing. Above all though, each would most like to do what the other does. If we look at their order of preferences for the evening, then the ranking of different outcomes is as follows:

	Her rank	His rank
Outcome 1: They both go to boxing	1	2
Outcome 2: They both go to ballet	2	1
Outcome 3: He goes to the ballet, she goes to the boxing	3	3
Outcome 4: He goes to the boxing, she goes to the ballet	4	4

Clearly, if they spend the evening apart (outcomes three or four), there has been a breakdown in communications, as there are two alternative options that both of them prefer. But there may be a struggle between them to achieve their own particular favourite of the two preferred options; they might end up making mistakes that lead them to an unpreferred one. He might say 'I'm going to the ballet come what may', to convince her she has to follow, and she might try the same trick. The result will be Outcome 3. Or even sadder, he might attempt to show goodwill by turning up at the boxing, only to discover she has done the same thing, and gone to the ballet. The worst outcome of all.

The battle of the sexes is a parsimonious means of characterizing certain forms of difficult political debate. Take the following example, a game we might call 'the reform of the overwieldy Italian public pension system':

	Conservatives' ranking	Socialists' ranking
Outcome 1: Cut pensions drastically	1	2
Outcome 2: Cut pensions a bit and make the rich pay more	2	1
Outcome 3: Stick with the status quo	3	3

The problem is that each side can threaten to block the move to the opponent's preferred outcome, by tactically supporting the status quo as a blocking device. The result can easily be political paralysis, even where there is a broad agreement that something does have to change.

Conclusion

The power of all these mechanisms has long been recognized by theorists and also by those who work in the Treasury, negotiating spending decisions. Many have reluctantly come to the conclusion that the arbitrary nature of the spending which results from all these processes has to be countered with equally arbitrary controls on how much can be spent. They believe irrationality has to be met with irrationality – targets for getting spending down, arbitrary limits on how much can be committed. This is an issue we take up later: suffice it to say that if the account of the spending process outlined here is right, the problem is not so much *too much spending*, as *the wrong type of spending*. Money is wasted, and inviting us to spend *less* is no solution unless it somehow involves spending less of the wasted money in particular. The best solution must involve means of discriminating between good and bad spending, and one needs to be suspicious of those who define the problem as one of merely excessive spending in general, as that invites the implication that cutting spending any old how is worthwhile.

Or to put this another way, one of our great problems in public spending is that inadequacies in our political discourse mean badly spent money absorbs scarce resources from worthwhile projects. The response of both those on the left and on the right of the political spectrum has been inadequate. On the right, the solution is to cut spending in the hope that the worst spending goes first. On the left, there has been a tendency to defend public spending of dubious value. They have done so in the belief that even dubious public spending is better than none. That is wrong. Dubious public spending, in an era when the ability to spend is limited by public tolerance, crowds out good public spending. Both the left and the right should agree on one thing – that if we can extract more out of the money we spend on public services, then there is more money to go round. They can then disagree about whether the spare resources created should be spent publicly, or given back to the public to be spent privately. But let's create those spare resources where we can.

Additional Reading

Bazalgette, Peter (1996), 'When Pressure Groups Get it Wrong' in *Pressure Group Politics in Modern Britain*, Occasional Paper, Social Market Foundation, London.

Bosanquet, Nick (1995), *Public Spending into the Millennium*, Social Market Foundation, London.

Buchanan, J.M. and Gordon Tullock (1962), *The Calculus of Consent*, University of Michigan Press, Ann Arbor, Michigan.

Buchanan, J.M. (1967), *Public Finance in Democratic Process*, University of North Carolina Press, Chapel Hill.

Buchanan, J.M. (1977), 'Why Does Government Grow?' in *Budgets and Bureaucrats: The Sources of Government Growth*, Duke University Press, Durham, North Carolina.

Cooper, Andrew (1995), *Costing the Public Policy Agenda: A Week of the* Today *Programme*, Hard Data Series, No. 2, Social Market Foundation, March.

Ham, Christopher and Michael Hill (1993), *The Policy Process in the Modern Capitalist State* (2nd edition), Harvester Wheatsheaf, London.

Niskanen W.A. (1971), *Bureaucracy and Representative Government*, Aldine, Chicago.

Niskanen, W.A. (1973), *Bureaucracy: Servant or Master?* Hobart Paperback No. 5, Institute of Economic Affairs, London.

Oates, W.A. (1975), 'Automatic increases in tax revenues – the effect on the size of the public budget' in W.E. Oates (ed.), *Financing the New Federalism: Revenue Sharing, Conditional Grants and Taxation*, John Hopkins University Press, Baltimore.

Sutherland, Stuart (1992), *Irrationality: The Enemy Within*, Penguin, London.

Willetts, David (1993), *Deregulation*, Social Market Foundation, London.

7 Collectivism and Uniformity?

The limits on expression of consumer choice

A man is called selfish if he lives in the manner that seems to him most suitable for the full realization of his own personality; if, in fact, the primary aim of his life is self-development. But this is the way in which everyone should live. Selfishness is not living as one wishes to live, it is asking others to live as one wishes to live. And unselfishness is letting other people's lives alone, not interfering with them. Selfishness always aims at creating around it an absolute uniformity of type. Unselfishness recognizes infinite variety of type as a delightful thing, accepts it, acquiesces in it, enjoys it. It is not selfish to think for oneself . . . Under Individualism people will be quite natural and absolutely unselfish, and will know the meanings of words and realize them in their free, beautiful lives.

OSCAR WILDE, *The Soul of Man Under Socialism.*

The Scope of Collective Finance

As if spending too much (or too little) on the wrong things wasn't bad enough, it is also arguable that government's seduction by the traditional model of public sector provision has led to spending beyond the *scope* appropriate to the state. In choosing to use taxation to provide items best left to individual consumers, government has inevitably imposed a uniformity of service levels across the population, even though tastes for services across the population vary.

Let us return to the example of government-supplied cars from Chapter 1: the world where no one bought their own car, but instead there was a national car service that provided each household with a

Ford Escort, financed out of taxation. (Some households, which were deemed particularly needy, maybe got two cars.)

What, if anything, is wrong with this society where such needs are financed and purchased collectively, and wants serviced uniformly? If education, health and much of public transport can be paid for by the state, why not cars? After all, imagine the deal that we could get if the state were buying on our behalf. Ford would give a substantial discount to snatch the biggest order for cars in its history. Moreover, think of the government's costs of borrowing. It only has to pay 5 to 10 per cent for its finance – far less than the 10 to 20 per cent hire purchase rates we pay if we borrow to buy a car.

Presuming you are not convinced that government should provide cars for people, the question is why? For example, if you are heavily imbued with a sense of the argument outlined in Chapter 5, you will recognize that we wouldn't want the government necessarily to *make* the cars it was handing out. That would be a recipe for everybody to have a Trabant. But that is not the way the issue here has been framed. It would be *Ford* who would be designing and making the cars in a world market that is by and large competitive, so none of the arguments about the poor quality of publicly-governed products need apply.

If, instead, you think back to Chapter 3, you will find yourself saying that it depends on what the public wants. If people prefer cars to cash, then cars they should have. Indeed, if they prefer the extra luxury of a Mondeo to the money saved on buying an Escort, government should buy Mondeos. That is correct. But it misses the important points:

Uniform provision of a private good almost always breaches the efficiency principle because people have varying tastes. (Not everyone wants an Escort.)

Tying up the quantity of redistribution in society to the provision of private services almost always leads to breaches of the efficiency principle too. (People's behaviour in voting for the nationally-provided car to be an Escort or a Mondeo will be distorted by their view of whether the outcome will affect the overall amount of distribution.)

Removing incentives at the margin of consumption – making it free to use a service – occasionally leads to breaches of the efficiency principle. (People will claim they need two Escorts, even if they only need one.)

Providing a private service publicly removes the incentive for service recipients to explore imaginative solutions to the problems the service is designed
to overcome. (People will not think as carefully about where they live or
how they travel, if they are given a car.)

Let us amplify these arguments.

Uniform Provision in a World of Heterogeneous Tastes

The efficiency principle tells us that if government buys us what we
are willing to pay for, government is doing its job well. This deduction
is correct, and although it is tricky to implement, it does at least guide
us to the right answer on how much to spend in principle. It is an
especially helpful idea when we are looking at what we might call *public
goods*, things like defence, where we effectively have to make one single
decision on the level of spending to cover all of us. Mr Jones at number
43 may not like the decision the government has come up with, but
because we can only make one decision on defence spending, Mr Jones
simply has to put up with it. As long as the government has done its
best in aggregate, the efficiency principle should be the guiding light
of government decision-making.

When it comes to cars, though, we are talking about *private goods*,
and life becomes a little more difficult. The efficiency principle still
applies – but it applies at the individual level. If *I* value a car more than
the cost, then under the efficiency principle, I should get a car. But if
you do not value the car sufficiently, then you should not get one, and
under the efficiency principle it would be wrong for you to get one.
And as long as some people do not want one, then efficiency is breached
if everybody is given one. In effect, if the government was buying cars
for us, it would be making twenty million separate spending decisions
– that would be the decision on whether to buy a car for each individual
household.

No government can make that many decisions very well. Some
people want a Ford Escort, some want a Rolls-Royce, and some want
to take the bus. One might argue that engaging in tortuous national
debate about whether the national car should be an Escort, a Mondeo,

or a Jaguar is pointless – why not just let people choose their own?

In practice, the conflict between efficiency and uniformity is a rather severe one to cope with, because the very reason many people like collective finance is precisely to ensure uniformity of provision. That is not a side effect, it is a desirable feature of the traditional public sector model. This leads to one of the great paradoxes of government provision:

> If we are all the same in what we can afford and what we want, there is little demand for government intervention to buy things for us, and there is little cost from government buying things for us.

> If we are all different in what we can afford and what we want, there is more of a cost to government buying things for us, and more of a demand for it too.

If we all chose to buy a Ford Escort each year, the cost of government raising taxes and buying one for us would not in fact be too high. But if we all chose to buy a Ford Escort each year, there would be no pressure for the government to buy one for us.

How far in practice tastes do vary can be observed from private spending. The Family Expenditure survey allows us to break down spending – by proportion – in different types of household. Table 1 shows that when we compare different types of household – young and old, or rich and poor, or large and small – we do see a fair bit of variation. It is just not the case that we all choose to spend our money in anything like a uniform way, and thus if a government imposed a uniform shopping basket on us, it would be bound to be buying the wrong shopping basket for some households. Diversity in tastes is an argument against the collective principle.

For example, a practical problem that has come up in the NHS: should the state pay for expensive drugs to cure cold sores? We know the sores will cure themselves; we also know that we can expedite the departure of the ugly and uncomfortable sores with the help of Zovirax. When that was a prescription-only treatment, it cost the government tens of pounds per tube, an expensive cure for discomfort. It is pretty clear that very poor people would rather have the money than cure the cold sore. It is equally clear that rich people typically would cure the cold sore rather than have the money. So we have three choices here:

Table 1: Variety in Expenditure Patterns
average weekly household spending in pounds

	London	Scotland	Wales	Ratio of highest to lowest
Restaurant meals	9.47	7.19	7.61	1.32
Alcoholic drink	10.81	12.28	11.63	1.14
Furniture	11.11	7.53	8.47	1.48
Books, maps, diaries	1.73	0.8	1.15	2.16
Motoring	33.98	41.98	40.21	1.24
Foreign holidays	8.32	6.38	6.3	1.32
Total on these items	**75.42**	**76.16**	**75.37**	

Source: *Family Expenditure Survey 1996/97*, Office for National Statistics.

> We force the rich to go without the Zovirax, even though they would be happy to pay for it [a breach of the efficiency principle].
>
> We give Zovirax to the poor, even though they would rather have the money [again, a breach of the efficiency principle].
>
> We allow inequality in health care – the rich get the Zovirax, and the poor do not [breach of much-cherished principle that health care should be provided equally].

Getting a straight answer out of people on this vexing issue is difficult. Some like to avoid the question by suggesting that cold sores can be serious, so everyone ought to have the Zovirax. Many see the dilemma, but like to err on the side of saying that everybody should get the drug. A few argue that the NHS should provide a kind of basic service that does *not* provide the drug, and that people who want non-essential drugs like Zovirax should pay extra for them.

The third group come closest to solving the problem, and come closest to describing the system we *now* have, in which the drug is now available over the counter: the NHS does not automatically provide the drug, but does allow you to buy it yourself. (The drug is also somewhat cheaper now.) The Zovirax problem was quite simply created by the fact that we collectivized – and as a result harmonized – a decision in which there is room for sensible divergence.

For those of you who incline to the view that the poor should have the drug on the NHS, it is time to examine your reasoning. Is it that you think the poor *should* want the drug and we need to be paternalistic and give it to them? Or is it that deep down you really think the rich will actually pay for the drug, so you might as well give it to the poor? If that is so, would you not rather spend the money generously donated by the rich on things that the poor really want? Why use up the largesse of the rich on things of marginal value?

In short, public finance of private consumption in areas where we have diverse tastes almost certainly has a cost, in terms of avoidably breaching the efficiency principle for a large proportion of the population. Breaching the efficiency principle, incurring deadweight costs, is not just a problem for the rich. A waste of resources is a waste of resources, and if the resources were not wasted, someone else – rich or poor – could enjoy them.

Of course, it is difficult to serve the efficiency principle in the context of diversity of tastes without diversity in the level of provision – the idea that some people may have Zovirax while others do not. And it is difficult to foster diversity in the level of provision while also preserving the idea of equality of provision – the idea that if some people have Zovirax, then everyone does.

The only conclusion to draw is that we should limit uniform provision of services to those areas where there is some particularly good reason for it; and that where government does need to provide a service, it should do so to a level that tends to suit those with a minimum taste for the item in question, and it should let others top up that provision at their own cost.

The Problem of Zero User Costs

There is a solution to the provision of uniform levels of service; that is to allow varying levels of service. We might give certain categories of people, or certain more demanding people, more of the service than everyone else. At its most extreme, we might simply let people use as much of the service as they choose, as we allow people to walk in the park as much as they like, for example.

This ensures that demand drives the level of service provided, and is more flexible than a uniform supply, but it gives rise to another cost: it is one that most economists would probably consider the most obvious and the most damning. It is the problem of there being no direct cost to the user of a service.

To understand the magnitude of this problem, suppose you live in a block of fifty flats, where the heating and hot water bills are shared among the tenants – no one has a meter of their own, the total energy bill for the whole block is just split up and divided evenly. Suppose too, just to make the point clear, that each flat has an identical taste for energy – this is a block of Stepford families in which everyone has the same income and the same desire for warmth and hot showers. As a result, there is no heterogeneity of tastes, and as everyone is the same, there is no redistribution to obscure the choices made by different types.

The heating system in this block is a disaster, because each individual flat chooses to overheat their property because they are not facing the full cost of their decision. What you will observe in such a flat is the heating turned up to maximum and the windows open to allow plenty of fresh air to blow in. The precise calculation that most of us do – more or less roughly – when setting the temperature of our property is whether we value that extra degree of warmth more or less than the extra cost of heating the property by that extra degree. In this building, for any one dweller, the cost of turning the heating up is borne by forty-nine other people. Each individual only pays one-fiftieth (i.e., 2 per cent) of their extra heating. In the end then, people will be heating their flats up far more than they would choose were they paying the full cost themselves.

Now, the crucial condition that makes the heating problem so severe is that the occupants of each flat can in effect demand as much heating as they want. If the level of demand can be controlled centrally – the temperature of the building is controlled by the caretaker – the problem of zero user costs obviously does not arise. But this is achieved only by worsening the problem of inefficiency created by uniform provision. We may not all want the same temperature in our flats.

Of all the major services government provides (I exclude social security for now, although this general argument does apply to it) there are a couple which appear – or which have appeared – to meet all these conditions: health care and legal aid in civil cases. Because it is we who decide whether we are ill or not – and because a good deal of expense is involved in ascertaining whether or not our own diagnosis is correct – each citizen in a system of free health care has the power to run up costs. We can make gratuitous trips to our GP, for example. This is not the only form of self-determined demand in the system. Some people choose to use the relatively expensive casualty services for minor ailments, when they could use a GP. They do not bear any proportion of that cost. Moreover, health complaints on the margin of what is covered by the NHS – cosmetic complaints for example – are essentially dealt with on the basis of patient persistence. You may or may not bother to get the problem dealt with. There is no reward – no cash-back scheme – for those who opt not to pursue treatment.

With legal aid, *in civil cases*, it is we who primarily make the decision as to whether to sue someone; and it is we who decide how much legal advice to buy (although this is a choice made on the expert advice of a person selling legal services), but in the case of those eligible for state aid, it is a third party – the Legal Aid Board – who picks up the bill. It is no wonder that change in the legal aid system has been proposed.

Even if the price signal of these items – provided free to the user – were not a problem in generating demand, there is an additional cost resulting from the fact the users pay nothing. They become less interested consumers. It is popularly supposed – with good reason – that we feel more comfortable leaving a play if we haven't had to pay for our tickets. This may be irrational – we should be comfortable leaving a play if it's no good, even if we did pay for the tickets. There is no point in piling the cost of wasted time on to the regrettable cash outlay. But the fact is we do feel less of a connection if we don't pay, and as a result we feel more inclined to walk away from the service, and less inclined to assert our rights as users. We can hardly demand our money back if we haven't paid for a ticket. But the possibility that if we *have* paid we *could* demand our money back gives an incentive to the theatre not to stage absolute rubbish.

The power of the direct financial relationship in establishing a framework of rights and responsibilities, expectations and interests, is not to be underestimated. If the old model of public sector delivery has turned that power off, that is to be regretted. The reform agenda obviously

then has to look at regenerating it. Such was the objective of the
Citizens' Charter initiative. Whether a hundred pages of charter are
worth £1 of direct financial relationship is an empirical question. I
confess to having doubts on this score.

If there is a solution to the problem of zero user costs, it is to avoid
such situations by charging people at least some proportion of the cost
of the service they incur. (The charge does not have to be a positive
one: people could be given cash-back not to take up a service, as well
as being charged to take up a service, although governments might
rightly be wary of handing out money to, for example, people who say
they are sick but are willing to forgo a trip to the doctor.) But charging a
fee for such services unfortunately carries the consequence of unwinding
some of the redistributional effects of existing service provision.

The alternative approach is to allow varying levels of service to be
provided, but not to let the recipient be the judge of how much service
to enjoy. It means employing an intermediary – a fundholder – to
allocate the service on an informed assessment of different clients' needs.
This is an option that we shall examine in Chapter 9.

The Problem of Redistribution

The fact that we use benefits-in-kind as a redistributive tool generates
yet another problem with state spending: even if the tastes of the entire
population were homogeneous, the fact that we mix up redistribution
of living standards and the choice of level of service, means we entirely
distort everybody's choice about how much service to vote for. (Indeed,
Chapter 2 argued this was one reason for the existence of benefits-in-
kind.) To recapitulate, imagine that we live in a selfish state, where
everybody thinks about their own self-interest when they cast their
vote in national elections, and imagine the way the different groups
would be likely to look upon state services.

The poor, who in effect pay nothing for services, will vote for more
of them, even when they think there is little value to the services on
offer. The rich will be confused, but if there was no redistribution
would tend to support high levels of provision.

But in our political system, it is the *median voter*, middle Britain, who will eventually determine how much is spent. This is because the political parties, in order to win elections, will find themselves inextricably drawn to appeal to the tastes of those in the middle – a process outlined by Harold Hotelling in 1929. He used a famous analogy of ice cream sellers positioning themselves on a beach boardwalk. In a two-party race, anyone positioned away from the centre can gain share by moving towards it. This was also the observation of Anthony Downs, who is most closely associated with the median voter theory.

In Britain, what will median voters support? If we take a look at what middle Britain would want from Table 1 in Chapter 2, we see that the third quintile pay about £6,400 in tax each year, and get just under £3,400 in cash benefits back. From the net payment of £3,000, they get all the public goods that the government buys, plus they personally get £3,300 of benefits-in-kind. Clearly the median voter is going to be behind more and better services. Middle Britain is paying £1 for private services which actually cost about £1.10.[1]

So in a broadly redistributive system, therefore, the median voter is a net recipient of transfers. The median voter will tend to support a bigger state – even though what she may really want is simply more redistribution.

If this is the case, it is damaging for the country: median voters would support extra spending costing £1.10, when they only valued it at £1.00. That would represent a clear breach of the efficiency principle.

Now we should not exaggerate the impact of the median voter view of these things. The fact that median voters may like benefits-in-kind is not entirely helpful in accounting for policy choices. Median voters may choose to rob the rich, but they do not have to charge their health bills to the rich in order to do that; they could rob them in other ways – by taking their cash, for example. And there is another problem with median voter explanations for the extension of government – much discussed in the economic literature on it – and that is that median

---

1. How can average voters get more out of the state than they put in? The reason is that there is a difference between the median voter and the average voter. On average, obviously, voters have to pay in what they get out. But the median voter is poorer than the average voter as there are some very rich people who pull the overall average up, without pulling the median up.

voters' policy options are very wide. They could equally choose to clobber the poor, for example. Indeed, any minority is vulnerable when the median voter is dictator. Concerns that the poor are being hurt by median voters are heard in about equal numbers these days as concerns that the rich are being hurt by them.

Nevertheless, in our democracy we do tend to link redistribution and service provision, and it is commonly supposed on both the right and the left that a consequence of this is that government is bigger than it might otherwise be.

To reform the collective finance built in to the old public sector model, and to do so in a way that inspires confidence that people with middle and lower incomes are not going to lose out, the only route is to accompany reforms with packages of compensation for losers. This is, unfortunately, a route that has proven politically difficult in the past. The extension of VAT to domestic fuel was a sensible measure on almost any criteria of efficiency or justice – and could hardly be opposed by any rational human being – *as long as the losers were compensated*. In fact, because not every single loser was fully compensated, the existence of a small number of sufferers was allowed to interfere with the whole measure.

Crowding Out Private Solutions

There is one final problem that extending the scope of tax finance beyond its natural border creates: it removes incentives for individuals or groups to think of alternative, more appropriate means of support. It crowds out viable, private spontaneous activity that might otherwise emerge. For example, if the state provides childcare, you can be sure that individuals will be less inclined to leave their kids with their in-laws – even though the in-laws may be a cheaper and more satisfactory kind of alternative. If the state provides arts subsidy, you can be sure that the arts world will be lazy about finding sponsorship. If the state provides care for the elderly, you can be sure the relatives will be disinclined to take granny in and look after her.

In the long term, it is plausible to believe that if the state provides health care, alternative modes of treatment – such as prevention, or 'complementary' approaches to health care – will be one of the main casualties. If the state provides uniform education, parental effort will diminish: the desire of parents to organize fund-raising events, to teach their own children, to engage private tutors, will all suffer. Indeed, if the state provides social services, it is bound to displace private philanthropy. Charity will diminish in proportion to the belief that the state is already providing for the needy.

If the state provides overseas aid, building valuable roads or dams in poor countries, it absolves the governments of those nations from the task of building those projects instead. The result may well be that the foreign government devotes the resources liberated by aid to far less beneficial purposes.

In all these cases, the problem of displacement is very hard to measure: we shall never know how well the alternatives to government support might have performed in the absence of government. It makes it very difficult indeed to truly assess the benefits of government at all. Overseas aid provides an important example: we tend to look at how valuable the projects we have financed with our aid budget are, to deem whether they are a success or not. That does *not* tell us how effective our aid is, though, and we should not allow the fact that our projects do tend to be successful to persuade us that our aid has been useful. If we finance useful projects, what is it that the recipient government does with its money? That determines how useful our aid is.

If the recipient government is funding even more valuable projects than ours, then our contribution is measured by the value of our projects. But if the recipient government is funding less valuable spending, then our aid is simply liberating resources for less useful purposes. Our net contribution is, therefore, the value of those less useful projects. If the recipient government cuts taxes and allows a level of domestic consumption above that which would otherwise have prevailed, then our aid is simply financing consumption in the recipient nation, even though it may look very useful project by project. There is, in fact, some evidence that aid does do this.[1]

The need to take into account the response of those on whom policy operates in assessing the effectiveness of policy is an application of a particular economic principle, the so-called 'Lucas Critique', named

1. See for example, Peter Boone, *Politics and the Effectiveness of Foreign Aid*, National Bureau of Economic Research Working Paper 5308, October 1995.

after the Nobel prize-winning economist Robert Lucas. He coined the principle in an attack on the idea that governments could usefully raise growth in an economy by relaxing fiscal or monetary policy. He argued such policies would work only if agents did not respond to higher demand with higher wage claims, or higher prices. But assuming that the population did respond, the policies would not work at all. Indeed, assuming the population knew exactly how hard it wanted to work, and how willing it was to raise prices for a given level of demand, such policies would be entirely undone by private behaviour, which would turn extra demand into higher inflation, not higher growth.

In addition to the displacement of flexible alternatives to government provision, the existence of government support has one final side-effect: it creates an industry (which has very little social value at all) of those who make an effort to obtain government finance for their projects. One of the social benefits of tough government is the consequent reduction in the national lobbying effort, and the release of those resources to other purposes.

Conclusion

This chapter and the last have essentially looked at whether government is tempted to spend too much, or to buy too many different things on our behalf. Notice, however, what might be a surprising omission from the discussion. Nowhere has it been argued that government shouldn't spend money because it cannot afford to. How come? Why shouldn't we argue against government cars, or big social security benefits, on the grounds that they require resources beyond what government has to spend?

The reason is that in the account of government offered here, government is not, and should not be, viewed as just another private individual in the economy, with a set income and an expenditure to match. That is a leviathan view of government. But if we are in the business of designing good government, the direct debit view is more appropriate. We should not view the authorities as some kind of agent acting for itself, with money it takes from us, the public. Instead, government should see itself – and indeed, should be seen – as an agent acting on behalf of us. It is a buying agent, collecting cash and procuring those things for us which it is best placed to buy. We give it the money to buy those things, and if it cannot afford something, it is because *we* cannot afford it. Government can, in principle, afford anything we can afford – or to put it more precisely, anything we want to buy, given our income.

Anyway, and this cannot be overstated, *if there is a problem with government spending, it is not that it uses up money, it is that it uses up money badly: it is not the cost of government you need to worry about, it is the deadweight loss of government.* If government is spending money on things that we would like to have – and that we would choose to have given the money we have – then there is no problem with it. The problems arise when decisions to buy things are made on behalf of people who would rather have the money to spend themselves.

Apply this argument to a specific case: should government finance nursery education? In July 1995, when the government announced a nursery vouchers scheme to finance education (or, as some might prefer to call it, childcare) nationally for four-year-old children, lots of people argued that the government could not afford it; at least as many argued it should afford more – nursery education for three-year-olds too. And some argued that it was a waste to apply a new voucher scheme, as that effectively gave money to parents who were already spending money on their own children. They argued it would be better to spend the money on new local authority nursery capacity, for those children who were not getting nursery education. By spending it on the local authorities, you would get more new nursery places for your pounds.

How wrong this whole argument was. In the first place, we should be very suspicious of collectivizing this piece of spending – it is clearly of more interest to the private individual than the public that the private individual's child is sent to nursery school. In fact, there is plenty of evidence to suggest that there is almost no public interest in nursery education at all (other than in some rather exceptional and expensive cases).[1]

---

1. As far back as 1976, one writer said, 'By 1939 nine studies had been carried out. They all produced the same result. They showed that nursery school education sometimes has a temporary effect in raising the educational attainments of the children but that it has invariably disappeared by the time the child is eight or nine. Since the war numerous investigations, running into literally dozens of studies of this kind have been done and the results have confirmed the pre-war studies.' (Richard Lynn, in the IEA *Dilemmas of Government Expenditure.*)

If we *do* choose to collectivize this piece of spending, then vouchers are surely not a bad way of doing it. Why give cash to local authorities? We have little reason to suppose they are the best at providing nursery care, so that introduces a deadweight loss straight away. And what about the idea that it is a waste of money to give vouchers to those who already pay for nursery care? No, it may be an unexpected gift, but that group is the one group of parents we can be sure we are not wasting money on in handing out nursery subsidies. It is the parents who *don't* send their children to nursery school who we might suspect would rather have the money than the nursery place. They are the ones we have least reason to give them to.

Finally, what we mean by the fact government cannot afford to introduce a nursery vouchers scheme is that government would have to raise taxes to pay for it and *we* cannot afford to pay higher taxes or, more precisely, we do not want to. The concern of government in a case like this should thus be whether the population wants the item, and if so, if there is any reason why government should act as an intermediary in paying for it. It is as simple as that.

Additional Reading

Downs, A. (1957), *An Economic Theory of Democracy*, Harper and Row, New York.

Georgellis, Yannis and Harry Papapanagos (1997), 'Work and Non-work Related Childcare Costs and UK Mothers' Employment Rates', paper presented to the annual conference of the Royal Economic Society, Stoke-on-Trent, March.

Hotelling, H. (1929), 'Stability in Competition', *Economic Journal*, March.

Lynn, Richard (1976), 'A Case Study: How Effective is Expenditure on Education?' in *The Dilemmas of Government Expenditure*, Reading 15, Institute of Economic Affairs, London.

8 Economic Malaise?

The impact of government spending on the economy and growth

> *Saturn's Children* shows how a high-taxing, high-spending State devours individual liberty and self-expression, expropriates private property, damages material prosperity, displaces self-governing institutions, blights the prospects of the young, undermines the family and demoralizes or criminalizes the weak and the vulnerable.
>
> Apocalyptic inside-cover material summarizing Alan Duncan and Dominic Hobson's 1995 book, *Saturn's Children* (now out of print).

Small Government, Successful Economies

Much has been written in recent years about the apparently impressive economic performance of the Asian 'tiger' economies, in which growth has been fast, and government small. Even allowing for Asia's economic slowdown in 1997, Singapore and Hong Kong (pre-1997) are generally held to have overtaken the UK in per capita GDP – the best widely published overall measure of economic success. Government spent (in 1995) the equivalent of just 20 per cent of GDP in Singapore, and 17 per cent in Hong Kong (in contrast with the UK's 43 per cent). It is tempting to draw a connection. Does small government enlarge your economy? Just how could it do so? And is there evidence to suggest we could improve our economic performance by shrinking the state, or at least is there evidence more systematic than the odd exaggerated report of miracles in far-off places?

Most of the talk on the economic effects of government spending comes from those who are pessimistic about it, who think that by and large government should shrink to give the economy a boost. Unfortunately, much of the evidence supports the view that big govern-

Table 1: Economic Success and Size of Government

	Per capita GDP (1995, US $)	General government spending 1995 (percentage of GDP)
US	26,980	32.5
Japan	22,110	35.5
Germany	20,070	50.1
France	21,030	54.7
Canada	21,130	47.7
Italy	19,870	52.5
Hong Kong	22,950	16.6
Singapore	22,770	20.3
UK	19,260	43.0
Brazil	5,400	37.5
China	2,920	13.8
India	1,400	31.7

Countries selected: G7 (Group of Seven largest industrial nations); two frequently cited Asian success stories; three of the largest middle- or low-income nations. Values converted into dollars at purchasing power parity rates. Government spending excludes transfer payments.

Source: *World Development Report*. Oxford University Press for the World Bank, 1997, for column 1. World Economic Forum. *Global Competitiveness Report 1996*, for column 2.

ments are a feature of rich, rather than poor countries. As Table 1 demonstrates, the poorest countries generally have small government, and the European countries which have traditionally had the smallest state shares are Greece and Portugal. The core European economies may have their problems, but the post-war performance of Germany and France has not been so startlingly bad that they would be wise to emulate the policies of the Mediterranean economies without a lot of careful consideration first.

Optimists might interpret this stylized evidence as providing support for the assertion that high levels of government spending *cause* economies to succeed – the rich are rich because of the civilizing and progressive influence of their authorities. The optimists would be right up to a point: a country that has no law and order, or properly implemented property rights, or physical infrastructure, will not function well. The percentage of government spending in GDP in Russia early in 1995 was 14.2 per cent, probably well below the economically optimal level. Infrastructure matters too – one economist attributed the fall in US productivity growth in the 1970s to a cut in investment in public infrastructure.[1]

But wherever you spot an A and B tending to occur together, it must either be the case that A causes B; or that B causes A; or that some C is causing both A and B. It is hard to believe that marginal government expenditures – the kind which we are more familiar with in big-government developed economies – creates much of a long-term boost to national income. Beyond the Russias and Zaires, the causation is more plausibly reversed. It is not that big government creates high incomes, it is that high incomes lead to pressures for big government. If not, there is probably some other third, hidden hand of causation, that leads to bigger government and faster economic development.

It is difficult to test for causation by observing a correlation, but it is possible to at least see whether bigger government helps economies grow. Steve Dowrick, of Australian National University in Canberra, has looked at twenty-four developed economies in the 1950s and 1980s. He concludes:

> Re-estimating the growth equation using the two–stage least squares pro-
> cedure, with the government variables instrumented by their lagged values,
> the joint significance of the government variables disappears altogether.

Which just says that using proper statistical techniques, and controlling for all other factors, any apparent correlation between economic growth and big government evaporates.

It is never easy to identify the chain of causation. As nations get richer, they tend to become somewhat more democratic. This is the so-called 'Lipset hypothesis' after Seymour Martin Lipset, who articulated it in 1959. This implies that as they adapt from governing for the sake of 5 per cent of the population towards governing for 95 per cent of the population, there is far more spending on projects of interest to a far wider proportion of the population than had been occurring

1. David Aschauer, *Journal of Monetary Economics,* March 1989.

before. The result is bigger government, but that bigger government is observed in the precise phase in a country's history in which it is most successful economically, without there being any direct causal link. So, despite the superficial evidence of Table 1, maybe government is not good for you after all.

Having dispensed with the superficial attractions of either view – that big government helps or hinders an economy – we can search more deeply for any evidence that it creates problems. Whatever the effect of government, it is not a wicked witch, casting evil spells on the economy to make it less effective. If government has an effect, it somehow has to manifest itself through some economic mechanism. What mechanism could it be?

Public Sector Inefficiency

The adoption of the old public sector model in our economy, in particular the use of the public sector to deliver services that could have been farmed out to the private sector, may provide one route to possible economic stagnation.

We have seen already that although government in the UK spends the equivalent of 40 per cent of GDP, it actually produces at most only 15 to 20 per cent of the economy's output. We have also seen that *over the long term*, it is plausible to argue that the public sector way of doing things does tend to produce things less effectively than private sector governance. If we bravely thought that we could, say, obtain 20 per cent efficiencies in the 20 per cent of the economy government manages, then we might expect the economy to be about 4 per cent bigger than it is. We might enjoy growth that exceeded the normal 2 to 2.25 per cent annual rate, and get, say, 3 per cent for four or five years instead. That would be a welcome development – if painful for those in the public sector. It would, incidentally, be just a little less than the estimated benefits of the single market programme of the European Union.[1] If that 4 per cent gain showed up in the international statistics

1. Estimates based on the Cecchini report, published by the EC, were of a 5 per cent Europe-wide gain.

(and it might not, as much of the public sector's contribution to GDP is simply measured by reference to what is spent, rather than by reference to what is produced), it would also be enough to take Britain to within striking distance of the per capita GDPs of Italy and the Netherlands, both countries behind whom we currently lag (assuming these countries did not also squeeze more efficiency out of their public sectors).

But using that piece of the old public sector model to explain the failures of government will not do. Four per cent is not enough to change our long-term growth rate, nor is it enough to explain the difference between what we really regard as successful and unsuccessful economies. To explain the really big differences between national economies, we need a bigger theory. Fortunately for those who deal in big ideas, there is exactly such a theory.

The 'Investment Suffers' Hypothesis

Perhaps the best articulation of it came in the *Public Spending White Paper* of 1976, from a Labour government:

> When world demand picks up, more resources will be needed for export and investment. We must ensure they are available for that purpose. Unless we are prepared to see rising taxation reduce take-home pay, these resources can be made available only if we keep public expenditure at roughly the same level for several years. [p. 23]

The thesis was actually most powerfully publicized by Robert Bacon and Walter Eltis, two Oxford academics who spotted the problem before it was fashionable in their famous 1970s book, *Britain's Economic Problem: Too Few Producers* (recently republished). It argued that in Britain governments get locked into a cycle of creating jobs to boost the economy, only to find that the private sector shrinks as a result, and thus government must create yet more jobs to alleviate the consequent suffering:

> As the unemployment figures rise, extra jobs can only be provided outside industry and only the government can provide jobs where there is no prospect of profits. Hence governments are tempted to provide still more jobs in the public services, and as they raise taxation to pay for them, in due course company profits and workers' living standards are further squeezed

with the result there is still more pressure against company profits in industry. In consequence industry invests less, more industrial workers become redundant, and still more workers need to be fitted into the public sector. This ever-accelerating spiral leads nowhere except to total economic collapse and it is so deep-rooted in structural maladjustment that it is in no way amenable to tinkering. [p. 24]

At the core of the idea is that when government spends, private investment suffers, and that when private investment suffers, long-term economic growth is suppressed. In the Bacon and Eltis world, that incites government to dig deeper into the hole, boosting spending to boost growth, and hence attacking investment further. This is the story on which at least some of the attack on big government is based.

Certainly, if government is to finance its spending, it has to raise cash equivalent to about 40 per cent of GDP. What is the effect of this on the rest of the economy?

The best long-term assumption to make is that government spending neither augments nor diminishes the total amount the economy can produce. As a result, government is bound to *displace* some 40 per cent of private spending with alternative spending.[1] Now the case that government damages the economy relies heavily on the idea that the spending which is displaced is disproportionately private investment spending.

Why Investment Might Suffer

The precise argument offered by proponents of this view is based upon two important propositions: first, that the level of investment is directly linked to the share of profits in the economy, and secondly that profits

---

1. Of course, the fact government is spending money may raise the total output of the economy. In the short term, in a recession, government spending may re-employ unemployed resources, and kick-start private activity into taking off. In that case the government spending could be a free lunch. But economies do not by and large remain in recessions forever, so government cannot raise the level of activity that way for too long. In the long term, government may contribute so much to the economy – roads, education, etc. – that the potential output of the economy rises. In practice, this is likely to be a small effect, and at least for the sake of argument, it is worth accepting that government spending quite straightforwardly displaces private spending.

end up bearing a disproportionate share of any extra government spending. Both propositions can be argued at a level of some technicality: the link between profits and investment (and also savings, which is the mirror image of investment) is one of the most complex and ancient areas of economic discussion. Here it is not worth offering more than a broad sweep of the intuitions behind each idea.

That profit shares and savings levels are more than fortuitously linked to each other is just about demonstrated in Table 2, which, if nothing else, shows that Britain and Sweden have had a relatively low share of profits and a low share of saving, while at least one Asian 'tiger' economy has enjoyed the reverse. It's hardly compelling, though.

Assuming this does offer superficial support for the idea that profit and savings or investment are linked, it is not entirely clear which way the causation runs: one view (associated with the late Lord Kaldor), in the Keynesian and Cambridge University tradition, asserts that the level of investment determines the level of profits, and that the level of profits determines the national rate of saving. (On this account, investment is influenced by the growth rate, perhaps tempered by the animal spirits of investors. The resulting level of investment and capital affects the share of the economy devoted to profits, and as profit-earners save more than the rest of us, the consequent distribution of income – the profit-share – determines the national savings level. The idea is that profits are by and large saved, and earnings spent.[1]) In all, growth leads to savings and investment.

Under this view, investment is in one sense invulnerable – you can be relaxed about what happens to profits, as investment carries on its merry way. In another sense, though, this view offers grounds for fearing for investment. If it is dictated by animal spirits, then we need

1. The modern logic to such an idea is that companies prefer to invest out of profits, rather than enduring the hassles of borrowing money and persuading shareholders to put up more cash. On the other hand the people in society who live off profits are primarily the elderly through their retirement pension. Even if they observe the companies in which they hold shares investing, they can sell shares to take out their cash. In general, these are people who have a higher propensity to spend than those who are saving for retirement.

Table 2: The Relationship between Profit and Savings by Country
percentage of GDP

	Gross national saving 1981–95	rank	Capital income share 1981–95	rank
Korea	32.70	1	42.20	1
Japan	32.17	2	32.21	10
Portugal	23.00	3	35.75	5
Germany	21.47	4	34.63	8
Finland	21.04	5	28.96	14
Spain	20.57	6	34.84	7
Italy	20.38	7	37.22	3
France	20.01	8	37.73	2
Australia	18.67	9	35.95	4
Belgium	18.02	10	35.22	6
Canada	17.86	11	31.59	11
Ireland	17.47	12	26.49	15
USA	16.33	13	33.52	9
Sweden	16.31	14	31.32	12
UK	15.28	15	30.18	13

Source: OECD, *Economic Outlook*, December 1997.

to keep the animals happy, and not scare them with policies that look inimical to business.

Away from the University of Cambridge, mainstream economics tends to view the relationship between investment, profit and savings rather differently. The demand for capital for investment reflects the opportunities to earn profits. Savings, on the other hand, represent the supply of capital for investment, and the quantity of savings reflects our taste for enjoying ourselves now as opposed to thinking about the future. How much investment and saving will occur will depend on the interaction of these two. In this more traditional economic view, corporate profits are obviously important and are held to affect the incentive to defer consumption, and to look ahead by buying new plant or machinery. The greater the profit from investing and looking to the future, the more looking to the future there will be. If profits suffer, then investment will suffer. Indeed, economic theory goes further: in a simple, competitive economy – where all the usual, not very realistic, assumptions of economists apply – the level of profits will tend to *equal* the volume of investment.[1]

The implication of this mainstream view is straightforward: if government hits profits – with large taxes, for instance – then investment suffers. Crucially, if it comes along and takes extra resources away from some part of the private sector, the impact on investment will crucially depend on who pays the taxes. Is it investors who bear them? Or is it the workers? It does not matter who bears the tax in any formal sense (who it is that writes the cheque for the taxes). It is who *in the end* suffers from the fact the taxes are levied. If it is profits that suffer, then so do savings and investment. Alternatively, if it is the workers who suffer the burden of taxation from lower take-home pay, then profits and investment – and economic growth – can carry on regardless. This is where the second premise of the argument comes in – that it is profits which tend to fall as governments spend more.

The outcome of the game of 'pass the tax parcel' depends on the way the economy functions, and in particular the relative power of workers and their employers. Suppose income tax is raised. Are the workers able to pass their tax on in the form of wage demands? Or do they simply have to grin and bear their reduction in take-home pay? Proponents of the 'investment suffers' hypothesis believe it is the former.

If higher income tax does lead to successful higher wage demands, then profits take the hit; and if the hypothesis is right, the investment rate will fall, and the level of capital intensity of the economy falls as well.[2]

1. A situation that is described as conforming to the 'golden rule', and which carries the implication that society is just saving, investing, and earning from investment the same total amounts. This itself carries the implication that society is only borrowing to invest, and not to consume.

2. This can, in the eyes of those arguing this case, create a vicious circle. For the economy to adjust to a new level of less capital intensity, workers have to accept some cut in their private income to maintain their jobs: after all, if there is less capital in the economy, factories will be able to afford to lose employees unless lower wages make it more attractive to hire more staff per machine. Now, if workers do not accept their pay cut lying down – if, for example, they are able to resist wage cuts – then there will be

Quite apart from income tax, when governments do raise money there is plenty of potential for them hitting profits and investment. Taxes on investment income provide the most obvious case, typically reducing the net rate of return on a project and as a result rendering viable projects unviable. Sometimes, taxes are imposed on profits because it is considered politically or morally better for them to be taxed than earnings. Raising VAT can push up the measured rate of inflation, and thus again lead to pressure for wage increases which, if successful, invariably depress profits. Even borrowing cash from the private sector raises problems of its own: if capital markets are not open internationally, then the increase in the demand for capital by government could push up the price of capital – i.e., interest rates – and crowd out private sector investment. If capital markets are open internationally, interest rates should not rise. But any shortfall in capital locally can be met by imports of capital from abroad, which inevitably push up the exchange rate and lower the rate of return for exporting companies.

Implications of the Hypothesis

In all these cases, then, the basic finding is that to ensure high levels of government spending avoid economic damage, the population must accept cuts in day-to-day private living standards commensurate with the increases in day-to-day public living standards. This is really a rather simpler conclusion than one might have supposed: it just says if government consumes more, it should try and ensure that it displaces private consumption not private investment in doing so. The mechanism for ensuring that consumption suffers rather than investment is to protect the level of company profits.

The most important mechanism for protecting profits is to ensure that in the great bargaining game between employers and employees, employers can maintain a strong hand. And if one believes this argument, it supports one of the great paradoxes of government spending:

---

inflation; or if government maintains a tough macro-economic policy, there will be a higher rate of unemployment. And the danger is that the unemployment increases the burden of government spending, and sends the economy further into the mess it is getting into.

That governments who want to spend a lot and minimize the chance of serious damage being wrought upon the economy, should aim to ensure that workers end up paying for government consumption out of their private consumption, and should protect corporate profit levels. Failure could magnify the cost to the economy of the government spending.

The long-term costs to the economy of big government are likely to be smaller when unions are weak.

Another way of looking at this argument is to say that using both big government and trade unions as a device to help the 'vulnerable' in society is to use one instrument too many. The interaction of the two leads to economic problems. In a society lacking a consensus on what levels of wages and profits are appropriate, either big government or strong unions may be all right – but not both. Under this view, the idea that you can pay for bigger government by getting rich investors to pay higher taxes without damage to the welfare of the poor is well-intentioned but misguided. In most cases, profits are a good thing for investment, and investment is good for growth.

Investors can be protected, of course. They endure the least suffering in one of two different situations. First, when the power of organized labour is weak – because then firms can squeeze employees harder than employees can squeeze firms. Second, if there is an organized and responsible national 'social compact' that fixes shares to allow for a high level of profits and investment. In short, big government can be paid for most appropriately when there are weak private sector unions, or when there are strong but responsible private sector unions.[1]

The centralized route of strong, responsible unions has been practised in much of Europe. The combination of big government and weak unions is oddly not easy to find – the forces that lead to big governments tend also to lead to strong unions; and it is possible strong unions tend to campaign for, and succeed in obtaining, big government. The nearest candidate for this combination is now the UK, which by global standards is still quite a big-government nation, and for the size of its government

---

1. Public sector unions matter too, as they can have an impact in determining the overall level of wages, but their impact on the private sector is less direct than that of the private sector unions.

appears to have a relatively weak trade union movement. The worst world to be in, of course, if government wishes to be large, is the one that has strong but irresponsible unions. Italy and Britain, one might suggest, have been caught in this world in the past.[1]

Assessment of the 'Investment Suffers' Hypothesis

In effect, the 'investment suffers' hypothesis is about monopoly power in the labour market: it is about the fight between labour and capital; between bosses and workers. In general, the workers have taken the side of big government, even though the workers themselves stand to lose rather a lot if investment suffers in the long term. So why have big governments emerged, and not attempted to protect profits and investment? What defence could there possibly be for levying especially high taxes on capital in the hope that capitalists pay them?

In fact, the 'investment suffers' hypothesis does appear to have some validity, but things are never simple, and the hypothesis is not as clear-cut as the plausible-sounding case just made out for it implies. Governments have never wilfully damaged investment: if they have done, they were, in retrospect, acting understandably.

For one thing, the early development of big government – especially big government promoted by socialist parties – aimed at protecting the investment ratio through government spending. In that vision, government would not waste its money on big millennium parties, but spend it on big new factories – government investment would replace private investment, so the profit share and the level of private investment was a matter on which it could take a relaxed view.

Most of us would now tend to take the view that replacing private investment with public investment is far from desirable, although probably not as bad as replacing private investment with public consumption.

An alternative defence is that government and investment can happily co-exist, while profits suffer. That is based on the idea that not all profits are actually returns to investment: a lot of profits are in fact returns to property that only the Almighty can claim to have created – land and

1. In Britain the situation has primarily changed because the unions have become weaker; in Italy it has primarily changed because they have become more responsible.

North Sea oil, for example. If we could tax the returns to assets that are not the result of investment, that would clearly not carry the same implication for the level of investment in the economy as taxing people's savings. In the minds of many – like those around the time of Asquith who introduced the first tax premium on unearned income in the 1907 budget – it was those profits from land that were envisaged as being the target.

Traditionally, economists used the term 'rent' to describe that part of GDP which goes to those who own natural resources, and 'rent' is distinct from 'profit', which was a compensation for investment (among other things). In practice, the distinction between rent and profit is difficult to draw: it is not easily possible to distinguish the return to a piece of land, for example, from the return to the building which occupies it. One is – in the economic sense – rent, the other is profit. The national accounts do not attempt to draw quite such a distinction, but do separate out the profits of corporate trading activity, and the profits of property, and this is the best available proxy for distinction between rents and profits.

Unfortunately for this line of argument, if governments in the past hoped to finance expansion by placing a burden on property income, they do not appear to have been very successful: the category of income entitled 'rent' in national accounts took 4.8 per cent of GDP in 1856, and 6.6 per cent in 1973. Given the vagaries of the data, one might say these figures are just for fun. What they do illustrate, however, is how unlikely it is that governments would finance an expansion from, say, 10 per cent of GDP to 25 per cent, on the basis of taxing the income from wealth held in the form of land and natural resources. The figures also suggest (absolutely no more than that) that governments have had difficulty in doing so.[1]

A final line of defence of big government against the 'investment suffers' hypothesis is simply that government is not a necessary condition for investment to fall. After all, workers are well able to extract monopoly

---

1. The source of these figures is the book *British Economic Growth 1856–1973* by Matthews *et al*. Experts in public accounts should note that the figures *do* include a component of implicit rent on government property. The authors of the study do not consider this to explain the historical pattern.

returns without the presence of taxation, and investment may suffer in any case. Who is to say that if taxes had been lower, workers would not have bid the overall cost of labour up to the point they did in the presence of taxes? Government may facilitate the process, but cannot be necessarily blamed for it. This is a powerful argument, although again one cannot help but feel the burden of taxation *would* have put pressure on the labour market.

In all, it does seem that in as far as government increases its spending *without taxing the return to land or natural resources*; *without investing the proceeds*; and *while increasing the burden on profits and investment*, then government imposes costs on the process of economic development that must be added to the simple costs in terms of pounds spent on the goods. We want private consumption to pay for public consumption, since in any rational view of government the two should be seen as substitutes for each other. The choice really should be between shopping at Sainsbury's and shopping at Whitehall.[1]

The Evidence

If this rather heavy meal has left an inconclusive taste in your mouth, that is probably inevitable. We can attempt to freshen the discussion with a brief look at some evidence on investment levels.

Here, there is good news and bad news. If you want to believe that investment has suffered in our economy as government has grown, the good news is there is plenty of evidence that the growth of government historically has coincided with a large fall in the share of profit in the economy, and a large growth in the share of wages earned by labour.

On the other hand, if you are a supporter of the 'investment suffers' hypothesis, you have one challenge: to explain the fact that post Second World War investment and savings have been at high levels by historic standards. Indeed, they have been higher than during the era of British economic dominance in the thrifty Victorian age. Relative to our past, the years of big government – 1965 to 1973 – were in fact a golden age

---

1. The arguments for this approach to imposing the burden of government spending are similar to the arguments for consumption rather than income taxes in the public choice literature. These arguments are not conclusive but are persuasive.

Table 3: Investment and Profit Shares in Britain over Time
percentage of GNP

	Wages, salaries, other income for labour	'Rent'	'Profits'	Investment[1]
1856	57.8	4.8	25.1	12.6
1873	54.4	5.2	28.8	17.2
1913	56.0	6.4	26.7	18.7
1924	66.6	5.3	21.3	10.9
1937	65.1	6.4	23.2	12.0
1951	70.9	3.4	21.1	16.5
1964	71.4	5.0	20.9	20.8
1973	72.8	6.6	17.2	21.7

Source: *British Economic Growth 1856–1973*, Matthews *et al*; Tables 6.1 and 5.6.

1. Investment is equal to gross fixed capital formation (new physical capital), plus new inventories (stocks of goods), plus net overseas investment.

of saving and investment (even though Britain's rates of investment were low by international standards). Table 3 outlines the facts, drawn from a book on British economic history, *British Economic Growth 1856–1973*, by three authors who have painstakingly trawled the evidence. They observe that in the post-war period, relative to other periods, government contributed savings to the economy. And during the post-war era, the tendency for the public in general to save – as opposed to companies or government, for example – grew over time. The increase in the savings rate, in the view of the authors, explains the faster accumulation of capital assets – in other words, the increase in investment in that period. They comment, 'No generally accepted explanation exists for the rise in the personal savings ratio in the 1950s and 1960s, which is one of the curiosities of British economic statistics.'

The fact that savings grew while profit shares fell is not just a challenge for the 'investment suffers' hypothesis, it is evidently a challenge for the economic theory underlying it – and indeed, a challenge even for the views of Cambridge University, who did not deny a correlation between profits and investment, but just argued it worked in a reverse of the orthodox attribution of causality.

At the risk of sounding a little disingenuous, it is possible to escape the difficulties of the evidence by saying that traditional economics posits a link between profits, investment and saving, but for external reasons the nature of that link may change from time to time. There is a link between the quantity of food we eat and obesity – but that link can change if, for example, we exercise more. So the economist has to argue that something has changed over the last century. For example, it is quite possible that there has been a shift in the propensity to save as a result of a host of factors – the age structure of the population, the development of pensions as an institution, and the fact that in the 1950s incomes were growing faster than people expected, for example. These changes in economic preferences would mean the economy was not necessarily on a steady growth path, so the traditional relationship between profits and investment need not hold. And given these changes, there is no certainty that investment or profit shares should move together.

To save the 'investment suffers' hypothesis, we can only then argue that in as far as profit levels and investment are related, investment has probably been *lower than it might otherwise have been*.

So much for the long-term evidence. A number of studies have attempted to demonstrate the problem based on shorter time horizons or by comparing different countries. Table 2 sketches some of the evidence, but it is very crude because it does not control for other factors that might explain the differing levels of each variable between countries. There is the original Bacon and Eltis study itself: in the 1970s, they thought investment did suffer, but they became far more optimistic during the 1980s, given the weakening of union power in the UK. They now surmise that the power of labour to pass on taxes is perhaps three-fifths of what it was.

More recently though, Steve Dowrick, who was mentioned above, has suggested that a 1 per cent increase in government consumption in a developed economy leads to a 0.3 per cent drop in investment. Or to put it another way, increasing government consumption from 15 per cent of GDP to 20 per cent of GDP would reduce investment from, say, 25 per cent of GDP to 22 per cent, or thereabouts. This suggests that investment *does* suffer disproportionately – it would mean the capital stock in Britain (with a 2 per cent growth rate, and an

Table 4: The Wage Clawback of Tax Increases

	Percentage increase in wages in response to a 1 per cent increase in taxes[1]	Average percentage of poll respondents believing tax is too high on certain income groups
Australia	1.6	54
Netherlands	1.2	53
Italy	1.0	54
Germany	0.7	47
United Kingdom	0.6	50
United States	0.4	51

Source: Column 1: Knoester and Van Windt, 1987. Column 2: *British Social Attitudes*, 1989.

1. Other countries for which data in this column is available are: Canada 0.6; France 0.6; Japan 1.2; Sweden 0.7.

assumed 8 per cent depreciation rate) would fall from 2.5 times GDP to 2.2 times GDP. One might argue that the effect is tolerable.

There is another form of evidence, outlined for different countries in the first column of Table 4. It relates to the degree to which employees are observed, using econometric techniques, to pass the burden of tax increases on to their employers. It appears that a 1 per cent increase in the tax burden leads to about half a per cent increase in the wages negotiated. In other words, for every extra pound government spends, we appear willing to put up about 50p of it.

That 50 per cent appears a reasonable approximation for most developed countries, considering the statistical error inherent in this kind of estimate. Britain appeared to be close to the average at the time of the study – the 0.6 per cent figure shows we actually demand a little more than half the tax increase back in the form of higher wages. However, the figure may be a little out of date for the UK now, given that conditions in the labour market appear to have changed substantially. Putting that aside, one could heroically assume that at the time of the study, and with strong unions capable of passing the burden of tax on, we put a value on government spending a little less than half what it costs.

But there is one more interesting question: can we infer that some government spending is less likely to hit investment than other government spending? The great question is whether the macroeconomic effects of inefficiently large government – leviathan government – are more severe than the macroeconomic effects of popular, sensible government spending – 'direct debit' government? In short, is there a refined version of the 'investment suffers' hypothesis that says investment suffers when government spends money badly, but suffers less when government spends money well, in accord with the efficiency principle outlined in Chapter 3. Or does the unrefined 'investment suffers' idea hold: that investment suffers by an amount regardless of the merits or sense of spending?

Table 4 does provide anecdotal support for the idea. The second column in the table is taken from international poll findings on whether people consider taxes too high for different income groups. There is a clear – although rather rough-and-ready – relationship between how discontented people are with the taxes they pay, and how much they demand in extra pay when taxes go up. The US, a low-tax country, with less discontent in the polls about how high taxes are, has less tax resistance in the labour market too. Indeed, of the six countries for whom there is data in both columns, the three most tax-resistant are the three most antagonistic to tax in the polls.

We cannot read much into this, but it at least suggests an interesting topic of further study. In principle, one can easily imagine that where you have nationally negotiated pay rates and centralized bargaining, in countries like Germany, the ability of the social pact to withstand extra taxes is far greater when the union members *want* the taxes to go up, in order to pay for extra spending. So in the case of Germany, the refined version of the 'investment suffers' hypothesis – the idea that it suffers primarily when government wastes money – does seem plausible.

That might not be true in Britain: where you have a deregulated and decentralized labour market, it is dog-eat-dog, regardless of how many dogs each dog has eaten. The bargain struck between employer and employee reflects bargaining power, and the marginal worth of the employee to the firm. In principle, the *cost* of the employee and all the taxes that she bears makes a big difference to that negotiation – but not the benefits of those costs to the employee.

The tentative conclusion to be drawn from all of this is that the potential macroeconomic costs of government spending, in displacing investment, should make governments very wary of spending at levels in excess of what they know to be the desired level. That is perhaps more true in countries with strong unions than it is in those with weak unions. This is because where labour is weak, it is more likely to pay for the spending whether it is good or bad, and hence the spending is less likely to damage investment levels. The evidence on investment suffering is not strong enough to suggest that spending should be avoided if it is clearly desired by the population.

Investment and Other Effects of Government

There are other ways in which government affects the way the economy operates – it is not just that it changes the 40 per cent of GDP that is displaced; the 60 per cent left is also distorted to some extent. As if to add weight to the idea that investment takes a hit from government spending, it is possible to argue that one of the biggest distortions is the fact that government's existence and protection discourage us from protecting ourselves – and hence lowers the level of savings that we might accumulate to provide a cushion. In addition to this, the amount government spends can have an impact on the ability of government to manage the economy effectively. We can take a look at each of these arguments.

Reducing the Incentive to Save

When Adam and Eve were placed in the Garden of Eden, God did not enrol them in any general pension plan. If the couple wanted to prepare for retirement (a lengthy phase of life in the Old Testament), they would themselves have to build up reserves and savings. A big question emerges from this: if there had been a modern-style government in the Garden of Eden, offering a pension in retirement, would Adam and Eve have saved less?

Without entering into an emotive debate about personal responsibility – an issue of undoubted concern to the Garden's authorities – the important effect to examine is the disincentive for residents to build up reserves, with a commensurate fall in the funds available for investment that is *quite independent of the 'investment suffers' hypothesis already discussed*.

To put the argument in a modern context and at its most basic, if government had never given us a pension, would we not have saved more for our own? The question is, has government (in its actions rather than its words) effectively encouraged us not to save?

Adam and Eve can illustrate the principles of this discussion rather well.[1] The argument is less dramatic than it sounds, but nevertheless very real. Imagine that Adam and Eve saved just enough that over the course of their lives the amount of their savings they used up on bad days exactly matched the amount they had saved on good days, so they died with nothing. For example, we could divide their life into two simple phases: in the first phase, they saved, planting trees from which to eat in retirement. In the second phase, they would retire and eat off these trees. If Adam and Eve were alone, the 'capital stock' of the Garden of Eden (mostly apple trees) would have grown during the early part of their life, and diminished during the latter phase.

The picture changes though, once we allow for the fact that Adam and Eve started to beget children. In this case, the capital stock accumulates early in Adam and Eve's life, but then, just as Adam and Eve are ready to run it down again, the children will start planting trees themselves, in readiness for their retirement. The Garden (with what would amount to a privatized pension system) would enter something close to an equilibrium, with overlapping generations. From then on, the Garden's total asset base (its number of trees) would stabilize, that is unless the population grew steadily, or unless some great disaster – such as a flood – wiped out all assets and required the system to start again.

Now, had the Lord enrolled Adam and Eve into a government pension scheme, and had the government acted like most governments do with regard to pensions, then things would have been a little different. Adam and Eve would not have had to worry about their pension and possible misfortune. They would not have had to save, as the government would look after them when the need arose, by taxing their children.

1. Which is why I do not vouch for this exposition being entirely original.

As for the children themselves, they too would now not need to save, because they would have the support of *their* children. But they would have to pay tax, as the government would need cash to pay a pension to Adam and Eve. The net effect on the children would be to have simply swapped savings into taxes.

The net difference overall between these systems – the funded scheme where Adam and Eve save for themselves and the unfunded scheme where Adam and Eve do not – is that Adam and Eve (the first generation) enjoy a better life (without the duty to save); the children are really no better or worse off, since they pay in roughly what they get out under either system.

The impact on the *flow* of savings and the stock of trees is more subtle. Savings are lower in the first period of Adam and Eve's life. It is a first-generation impact only. Thereafter, the flow of savings is simply replaced by a flow of taxes. However, the impact on the capital *stock* of the garden is permanently lower – the trees that Adam and Eve would have 'saved' in that first period will not exist, and never will. The capital stock is reduced by the absent flow of savings from the first generation.

This is the worry about government insurance or pension schemes that are not self-financing from their inauguration. In as far as they displace private schemes, they leave a lower capital stock than would otherwise exist. That capital gap will grow when the population is growing; shrink when the population is falling; and grow when the schemes are made more generous.

Is this effect of government a large one? The economist who has been most worried about this effect is a right-wing American called Martin Feldstein, former head of the Council of Economic Advisors to Ronald Reagan. The economist who has been most relaxed about this effect is another right-wing American called Robert Barro. In this debate, an extensive one among academics, Barro has had more of the professionals on his side. The arguments and evidence are all rather interesting, but extremely complicated. Indeed, interpreting the evidence has generated one of the more dramatic battles of recent econometrics. Martin Feldstein originally produced some results purporting to show that the savings effect was large. Then, however, two other academics, Dean Leimer and Selig Lesnoy, attempted to replicate his results and discovered that he had made a computing error. Feldstein retorted with an apology:

> An error was made by the programmer who converted the specification of social security wealth into FORTRAN. Because of a mis-placed 'do-loop' in the sub-routine that incorporates the 1957 change in the benefits paid to surviving spouses, the calculated value of social security grew faster than the correct specification implied.

In fact, this rogue 'do-loop' meant his results should have been much smaller than they were. Interestingly, however, that was not the only problem in the original Feldstein paper: he had also been using data that was subsequently revised. Taking the new data into account, his results were actually only a bit smaller and a bit more uncertain than the originals. So, with all *known* mistakes taken into account, he proclaimed that each dollar of US government social security tax leads to a fall in personal savings of 92 cents. For the year 1976, he claims that private saving – at \$95bn – was \$58bn smaller than it would have been had people not enjoyed the security of their share of government's \$3,208bn of social security promises. One is left somewhat unsure quite how much weight can be attached to these results (and to any results of exercises too complicated to be transparent).

The counter-argument to Feldstein anyway is quite convincing. Barro argues that all we are talking about in this issue is the relative distribution of wealth from one generation to the next, and that government has no monopoly power to determine inter-generational gifts. If Adam and Eve had not had to save for retirement, for example – knowing that government would look after them using taxes paid by future generations – they might have saved anyway, and chosen to leave a bequest to their children. Or, even if there had been no government pension, Adam and Eve may have chosen not to save anyway, instead hoping to rely on their children's generosity. In either case, the existence of government itself would not reduce savings compared to a world of no government. Its main effect would simply be to formalize the intergenerational arrangement. As Barro says,

> An important effect of this type is the apparently strong influence of social security in reducing the fraction of retired people who live with, and

presumably receive support from, their children. When this sort of private offset to social security occurs, the downward effect on private saving would no longer be predicted.

Barro's own statistical work has led him to conclude that you cannot draw conclusions from statistical work on this subject – it neither supports nor refutes the hypothesis.

But taking the cue from Barro, that government merely formalizes the arrangements that would anyway exist between generations, there is still some evidence that government has an effect on the level of savings. This looks at the effect on those with families, and those without. In the context of the demographics of growing populations in the era after the Second World War, that coincided with large, unfunded government pension systems, the level of savings may well have been depressed. By what amount? In 1989, the American academics Douglas Bernheim and Lawrence Levin came up with estimates as follows: for married couples, the existence of US social security makes little difference to saving patterns. At a best guess, every extra dollar expected in social security leads to a 20-cent drop in other wealth that couples would bother to accumulate. But that is just a guess, and cannot reliably be distinguished from zero given the sample size. As for single people, the figure is much higher and statistically more reliably distinct from zero. A dollar of social security appears to reduce other wealth by about $1.21. Single people would save more in the absence of government, because they have fewer children to act as a substitute for a pension. These are results the authors describe as preliminary. The result justifies concern, but not panic.

The evidence as described concerns pension rights. We still have to worry about precautionary saving, against misfortune. Obviously, the existence of government-based social protection reduces the need for us to keep a reserve for ourselves. This undoubtedly means that government reduces the stock of savings that would otherwise exist. What is not clear is whether it is in some sense socially desirable that there should be a stock of savings for this purpose. The issues and merits of funding primarily relate to pensions.

Excessive Borrowing

Another great macroeconomic worry is that governments may borrow too much. This issue has arisen in several other contexts: governments will borrow instead of raising taxes in order to con the electorate (*fiscal illusion*); and when governments borrow, they may crowd out private investment by pushing up interest rates without companies enjoying the power of restoring profitability by passing the costs on to customers or workers ('*investment suffers' hypothesis*).

The name of Robert Barro arises again on this: and again he argues that governments have less power than you might think. If they borrow more, we the population will save more in anticipation of the higher taxes that we will end up paying eventually. Whether governments choose to tax or to borrow makes little difference to the macroeconomy. The argument has been written in technical and less technical form – a popular account of it is found in the Barro book of essays, *Getting it Right*.

There is one other important effect of large borrowing, however. If levels of debt rise fast, there can begin to be some risk attached to the possibility of default on that debt. This can mean that governments who wish to use fiscal policy as a tool for stabilizing the economy – running big deficits in depressed years for the economy and small ones in buoyant times – can face a premium cost for doing so. If you have used up your credit limit in the capital market simply financing spending that you didn't want to pay for immediately, then you have no credit left to use on stabilization policy when the need arises.

That big governments do borrow more is not entirely obvious. Deficits in Germany and France have not been systematically higher than in the US, for example. Deficits in both 'big government' Italy, and 'small government' Greece have been. The idea that big governments borrow a lot appears more convincing if one looks at the evidence across time, because deficits and spending grew in the 1970s in many countries. Deficits continued to be a problem in the eighties, even when inflation and other problems of the 1970s diminished. The IMF, in its *World Economic Outlook* of April 1996, argued that, 'Even when there may appear to be a case for a policy stimulus, large existing deficits have increasingly eliminated fiscal policy as a counter-cyclical policy instrument.' Certainly, big government is not helpful to efforts to keep government borrowing small.

The message of all this is that those governments who still believe in fiscal policy as a tool – governments mainly of a left persuasion – far from thinking that they are justified in borrowing to finance spending, have to be particularly cautious about borrowing. They need to preserve their tools for the jobs they really need them to do.

Conclusion

Investment is important because it is the seedcorn of economic prosperity and social renewal; it generates both wealth and welfare. Investment – by the public and private sectors, and by a partnership of the two – increases the future productivity of the economy. Yet for a long time we have failed to invest enough in ourselves – in the life-chances of all children, in our skills, in our industry and infrastructure, and in our communities. In the last fifteen years, consumption has boomed with private and government consumption together reaching 87 per cent of gross domestic product, compared to an EU average of 80 per cent. But our industry is weak, our public services neglected, our infrastructure is underfunded and our nation divided.

Social Justice Commission, *Strategies for National Renewal*, p. 97.

What does this paragraph from the report of the Social Justice Commission, set up by the late John Smith to inform Labour Party policy, tell us?

Perhaps first is that the centre left is enthusiastic about investment – indeed, a more gushing compendium of pro-investment clichés would be hard to imagine. The second point is that the centre left recognizes that public consumption is not investment, and might detract from investment. The third point is that the centre left is reluctant to admit that lower public consumption may be a necessary consequence of a policy to support higher investment. The report says that our public services are neglected and our nation divided with the levels of public spending we have. Think how much worse it will have to be if we want to raise the share of private investment significantly – unless private consumption can be cut very substantially, public consumption will have to suffer – i.e. public services will become more neglected, and the nation more divided as the redistribution built in to the services is trimmed back.

In short, one message of this chapter – a message which had evidently not been understood by the Social Justice Commission – is that tough decisions have to be taken. And it is those on the left with their enthusiasm for investment, not those on the right, who should be most inclined to take those tough decisions.

But perhaps the other – again familiar – message is that whether you think government has a benign or malevolent effect on the economy, on growth, on inflation, and on living standards really depends on that same old distinction between the view of government as a kind of agent for the public, acting more or less rationally; or as a kind of leviathan, robbing the public for its own ends.

Or to put it another way, if each individual decision taken by government is sensible, meeting the efficiency principle and with benefits outweighing costs, then the overall effect of government on the economy can hardly be damaging. If government decisions are well placed and efficiently delivered, and if spending decisions do not distort private behaviour in detrimental ways, then there is little reason to worry about the presence of government in the macro-economy.

Additional Reading

Bacon, Robert and Walter Eltis (1976), *Britain's Economic Problem: Too Few Producers* and (1996) *Britain's Economic Problem Revisited*, Macmillan, London.

Barro, Robert J. (1996), *Getting it Right: Markets and Choices in a Free Society*, MIT Press, Cambridge, Massachusetts and London.

Barro, Robert and Glenn MacDonald (1979), 'Social Security and Consumer Spending in an International Cross Section', *Journal of Public Economics*, Vol. 11, pp. 275–89.

Bernheim, Douglas and Lawrence Levin (1989), 'Social Security and Personal Saving: An Analysis of Expectations', *American Economic Review*, Vol. 79, No. 2.

Coates, David (1994), *The Question of UK Decline*, Harvester Wheatsheaf, Hemel Hempstead.

Dowrick, Steve (1993), 'Government Consumption: Its Effects on Productivity, Growth and Investment' in Norman Gemmell (ed.), *The Growth of the Public Sector: Theories and International Evidence*, Edward Elgar, Aldershot.

Feldstein, Martin (1974), 'Social Security, Induced Retirement and Aggregate Capital Accumulation', *Journal of Political Economy*, Vol. 82, No. 5.

Feldstein, Martin (1982), 'Social Security and Private Saving: A Reply', *Journal of Political Economy*, Vol. 90, No. 3.

Knoester, Anthonie and Nico van der Windt (1987), 'Real Wages and Taxation in Ten OECD Countries', *Oxford Bulletin of Economics and Statistics*, Vol. 49, No. 1.

Leimer, Dean and Selig Lesnoy (1982), 'Social Security and Private Saving: New Time Series Evidence', *Journal of Political Economy*, Vol. 90, No. 3.

Liebfritz, Willi, *et al.* (1995), *Ageing Populations, Pension Systems, and Government Budgets: How Do they Affect Saving?*, Organization for Economic Co-operation and Development, Economics Department Working Paper No. 156, Paris.

Matthews, R.C.O., C. H. Feinstein and J. C. Odling-Smee (1982), *British Economic Growth 1856–1973*, Clarendon Press, Oxford.

Roll, Eric (1995), *Where Did We Go Wrong?*, Faber and Faber, London.

World Bank (1993), *The East Asian Miracle: Economic Growth and Public Policy*, Oxford University Press, New York.

Part Three
Possibilities for Reform

We have so far romped through some problems in the design and application of public spending decisions, and in particular we have seen that a number of these problems have been created or exacerbated by the use of the monolithic public sector model as the choice of delivery vehicle. This conclusion is now surprisingly widely held and it is not surprising, therefore, that reform of the public sector, and an examination of all areas of public spending, is prominent on the policy shelf.

One of the first actions of the new Labour government elected in 1997 was to announce a comprehensive review of all government spending. All departments would look at all their spending, reviewing all functions from scratch. The process, under Treasury control, is set to take about a year. As the Budget 'Red Book' in July 1997 said,

> The review will take nothing for granted. It will examine each department's objectives and look at every item of spending to ensure that it contributes to the government's objectives as effectively and efficiently as possible.

The words are not so different from those of Michael Portillo, Chief Secretary to the Treasury under John Major, who launched the so-called Fundamental Expenditure Reviews (FERs) in February 1993, 'Which in the lifetime of this Parliament will scrutinize every government department to identify areas of expenditure which are inappropriate for the 1990s.' Indeed, the objectives are not that different from the launch of the Programme Analysis and Review process (PAR) in 1970. Edward Heath said at the time, 'What we are trying to do is take each aspect of work in a department and say, "Right, for this year we are going to analyse this, see what its origin was, what its purpose and cost are."'

These two earlier attempts at reviewing the functions of government both failed. The obituary of PAR was written by Heclo and Wildavsky in their masterpiece on the workings of the civil service, *The Private Government of Public Money*:

> A host of government policies have been subject to special reviews in every department, with few discernible results . . . Whitehall, as it turned out, was not much interested in producing critical evaluations of its own work. For that, one needs to look outside. Something like PAR is still needed, because the reborn annual budget process does little to disturb the inertia of existing policy. Worse, it tends to displace any concern for policy contents with a preoccupation with cash controls.[1]

No one has ever written an obituary of the Fundamental Expenditure Reviews. It appears they fizzled out. In the last Budget 'Red Book' of the Parliament, they did not even merit an honorary mention. Several departments, most notably the Department of Social Security under Peter Lilley, and the Treasury itself, did make changes associated with their FERs. But programme cuts were simply not the order of the day.

In this section, we can attempt our own 'comprehensive spending review'. But there is a crucial way in which it differs from the attempts of various governments to review their programmes. Instead of asking a general question − 'Should the state do this?' − it is likely to be more effective to ask various specific questions. In particular, the most interesting question for most programmes is not 'Should the state finance this?'. It is 'Should the state deliver this in the way it has chosen to do so?'. In short, as before, we need to be as concerned with the way we *supply* public services, as we do with the way we *finance* them. We want to control government value added, as much as we do government spending.

The first question we need to ask, then, is whether the traditional public sector model is the right model to deliver public services on which public money is spent. This is the subject of Chapters 9 and 10. In particular, they look at potential reform along the lines of the

1. Hugh Heclo and Aaron Wildavsky (1981), *The Private Government of Public Money* (second edition), Macmillan, London. Pages xlii−xliii.

purchaser−provider split, one of the more fashionable methods of remodelling the state. Chapter 9 looks at different possible designs of the purchaser−provider split, and where each might be most appropriate. Chapter 10 looks at the issue of capital and investment. It argues that the greatest benefits from the purchaser−provider split are that capacity and investment decisions can be left to the capital market. This should allow the kind of entrepreneurship, progress and innovation that has been lacking in the public sector to emerge. At the same time, it outlines the difficulties of that route. These chapters are an attempt to sketch solutions to the problems outlined in Chapter 5.

The demand-side agenda − how we pay for programmes − is not to be ignored. We need to ask whether collective finance is necessary for programmes, or whether private money could be expected to pay for them instead, in whole or in part. This is the subject of Chapters 11 and 12. The former looks at specific areas where the government could attempt to withdraw its spending to some extent. The latter looks at budgeting and control more generally. These provide a somewhat inconclusive guide to the potential for cutting public spending, and the numerous obstacles and problems inherent in that path.

9 The Purchaser–Provider Split

Reforming the delivery of services

For the last 50 years, political debate in America has centered on questions of ends: what government should do, and for whom. We believe such debates are secondary today, because we simply do not have the means to achieve the new ends we seek. After 10 years of education reform and $60 billion in new money, test scores are stagnant and dropout rates are higher than they were in 1980. After 20 years of environmental legislation to clean up our air and water, pollution is as bad as ever. After only a few years of the savings-and-loan clean-up, the projected cost has skyrocketed from $50 billion to $500 billion. We have new goals, yes, but our governments cannot seem to achieve them. The central failure of government today is one of *means*, not *ends*.

DAVID OSBOURNE AND TED GAEBLER,
Reinventing Government (preface).

The Basic Principle

Public libraries are a good thing. After all, people like to read; usually they like to read each book once and only once, but the technology of books means it is inefficient to throw them away (or stack them uselessly on a shelf) after one read only. How sensible then, to have a polygamy arrangement for books, under which one copy of a book is read many times over by lots of different people (with, thanks to a sensible collective arrangement, the author duly compensated). Anyway, regardless of the technology, libraries are community centres and a form of opportunity for those who wish to raise themselves up, but who cannot afford the books that might help them on the way.

In the UK today, there are about 4,400 public libraries, lending 500 million books out each year (about nine for each person in the country) and absorbing 380 million visits, at a total cost of a little under £1bn a year. The budget is distributed by local authorities who provide buildings, hire staff, pay them to run the libraries, and give them money for books (or, sometimes, give them books direct).

But do we really think our libraries are as good as they could be? Do we know whether libraries are efficient or inefficient? Do they select the right books? Offer the right services? Display books in the right way? Offer the right balance of space to shelves and seating? Lend out for the most appropriate length of time? Devote the right balance of resources to fiction and non-fiction? Occupy the right locations? Market themselves appropriately? Recruit the right staff? Open for the right hours?

And what about imagination? Have they explored the idea of offering other services? Do they sell you a cup of tea, for example? Or make rooms available for local groups' meetings? Or deliver to your home books ordered from a catalogue? Or arrange book readings? Or provide centres of excellence in particular subject matters? Or have computerized catalogues of book reviews? Or sell new books? Or experiment with alternative opening hours?

The answer is that not many do. And that may be because these are all bad ideas; or it may be because the library sector is slow to change and innovate. More likely, it is a combination in which these two factors reinforce each other: libraries have adapted reasonably well to their (often elderly *Daily Telegraph*-reading) clientele. They have used some imagination in offering the right services for this constituency (large print books, for example) and have been a good deal more entrepreneurial than they might have been in offering interesting new services (mobile library services, lending out CDs, exhibitions of big town planning proposals, and so on).

But it is hard to know whether they have been as effective at thinking outside the boundaries of their norms as we would like. And it is hard to know how effective they are at making good management decisions about what they do.

This chapter is not actually about libraries, but the example of them will be used recurringly. It is about how to ensure the best is extracted from public money. How to ensure that if the state pays for our libraries (I am not concerned here with the size of the overall budget), it gets the best for that money, and ensures innovation and progress. It is a chapter concerned with countering the problems of the monolithic traditional model of state-run services.

One does not want to propose changes to the structure of the public library service that gratuitously stir up anxiety and fear. But equally, one should challenge institutions to offer the best, to adapt, and to maintain a verve and spirit. This is not to say institutions should eschew conservative practices (Radio Four does very well at being traditional, and would suffer badly if it tried to be Radio Five Live); but it is to argue that thought should be given to the practices chosen; that if tranquillity and tradition are the right characteristics, then these should be pursued in a thoughtful and positive way.

It may be that the monolithic model of tax-financed, public sector delivery (for example, the public library) is the only means to achieve those ends, and if this is right, that provides a strong case for the existing structure of provision. But let us explore alternatives. And the most general form of alternative is that of the *purchaser–provider split*. It is based on the following argument:

> Government does not *do* things very well.
>
> Government should *pay* for things out of taxation, to ensure a fair distribution of income and universal access to services.
>
> Ergo, government should buy services for us, but should not provide them.

Of course, government purchases library services, education and hospital services for us already, so what does the purchaser–provider split really mean? There are various different ways of looking at it: the core is that the government's funding role should be detached from its provision role. Instead of paying for libraries, hospitals and schools directly – just for being there and doing their best – government should pay libraries, hospitals and schools on an arm's-length basis. It can be seen as a move towards *payment for services on the basis of outputs rather than inputs*. Another way of looking at the purchaser–provider split is as a shift towards the use of *contracts* in public services – you hire libraries, schools and hospitals to provide services as per a contract, rather than as a member of the public sector family.

These different concepts will usually go together. At the moment, local authorities give libraries, for example, a budget – a certain power over a set of resources. The budget-holder responsible for the library aims to maximize the output of the library, given the constraint of the budget supplied. Under the purchaser–provider split, the state offers to pay the library for what it actually achieves; for its output. For example, this might be defined as the number of books lent in the year, plus the number of visitors coming through the door. If the library has no visitors, or lends no books, it produces nothing, and in consequence it would get nothing. (In this event, it would very likely quickly go out of business.) If the library is popular and attracts the punters, then it gets paid a lot.

To put some specifics on the idea, one simple tariff arrangement could be to pay libraries a pound for each time a book was borrowed; plus a pound for each visitor through the door as well. If the same number of loans and visitors occurred as now, then total spending would be about the same. But the distribution of the budget would be linked very directly to those libraries that attracted visitors and that lent books.

Observe what would not change in this new world of public libraries: they would still lend books to the public free of charge (except for modest fines for overdue returns) and they would still be paid for by taxation. In effect, the public library user need not notice any change whatsoever. It is the *supply* of library services that would be affected, not the demand. We would still suffer all the problems (discussed in Chapters 6 to 8) of lobby groups, of collectivized spending, and of any potential damage to the macro-economy from taxes. What we might hope to achieve would be an improvement in the quality of libraries and library services, because in principle the libraries would be so keen to attract customers that they would stock the most interesting books they could find, offer cups of tea, arrange special book readings, install post office facilities, introduce computers, and rent out rooms to counselling services and the like. Anything that drags readers through the door. They would also attempt to minimize the cost of whatever they were doing in order to generate cash that could be invested in services to keep attracting customers. The only difference for the customer, then, in this new world of libraries would be the improvement in service that would follow.

Or would it? The purchaser–provider split is already on its way to being implemented for various services and it remains the most plausible means of overturning the old monolithic model of state spending. Unfortunately, in practice it raises a number of serious implementation problems. If those problems can be overcome, however, there is no reason not to believe it can generate benefits equivalent to those we have seen in contracted-out local authority services, say, or privatized industries.

Implementing the Purchaser–Provider Split

The purchaser–provider split can come in a number of quite different forms but they all have the same essential ingredients: producers are selected competitively and paid at arm's-length, on the basis of their outputs. Nevertheless, a desire to introduce the purchaser–provider split into any sector gives rise to a number of different choices.

The first crucial choice in implementing the purchaser–provider split, is whether in application it is pure – the payments for outputs cover *all* costs, including the cost of servicing capital and capacity. Or whether it is partial, and the output payments cover only some costs, for example the day-to-day running costs, while other costs (such as the cost of the capital tied up in the business) are provided by the state. We could, for example, keep the library building in state hands, while moving to some kind of purchaser–provider split in the flow of resources needed for the books and heating of the library. Indeed schools, for example, are already funded on a mixed basis – their capital is provided by the state; their running costs are covered by payments for each student they attract.

The issues surrounding pure or partial purchaser–provider splits are complex and important. The most important case – that of whether capital and investment are handled on an arm's-length basis, or whether they are kept in the hands of the state – is so important it is covered fully in the next chapter. In the musings here, we shall by and large forget about the finance of capital.

The second crucial choice in implementing the purchaser–provider split is whether players in the market created face real or just 'pretend' budget constraints. The purchaser–provider split can be implemented in the form of contracting out functions to genuinely external suppliers, to whom the purchaser feels no obligations at all, and who have to deliver within budget. Equally, the purchaser–provider split has been associated with a set of policies loosely called 'internal markets' in which the purchaser and the provider are essentially part of the same organization. In the BBC, for example, the 'producer choice' system of management is a market-based system, but it is one in which real choice is limited by the knowledge that we are all part of the same organization, and more pertinently, by the fact that if one unit loses money, those that make money will effectively bail it out. Like the first point about capital, and pure or partial purchaser–provider splits, this one is too important to be dealt with here.

Purchaser-provider schemes – and potential schemes – can also vary, by who it is that makes the purchasing decision. Is it a state agency (the Home Office, for example), or is it individual members of the public? If it is us, as members of the public, who do the purchasing, then there are still various different ways of effecting our market presence: it can be direct (with a voucher, say, as was once proposed in the case of nursery education) or indirect (as in the case of per capita based payments to schools, determined by a formula and the number of children who go to the school). Or, there is the intermediary option of a fundholder who purchases on behalf of the public, but at a far more decentralized level than a local or national government (for example, fundholding GPs, who hold a budget for each NHS patient in their practice).

Thirdly, it has to be decided whether purchasing in this world is based on open, continual competition in the market (as in the nursery voucher scheme), or whether competition is an occasional occurrence (as in franchising of railway routes, or contracting out of local authority services). Is it competition *within* the market, or is it competition *for* the market?

Adding up the varieties of purchaser–provider split implementation strategies, one can see that there are $2 \times 2 \times 4 \times 2$ which equals 32 different forms. There is an additional mixed case which makes 33 varieties in all, although in most industries, not every one of them will

Table 1: Permutations of the Purchaser–Provider Split in Public Libraries

Who purchases?	How open is the contest?	
	Long-term contract (competition for the market)	Open, continual competition (competition in the market)
Individuals		
direct	Subscription scheme: we each 'join' a library, and the state gives us a token to pay our sub	Library voucher scheme: we each get, say, £10 worth of library tickets to use a year
indirect	Subscription scheme: state pays libraries for every sub they obtain	Tariff system: state pays any library a pre-fixed rate for attracting customers day-to-day
Government	Library franchise: state offers to finance a library for a set period	Tariff system: state pays any library a pre-fixed rate for a range of outputs, broader than mere attraction of customers
Intermediate agent	Library clubs scheme: we each join a club, paid for by government; the club buys library rights for us	
Mixed	State selects a franchise-holding library; but it then pays that library by reference to day-to-day usage by customers	

be feasible. Table 1 lists the possible permutations of schemes, applied to the example of public libraries. Ignoring for the moment the division between pure and partial applications of the purchaser–provider split, and internal markets versus real budget constraints, we are left with eight practical varieties of purchaser–provider split for public library services, out of which four broad types of scheme can be discerned:

Voucher schemes under which the final consumer buys library services, or subscribes to a library, paying with government-issued vouchers; government reimburses the library with real cash for every voucher it obtains.

Franchise schemes, under which government contracts with libraries to offer library services under pre-specified terms and conditions, for a pre-set period.

Tariff schemes, under which government pays any registered library a pre-set amount for pre-specified services, but in which there are no continuing obligations.

Fundholder schemes, under which consumers choose a fundholding club to buy library services on their behalf.

Broadly, this list could equally apply to a number of government services. But each method has pluses and minuses.

Vouchers

The word 'voucher' arouses oddly passionate feelings in public policy debate, even though, of course, vouchers do not have to take the physical form of paper coupons (indeed, the most likely practical voucher in the public library case would be a plastic card stored with credits). The word stands for consumer sovereignty in the eyes of some, and an ill-disguised attempt to bash public servants in the eyes of others.

Voucher schemes have the advantage of allowing the final consumer to make a purchase choice and they thus minimize any feeling of disconnection between the public and their services. As long as you believe the public knows what it wants from libraries, and does not need the state to choose its reading material, vouchers are a reasonable choice. Indeed, you might actually *promote* the use of libraries among the currently uninterested mass of the population by enshrining the library-entitlement in the form of a piece of paper, or a plastic card.

Depending on the taste of libraries themselves, vouchers could be used to pay for specific services – like borrowing books, or entering a library; or it might facilitate planning and simplicity for libraries to adopt subscription schemes, under which vouchers were used to pay for membership of a library, bestowing certain borrowing and visiting rights.

Either way, the voucher scheme maximizes the competitive pressure on suppliers to satisfy the public. Anyone would be allowed to open a library. There would be no let-up at all in pressure – every day, libraries would be competing for business. The book police would have no place in this world, dictating that Mills & Boon are not worthy of subsidy; only the public would be the judge of what they wanted to read. And because there are so many members of the public, the libraries would not be subject to the capricious whims of the local or national government. It is far more preferable to be in a market with a multiplicity of potential customers, than just one.

Vouchers have an additional advantage in avoiding the necessity of an elaborate bureaucracy to draw up contracts, assess compliance and the like. But they do not obviate the need for bureaucracy entirely. If people were being given library vouchers, we would have to ensure that they were only using them to purchase library services. Many bars would be happy to stack a few books on a shelf outside the toilet, call themselves libraries and exchange drinks in return for vouchers. More to the point, many customers would be happy to use their vouchers to purchase drinks in such establishments. Taxpayers may justifiably feel that, whatever they were subsidizing libraries for, it was not for this, so there would have to be a small bureaucracy to register libraries as libraries (Ofbook), and ensure that library services were what they offered.

This of course undermines a great deal of the appeal of vouchers: for a start, the book police re-enter the fray; if libraries who choose to offer popular books or innovative services are deemed to be straying from their brief as a library, then they will lose their voucher-refund entitlement. Suddenly the whole development of the industry depends on bureaucrats again – rather as it does today.

Voucher schemes are, however, advantageous in a number of other respects. They effectively impose a cost to the user of libraries – when you use the library, you lose a voucher. That has the comforting incentive effect – at least comforting to economists, but probably not to anyone else – of making people think about their use of the library, rather than assuming that it is a costless facility. Under a voucher scheme, libraries could set tariffs as they please – they could charge any number of vouchers of their own choosing for particular services, so they would be able to offer an extensive and imaginative range of services, priced sensibly. Crucially this means suppliers can themselves initiate market developments, by offering services at given prices, and seeing whether there are any takers. There would also be price competition – libraries would have an incentive to keep prices low to win business. In a voucher world, it would be easy to mix voucher payments with the acceptance of cash and credit cards, for those who have run out of their voucher allotment.

But herein lies one of the biggest problem with voucher schemes, at least in the case of libraries: the impact they have on the current distribution of library purchasing. We all know that not everybody uses public libraries. But we also know that vouchers would have to be distributed in a relatively arbitrary and uniform way. It would not be easy to give people vouchers in proportion to their existing use of libraries. As a result, any library voucher scheme would inevitably have the disadvantage of offering far too small a voucher for those who actually use libraries, and far too big a voucher for those who do not use libraries at all.

This is unfortunately almost a fatal factor when it comes to library vouchers. It means vouchers are only useful where government has as a specific goal of policy that big library users should have their library entitlements capped and a library market be developed, in which top-up library services can be purchased with cash as well as vouchers.[1] There may be merits in mixing library services available free to the user and those charged to the user, but that is beyond the scope of this chapter, in which the challenge is to identify changes that do not upset the current distribution of living standards.

Vouchers, then, are probably not very plausible for the use of public libraries – not without a fight against the good library-users of Tunbridge Wells at least. And indeed, they do not work well wherever the legitimate demand for a service varies in unpredictable ways among different people. Vouchers for legal aid, for example, make little sense

---

1. You could issue vouchers to a total face value vastly in excess of the current total spending on libraries, in the hope and expectation that not all vouchers would be redeemed. That way, the big users would have enough vouchers to support their library habit. But it would be a risk, as you might find spending on libraries out of control if too many vouchers were redeemed.

as the vast bulk of us need none, and a few of us need a lot. Only if you can tailor your voucher payments to pre-identified groups, such that within each group demand for the service is uniform, can vouchers work.

But voucher schemes do have a potential place in some very large public services. They are clearly most desirable in those situations where customers are in a good position to make their own choice of supplier, and also where levels of consumption among the target population are uniform, or at least identifiable by government. The obvious cases are those around which the vouchers debate has been most active – schools, training and higher education, nursery care, and care homes for the aged.

Vouchers are not entirely untried as a concept. Britain tried a quasi-voucher scheme for nursing care for the aged between 1981 and 1993. The scheme – described by the OECD in a useful reference on purchaser–provider split schemes, *Managing with Market Type Mechanisms* – was judged to have been successful in one regard, and unsuccessful in one regard. The good news for vouchers was that they stimulated a market in nursing homes – 'market providers responded by quickly expanding and diversifying the supply of facilities'. The bad news for vouchers was that they ended up costing a lot – 'the very dynamism of the expanding industry catering to these needs meant that publicity stimulated demand'. In short, vouchers worked a bit too well for the comfort of a penny-pinching government.

But they also suffered another problem: vouchers were redeemable against care in residential nursing homes. That may seem fine, but it distorted the choice people made as to cheaper alternatives, such as lighter-touch care in the elderly person's own home, for example, or in sheltered housing. In other words, the quasi-voucher and the way it was designed, did a lot to suppress the exploration of imaginative solutions to problems that the market is designed to foster.

Franchising or Contracting[1]

Imagine instead that we went for a franchise or contracting scheme: in this case, it is government – local, central, or some agency – that does the choosing, and it does so every few years rather than continuously.

In the example of libraries this is the closest arrangement to the current system. But instead of just building and operating a library, and selecting the staff on a competitive basis, the council would put the library service out to tender, with different operators writing up a specification of what they would offer, and for how much. One, or several, operators would be given the contract and would provide the service.

The basis for paying library operators would have to be predetermined – an annual amount for the duration of the contract, for example. Or it could be based on a pre-determined formula, for example the library might get an annual subsidy plus an amount for each visitor or each book lent. In this latter case, the action of consumers would at least have some bearing on the success or failure of the library. Otherwise, however, the pattern and nature of demand for a service would not be affected by franchising.

Franchising appears to be an advance on the existing system because although competitive pressure is applied only spasmodically, it is at least applied. It does at least allow a competition for library management every few years. Moreover, it has some power to keep operators on their toes, because they want to avoid losing the contract at the next point of competition. But we have to remember that the downside of franchising is that competition is limited. Effectively, new entrants are banned from coming in to the game except at the key junction points of franchise award. They are not able to try their hand at the service speculatively, or to experiment with it. They either get the work, or they do not.

1. Some use the term 'franchising' to refer to a concession offered in which direct user fees will be paid (like the franchise to sell lottery tickets) and contracting as a term to describe the situation when a private company has the right to provide a service paid for by a buying agency (like local refuse collection). However, I use the two terms indistinguishably.

So what are the advantages of limiting competition in this way? Why might you rather select one monopoly supplier than continuously leave your options open? Why would you be willing to pay one library – a franchise winner – a subsidy, but not another library, even were it willing to offer an identical service on an identical day?

One reason might be that we prefer to limit the number of suppliers. Maybe we feel that one library with a wide selection of books is better than two with a narrow selection. In this case, we are saying that libraries are what economists like to call a *natural monopoly*, and we might feel justified in restricting the largesse of the state to paying cash to just one library, rather than any old one that chooses to open.

Natural monopolies are perhaps more pervasive than is sometimes imagined. Even if we all agree that we want one local library with a wide range of books, individual choice in a quasi-market may still give us two libraries with a narrow range, simply because in a market system, we may not all agree which local library should be the local monopoly – so there is a role for government to intervene and decide for us.[1] That is what a franchise or contract system does.

Even if the argument seems implausible with regard to public libraries, it is surely plausible with respect to refuse collection services, and it is not surprising that these are organized on a collective basis, and conducted through contracts.

And refuse collection also gives us the second factor that determines the desirability of long-term contracting rather than continual competition. With regard to refuse collection or libraries, we could increase competitive pressure by having very frequent franchise contests. Even if there is to be only one library or refuse collector in any town, we can apply continuous pressure to the winning supplier by limiting the length of its franchise to a very short period – a week for example, rather than for the more typical five-year contract. The reason we do not do that – even though it would impose extra competition on to a natural monopoly – is that there are costs that suppliers incur on serving a contract, and many of these costs are irrecoverable once incurred – they are 'sunk costs' of, say, obtaining books; or learning routes,

1. This kind of market pathology can be characterized by reference to game theory, and the 'battle of the sexes' game, described in Chapter 6.

organizing systems and obtaining local staff. These are far more worrying to potential entrants than the costs of, say, labour, which can be redeployed fairly easily if the contract is lost. Sunk costs render it unattractive to serve these contracts for as little as a week. You will find weekly contractors, but you will pay a lot more for them.

So we have two reasons for limiting competition and engaging in a franchise contest – natural monopoly and sunk costs. In effect, what both of these effectively say is that there is some minimum efficient definition of the service being offered; that it is not sensible to divide the library service into two, or refuse collection into weekly chunks. The minimum bite size is a very large bite, in other words. It is then possible to derive a general rule of franchising taking this argument on board: aim for the maximum possible competition compatible with the minimum efficient specification of what the service entails.

We do have some experience of the franchising option, in for example local authority competitive tendering, and in the running of the National Lottery. That evidence is generally favourable. Costs have fallen for local authority services by about 20 per cent where tendering has occurred. And Britain's lottery – a rare profit-oriented private sector one – appears to perform extremely well by international standards. Unlike some of the other forms of purchaser–provider split, franchising has almost no limits in principle. Almost any task of the state can be subject to its disciplines. Schools, hospitals, all could be put on time-limited contracts with some consequent pressure to perform.

The ease with which it can be implemented makes it tempting as the first and last option to be considered. But we should not forget that the essence of a franchise is to put a limit on competition and new entry to a sector. That is an effect that we should aim to impose sparingly.

Tariff Systems

The next of our systems – which I awkwardly describe as 'tariff systems' for want of a better name – is simply one in which government publishes a set of prices for different outputs, and pays those pre-set rates to *any* provider producing those outputs. The archetypal scheme applied to libraries would be a £1 payment for all visitors to a building containing lots of books, or a £1 payment for all books that are lent under something that looks like library conditions.

If the payments are based specifically on customer use of the library – for visits or loans – then in fact you have a scheme rather like a voucher scheme – it is the customer who calls the tune, even though the customer never sees or makes the payment. There are two important differences between tariff-based systems and vouchers, however. First is the distribution of benefits they bestow on users. A voucher effectively caps the entitlement of an individual, whereas a tariff system does not: the library gets its cash, regardless of who its customer is. There is no limit on the amount an individual can demand. The second is that pre-published tariffs remove price competition: all providers are paid the same for a particular service.

The tariff scheme is rather like a 'spot market' in library services – it's like paying libraries on piece-rates, rather than employing them to do a job. The big advantage of this way of doing things is that it maximizes the opportunity for those who think they can run libraries well to enter the market for libraries: they do not have to get permission, win a contest, or wait four years. All they have to do is collect customers and win. If their judgement that they are good at running libraries is right, they will be rich. If their judgement is poor, they will not be. It is all very simple. Just like its close relative the voucher scheme, the published tariff promotes a rapid responsiveness to customer preferences.

And just like vouchers, tariffs have the problem that the product being purchased may actually be more complicated than the spot market implies. You do not necessarily purchase the loan of one book, or a visit to the library; you purchase a whole package, a set of library services that are best thought of – and best marketed – in one big bundle. If that is right, you want the purchasing decision to match the product being purchased, and not to artificially break it down into unreasonably small components.

But even if this factor did not apply, there is a particular reason for doubting that a tariff-based spot market approach is as desirable as it may seem: somehow, we want suppliers to offer a choice of services available at specified prices. We want that choice to be unconstrained to maximize the opportunities for innovation. In a well-designed voucher scheme, suppliers can offer services as they like, and individual customers can choose to buy them or not. In a franchising system, negotiation over a contract between a buyer and a library involves a two-way process of specifying potential outputs and the prices that are attached to them. The supplier can nominate services in this interactive process, and government can choose to pay for them or not.

However, a published tariff has to be openly available to all. This is a problem, because there may be suppliers who have an innovative idea for an unusual output – computer terminals in the library for example. But suppose that government has not published a tariff rate for computer terminals – all it counts, say, are book loans and visits – then the imaginative library is unable to capture a market that you might well want it to capture.

We shall discuss the issue of how to pay suppliers later: suffice it to say that if a purchaser–provider scheme does not have any mechanism for entrepreneurial behaviour to be rewarded, then it scores a large negative. If government knows that it is offering a tariff that applies a price to every possible output that could emerge from a library, there will be no problem. But in the imperfect world which justifies the purchaser–provider split kind of scheme anyway, government does not know every possible library output, and nor is it likely government will be the first to anticipate new outputs. As a result, government must leave the library door open to suggestions from independent suppliers.

Fundholding

The final broad direction of purchaser–provider split in libraries is for there to be a purchaser intermediary between the public and the library. The purchaser – call it a sort of book club – would, in the jargon of the purchaser–provider split, be a *fundholder*. It would get a budget from the government for each member it attracts. It would use that money to go out and buy library services from the market – it might do a deal with one library or another, or with a national chain of libraries, and offer certain facilities to members. The club may not itself run libraries – although there is no reason for it not to be allowed to. You might view this route as the establishment of a PPP or a BUPA of the book world.

It is arguable that local government itself is already exactly such a book club (among other things). It gets a per capita fund element, and is expected to obtain library services with that. And, by and large, local government does already provide library services, albeit it tends to run them directly rather than purchasing them from independent suppliers.

The purchaser–provider split fundholder idea is rather similar. However, the assumption would be that the fundholder either has no local monopoly (you could choose your fundholder); or at least would be steered towards buying services rather than providing them; moreover, they would not necessarily be geographically confined. Clubs could cover multiple jurisdictions, and there could be multiple clubs per jurisdiction.

Now in the library world, there is probably a rather weak case for inserting a new layer of purchasing bureaucracy between the public and their libraries. Book clubs are not really worth the trouble. But let us just be clear what the benefits of this scheme can be in other sectors.

For one thing, if we wanted to allocate access to libraries on the basis of some kind of need (a desperate desire to read books, for example), then the intermediary could act as the go-between in determining what an individual member's library entitlements are, based on a close and objective reading of the individual's need. For another, the fundholder is especially helpful in cases where the individual does not know what to demand and a supplier paid under any of the other schemes would have an incentive to sell the individual something even if it is the wrong thing. The fundholder thus acts as an intelligent intermediary – a broker or agent in a market where we ourselves are likely to get lost.

These arguments pretty clearly lead to the conclusion that if you want a purchaser–provider split in health care, the fundholding model is appropriate, and it is not entirely surprising therefore that the fundholding model was adopted in the UK health reforms of the late 1980s. What was odd was the strange mix between competitive fundholding at the level of the GP (for half the population) and a mix of fundholding and agency buying at the level of the health authority (for the other half of the population). There was an element of choice for consumers – because most of us could select a fundholding GP – but it has always been a rather opaque choice, and it is not clear that fundholding GPs would be able to offer the service they do, were all GPs fundholders.

The idea of fundholders has also, quite appropriately, been explored for adoption in the area of subsidized legal aid.[1]

There is another large advantage to the fundholder scheme: markets work much better when there are multiple players. So, in contrast to one government agency or local council awarding library franchises, the club idea means that libraries would face far more potential customers, and would be far less in the hands of one, possibly capricious, buyer. Markets ideally need five buyers if they are not to be dominated by any one, or distorted by strategic behaviour. If we reject letting individuals have the power of choice, the next best thing is to have a number of purchasers.

The use of multiple purchasers also fosters a multiplicity of contract forms and transactions. It would mean that no single decision would have to be taken about whether the contracts are long, short, spot-market, all-embracing or narrow. Innovation could be rewarded, as suppliers can offer services at a given price in a world of multiple buyers.

Applying the Purchaser–Provider Split

The set of factors discussed here sets up a tangled web of arguments and factors to highlight the advantages and disadvantages of different types of purchaser–provider split, if that is the reform strategy of choice. Even this discussion is not comprehensive (you could have a franchise system based on continually open contracts, for example), but it does cover most of the tricky principles of selecting an implementation strategy.

The basic principle, however, is simple. In the world of the purchaser–provider split, providers – be they libraries, schools, hospitals, or prisons – are private, or at least told to run as though they were private. They run themselves; they can fail or succeed; and they have to market their services to the purchaser. The purchaser is funded by the state, and can be either the state itself; the ultimate client of the service; or some intermediary.

For schools, the arguments would point to a voucher scheme.

1. See the Social Market Foundation memorandum, *Organising Cost Effective Access to Justice*, by Gwyn Bevan, Tony Holland and Michael Partington, 1994.

Demand is uniform among those with children of school age; parents can make a reasonably informed choice; there are no natural monopoly features; and sunk costs are low.

For health care, as argued above, the fundholding system appears to be the most logical system of splitting purchasing from providing. Demand varies unpredictably, so the purchaser has to assess the customer's need as well as the supplier's ability; it is economical anyway for there to be a layer of screening between hospitals and patients, and that layer might efficiently be a fundholding layer. But there are local natural monopoly features in aspects of health care – in accident and emergency cover, for example – so some contracting might be appropriate too. A mixture may be appropriate for different types of health provision.

There are more complex cases than these, however, such as prisons and custodial services. We do not want to give a choice to prisoners themselves, as they are likely to veer towards the most luxurious and least secure establishment. So vouchers are to be excluded, unless they are given to judges. Franchising is clearly possible – and indeed appears to be the model chosen for privately financed prisons. But this is not the only option. We could create a market in custodial services by randomly assigning prisoners to one of, say, five fundholders who purchase custodial services on their behalf. The fundholders would not be permitted to reject prisoners, unlike individual prisons. And the funding of the fundholders could be fairly crude, based on a simple formula in the expectation that high-cost and low-cost prisoners would roughly cancel each other out.

How about the administration of social security benefits? Ideally, one would let recipients have a choice of administration system. But again, there are problems in letting claimants choose a system, unless the systems are all equally rigorous at enforcing the benefit rules. In principle, however, it would be possible to adopt a mixed system: we could offer franchises to, say, four national benefit claimant systems (the Benefits Agency could be cut into two, and a bank or building society or the Post Office could be encouraged to enter the business as well). We could let claimants choose their benefit office, and the franchise could simply state that the administrators get paid for every claimant to whom benefits are paid, but on the basis of spot checks, face large penalties for false recipients.

A more limited option would be to award regional franchises, an idea introduced in the US state of Wisconsin. Private companies do not compete for the custom of claimants day to day – they had to compete with the old state benefit offices and each other for the contracts to serve. The experience is too young to assess, and was introduced with other (very radical) reforms that complicate the task of assessing its impact, but certainly some of the drive demonstrated by the new welfare administrators is encouraging. The companies have been placed on incentive contracts to get claimants into work, and keep them there.

Finally, to emphasize the potential for the purchaser–provider split to reform spending across government departments, take overseas aid. Could that be subjected to the principle of purchasing? It could be, and would very likely improve if it was (its effectiveness record is poor at the moment). How would it be done? Most of the Department for International Development would have to be hived off into separate agencies, bidding for project work. The remainder would become purchasers – assessing bids, creating an aid strategy, and monitoring the delivery of services bought. Anyone would be able to bid for funds, not just the former D f I D spin-off groups, provided they met a number of criteria drawn up by the aid purchaser. Much larger quantities of funds would undoubtedly pass into the hands of non-governmental organizations like Oxfam and Save the Children.

In a host of areas, it is possible to conceive of sensible systems of dividing the provision of a service from the finance of it. But just as all the implementation schemes have common features, they usually share a common problem.

Bureaucracy and the Problem of Measuring Outputs

Under any purchaser–provider split, we pay providers at arm's-length for what they do, and thus under any purchaser–provider split, at some stage we have to actually measure what providers do. And this is not easy – it involves an inconvenient process of administration, just as privatization of monopoly utilities involves an inconvenient process of regulation. Either you measure outputs in a crude way, and hence encourage providers to provide those crude outputs (a problem exactly analogous to that of central planning in former Communist territories, where setting production targets in terms of output quantities led to an abysmal deterioration in the quality of production). Or you measure output in a sophisticated way, and endure the administrative cost involved.

So here is the unfortunate rule of purchaser–provider split implementation: the purchaser–provider split involves an unpleasant choice between bureaucracy and distorted incentives.

Take an example: it would be relatively easy to measure the number of books a library lends (although as soon as the number of books lent becomes important, we have to start checking library systems against fraud in a way that does not bother us now). It would be relatively easy to measure the number of visitors to a library. But neither really embraces the work a library does or the quality of its outputs, which involve a far more subtle delivery of community services. Of course, a high quality library may lend more books, but who is to say it would do that in exact proportion to the extra value of its general services? And a generally worse library could look far better by putting more effort into the task of getting books out the door.

The challenge of measuring outputs is discussed extensively and usefully in the great bible of public sector reform, *Reinventing Government*, by David Osbourne and Ted Gaebler. They make the point that outputs are only a small part of the story – what you really want to measure is *outcomes*. In the case of a library, it is welfare of the local community; in the case of prisons it is reductions in crime; in the case of overseas aid it is enhancements to the living standards of the world's poor. It is, however, very difficult to measure these outcomes in a way that directly ties them to the work of service providers.

The problem is that if you do not measure outputs that reflect the outcomes you wish to purchase, then you really have no basis for a proper market. This has led to the criticism, for example, that contracted-out cleaning services were cheaper, but lower quality than direct labour ones. Or the criticism of school league tables that they measured the quality of pupils entering schools, rather than the quality of teaching at schools. Or the idea that when a purchaser–provider split is implemented, the accountants take over, knowing the price of everything and the value of nothing. Design goes out of the window, as the accountants end up measuring things that are easy to quantify – quantities rather than qualities. We all end up impoverished as a result of cack-handed implementation of pseudo-markets that have none of the desirable features of real markets.[1]

Measurement is a real problem. It is not surprising that in every area where purchaser–provider split attempts have been made – be it in the internal market of the BBC, in the NHS, contracting out local services, or the Private Finance Initiative – accusations have been made that the whole process is bureaucratic and costly. It is particularly costly where a decision is taken to monitor each individual output on a precise basis.[2]

There is some worrying empirical support for the idea that transaction costs offset any benefits of reform. The cases of highway maintenance in Massachusetts, and vehicle maintenance in Albany, written up by Elliot Sclar, apparently suggest cost increases after privatization of services. He suggests simply reforming the directly employed state or city workforce can yield larger benefits. He may be right, although his cases only covered four years of experience so any very long term gains from a more competitive environment would not have had much time to operate. If the gains of reform are of the magnitude, say, achieved by the contracting out of refuse collection services, the costs of monitoring what the supplier does is easily a price worth paying.

Indeed, an earlier example from this book demonstrates the true nature of the problem. Suppose that government did all the buying of cars in the economy, and disbursed them among us on an equitable basis. This would be a major procurement task for the authorities; the quantity of cars would be easy to measure, but the quality would surely be important too. Now, we could have a great national debate on the whole subject of which aspect of quality was best; we could design complicated contracts, offering a price for them based on a formula depending on how many cars broke down, or how much petrol they used, or how long they lasted. We would bemoan the fact that buying

1. This was a fear expressed by a number of public servants at a Social Market Foundation/ Design Council conference, written up in *Design Decisions: Improving the Effectiveness of Public Purchasing*, by Mark Fisher et al, SMF, London, 1996.

2. With the exception of voucher schemes, which obviate the need for any central output measurement.

cars was very difficult because it is so hard to specify precisely what you want to get out of a car. Indeed, if government bought baked beans, we could have a tortuous debate about those too.

But these problems do not disappear just because government is not buying cars or baked beans. They apparently fade away because they are reduced to a very large number of problems sufficiently small that they can be ignored. (Which car I buy is not a problem the nation needs to debate, but it is one to which I devote quite a bit of attention.) The amount of total effort expended in making decisions over car purchases and over baked bean purchases is probably quite large: it is probably large relative to the effort government expends in measuring outputs in sectors of similar size. Indeed, if government took over the purchasing function, it is not obvious it should expend less effort in choosing brands than we do. Why would it pay to make a random rather than a considered purchasing choice, simply because the decision had been centralized and hence the cost of selection made more transparent?

In short, in areas where government does the buying, government has to do the selecting, and the assessing. That is an expensive process – but no more expensive than in individual decisions, and possibly less. These costs are surely worth incurring at the individual level, and they are surely worth incurring at the national level too. The problem of selecting what we want is a real problem that can only be solved after real work. That is all the measurement of outputs is.

The Shortage of Management Skills

This discussion brings us to a second potential problem of the purchaser–provider split as a concept: what it aims to do is to establish incentives to efficient and effective performance. But incentives do not work by magic (just as we said that privatization does not work by magic). Incentives can only work because people respond to them in some way. The great hurdle which the plan may not overcome, therefore, is a dearth of people capable of responding to the incentives you apply.

This is serious. Reforms along the lines of a purchaser–provider split are only likely to work if, at the very minimum, their logic is understood by those expected to implement and carry them to fruition. Yet are we really going to be able to find managers for all our public libraries, hospitals, schools, and prisons who are capable of running them like small companies – drawing up contracts, setting internal budgets, making strategic decisions? Where are we going to find the purchasing skills necessary in the residual public sector? The logic of the purchaser–provider split and the desirable pattern of incentives it imposes apparently elude many in the Palace of Westminster, let alone in town halls across Britain; if senior officials in the Department for Education exhibit an ignorance of the idea that capital has a cost, what expectation can we have that the average school administrator will understand things any more clearly?

Indeed, one interpretation of the failures of the public sector in the past is not that the incentives have been wrong, but that town halls and public organizations have been led by a mediocre cadre of executives – underpaid, poorly motivated and completely untrained. On this interpretation, the solution to the problems of the public sector is to employ decent managers: without that step being taken, no other reform will work; with that step being taken, any reform will work.

It would be a mistake to resist this line of argument. The evidence for it is the same as the evidence for public sector reform generally: wherever we have seen success, there does appear to have been a large and more intelligent input of management skills. No one can definitively say that is not the magic ingredient of any improvement in performance. However, there is no real conflict of position between the 'better management' school of reform, and the purchaser–provider split school of reform. What *can* be said is that reforms along the lines of the purchaser–provider split have tended to promote the more effective deployment of management in the public sector. Paying managers more, bringing them in from the private sector, sending them on courses – all these changes have gone with the process of reform. Indeed, the process of reform appears to concentrate the minds of management, so that people who may have appeared to neglect the idea of strategic thinking are challenged to start performing it once they see a need to. The purchaser–provider split is at least arguably one route to better management, not an alternative to it.

Conclusion

The choice of whether government should *do* things, or should *buy* them is exactly analogous to the choice faced by private companies all the time. Should they employ people to clean their offices, or should they hire a firm to do it? Should they make the product they sell, or should they sub-contract it to a small assembly plant in South Korea? The idea of the *virtual firm* – an organization that is simply a bundle of contracts with independent suppliers – is the concept that emerges from taking the 'contract out' route very seriously.

But just what is the difference between doing and buying? What is the difference between writing contracts with external suppliers, and writing contracts of employment with your own staff? Is not the firm just a big bundle of contracts anyway – hasn't it always been that?

Of course it is true that firms are really bundles of contracts – with lenders, employees, suppliers and customers. But the truth remains that there is a difference between the type of contract typically signed with an employee, and the type of contract typically signed with a supplier. The employee contract tends to have a looser set of obligations – the workload is to some extent flexible, and the contract tends to run for an indefinite period. The employee contract can get away with being more vague precisely because employees and employer are not expecting to just be together for one or two days, but instead interact in the expectation that they will still be working together in a year's time. This has a disciplining effect on behaviour that can substitute for tight specifications of contractual duty.

It is clear that there are reasons to sign both vague, flexible contracts, and tight, specific contracts. You probably need some people in an organization to know that they will be fed in three weeks' time, to get the best out of them. But you equally need everybody to realize that food in five years' time depends on hard, effective work now. People need to operate in an environment in which they feel accountable, but not so accountable that they can't relax.

Now, of course, some employee contracts end up looking rather like some supplier contracts – the boundary between the two is not well defined. Indeed, the tax treatment of the two is not equal, and as a result the Inland Revenue and Customs and Excise have to police that boundary to ensure that suppliers are genuinely suppliers, and are not really employees.

All this makes the telling point that the difference between purchasing and providing is a subtle one, and that perhaps the best way of looking at the purchaser–provider split is as a form of management technique that simply swaps a lot of vague, open-ended contracts for quite a number of more explicit, time-limited ones. It is really about putting obligations and expectations into a more formal mould, and time-limiting the duration of the relationship between purchaser and provider.

One should not expect miracles of such a change in style, but it is probably a sensible way of organizing the deployment of resources. Simply remember that the alternative to the purchaser–provider split is to run public services on the basis of contracts that are open-ended and vague, and in which as a matter of policy, the measurement of outputs, the specification of priorities, the accounting of costs and the relationship between outputs and welfare are all ignored, simply in order to save money. The purchaser–provider split has problems, but those problems are inherent to the running of public services. They have not been solved by the old model of the public sector, they have just been ignored. For all the problems therefore, a more extensive use of external contracting in one or other of the forms outlined in this chapter seems desirable.

But that is not the end of it. Let us ask what the active ingredient to better performance needs to be. The argument of Chapter 5 suggested that one reason to expect poorer effectiveness from public providers related to the absence in the public sector of effective mechanisms for change. It argued that what is missing from the public sector are the mechanisms of the capital market for fostering entrepreneurship and punishing mediocrity. Now, if it is implemented in a half-hearted form, the purchaser–provider split will not impose the disciplines of the capital market. In its most limited forms – internal markets for example – the purchaser–provider split may generate some benefits, but it does not fundamentally expose providers to the capital market which is, in the long term, a means to ensure that progress occurs.

To understand the real challenges of public sector reform, we need to consider not just the relationship between the purchaser and the provider, but the corporate structure of the providers themselves, and the way in which that structure can be subject to the opportunities and constraints of the capital market.

Additional Reading

Mayer, Colin and Tim Jenkins (eds) (1996), *Contracts and Competition*, Oxford Review of Economic Policy, Vol. 12, No. 4.

Organization for Economic Co-operation and Development (1993), *Managing with Market Type Mechanisms*, Public Management Studies, OECD, Paris.

Organization for Economic Co-operatioin and Development (1994), *Perform-ance Management in Government: Performance Measurement and Results-oriented Management*, Public Management Occasional Papers No. 3, OECD, Paris.

Osbourne, D., and Ted Gaebler (1992), *Reinventing Government*, Addison-Wesley, Reading, Massachusetts.

Sclar, Elliot (1997), *The Privatization of Public Service: Lessons from Case Studies*, Economic Policy Institute, Washington DC.

Scott, Graham C. (1996), *Government Reform in New Zealand*, International Monetary Fund, Washington DC.

10 The Question of Capital

Decentralizing capital, capacity and investment

The key to the British financial system is to understand it as a *system*.

WILL HUTTON, *The State We're In*, p. 132.

Control of Capital and Capacity

Clarity of purpose, a sense of mission, well-defined tasks, and continually-monitored outcomes are all important. Any form of purchaser–provider split provides all those. But in this chapter we shall take a look at the mechanisms through which such a split can most significantly generate improvements in public services, and the area in which reform along purchaser–provider split lines raises the most significant resistance: in the control and allocation of capital.

In Chapter 5 it was argued that the main flaw in the traditional public sector was the absence of a capital market to drive innovation and progress. Entrepreneurship is hard to foster in a world of hierarchy and budgets; the expansion of those providers who are good at the expense of those who are not is hard to achieve in a world where politicians rather than capital markets drive the allocation of capital and investment, and where providers cannot go bankrupt. But in a world of private, or quasi-private, providers; in a world where providers are separate from government; in short, in the world of the full-blown purchaser–provider split, change of this sort can be driven by the capital market. It is competition for capacity in an industry that appears to matter as the decades pass, rather than competition for customers (although, obviously, the latter is the thing that drives the former).

There is one overwhelmingly obvious conclusion to the argument: to realize the full potential of the purchaser–provider split, government has to impose real budget constraints on providers, not bail them out when times get tough; it has to abandon its control of capital and capacity in the public services, and delegate that task to decentralized capital markets. It has to go further than internal market reforms, or partial purchaser–provider splits. In effect, it has to get politicians or administrators out of decisions about where to invest money, and let investors, banks, entrepreneurs and businesspeople in.

To effect this most radical shift in the delivery of services, government needs to make an apparently simple change in the finance of capital: instead of *providing* capital – and thus essentially having to allocate it – government needs to purchase services at rates sufficiently generous to support the cost of capital that independent suppliers would themselves incur.

To understand this, two points have to be remembered: firstly, that capital is an important component of total costs. Secondly, that the cost of capital can be expressed in two different ways: either as a one-off lump sum cost (like the price of a house); or as a continuous flow of annual returns (like a rental on a property). These two ways of expressing the value of a piece of capital are linked to each other in a more or less mechanical fashion. Give me a one-off capital sum, and using a Hewlett-Packard 12C financial calculator, I will convert it into an equivalent value stream of annual flows of income. Any particular investment can be expressed in as many ways as you want – it can be squeezed into one payment or a hundred payments. The present value of the one payment can be designed to equal the value of the hundred.

Indeed, it is not a bad habit to always think of capital sums in terms of their annualized equivalent payments. You want to know whether to buy the more expensive wide-screen TV set? Well, work out how much extra it costs per week over its lifetime, rather than staring blankly at the screen in the store, unable to decide whether £300 extra is a lot or a little.

All that the full purchaser–provider split implies is that government converts capital sums into income streams, and treats them like any other cost. To see how this differs from a partial purchaser–provider split, take the example of schools. At the moment, for example, government pays schools an annual running cost fee for each student they attract. But it does not pay an annual fee for the cost of capital tied up in education. Capital is thus provided by the government itself – the state pays for school buildings, new schools, renovation of schools, extensions of schools, the replacement of Portakabin classrooms and so on. It does this with a capital budget, and it rations its capital out to lucky schools that persuade the authorities they need more capacity or investment.

Under the full purchasing route, government would scrap the capital budget, and would expect schools to beg, steal or borrow the capital they need for new investment themselves. In return for the saving on investment costs, though, government would have to include a generous profit margin in the annual running costs fee, so schools could afford to support and repay the capital they have obtained. Schools would have to pay for extensions or replacements themselves, but if these attracted new students, then the schools would get extra revenues to cover the money borrowed from the bank.

As government would no longer be responsible for the capital of schools, the borrowing of schools could be defined outside the public sector borrowing requirement, and they would go to the banks (or indeed to whoever they wanted) to raise their funds. Investors would be compensated with the profit margin built into the funds paid to schools for teaching. As far as the consumer of education goes, nothing need change.

Such a switch has a very dramatic effect on the possibility of new entry into the market for education. In the world of the traditional public sector, you were not really allowed to open a state school without the permission of the state. If Richard Branson wanted to open a state school, he might sometimes have got permission (normally this would be easier if he was an established church, and if the local schools were already full so would not suffer from the new competition). But there was still a string attached: if he did open a school, he had to pay for some or all of the investment. Yet, where would that capital come from? Unless it was endowed free of charge by someone, it would have to be borrowed, and then earn an annual return. Yet there was no annual return to be made because however many pupils Richard Branson could attract, he would still only be paid a fee that covers the running costs – the teachers, the books and the heating bill.

So, in effect, in the traditional system, where the cost of investment and capital is met by the taxpayer, competition between private and public providers is impossible as the private providers have a cost – the cost of capital – that the public ones simply don't have to face. Under a pure purchaser–provider split route, the public and the private are financed on an even basis – as long as the public providers have to raise their capital themselves, and don't receive hand-outs.

In principle, once government has abandoned its direct control of capacity and started purchasing at arm's-length, then new entry into public services could be encouraged – anyone would be allowed to open a prison, or would be allowed to rent accommodation out for social housing. The government would simply buy services on the basis of quality and price. All the forces of the commercial world – forces that appear to be rather effective in extracting good performance – would be unleashed.

It is a seductively simple idea, with what look like modest implications. In principle, it need not even cost anything, because in principle in an efficient, steady-state, competitive, frictionless world, capitalizing capital assets into an annual stream of returns should not alter the lifetime cost of them. Indeed, under an obtuse piece of economic reasoning surrounding the so-called 'Golden Rule of Capital Accumulation', it so happens that the total returns from capital in a year should just be equal to the efficient investment budget. Yet implementing the full purchaser–provider split is no easy task, and it raises a number of serious problems.

Introducing Internal Capital Markets

If one seriously wanted to make the reform outlined in principle above, there are four basic steps that would have to be taken. Each on its own would represent as major a revolution in public services as we have witnessed in the last decade.

The first is to start charging existing public organizations for their capital. We would say to schools and prisons that they have to pay rent on their premises, for example. This would immediately cut them free from the umbilical cord of government support, and put them on an arm's-length basis from their source of funds. They would be getting nothing for free. The second, complementary step is to increase the budget available to such organizations, in order to let them meet their new capital charges.

Canny observers will have noticed that all this involves is taking with one hand, and giving back with the other. But crucially, the two changes between them would mean that organizations have incentives to economize on capital – to use it more carefully – and to make sensible choices between capital and other resources. In the past, decisions on the two have been taken under such entirely separate systems that no real connection or trading-off has been possible. Moreover, the fact that the running costs bill includes an element of return will mean that new traders – who have not been given capital by the government – will be allowed to compete on level terms.

And that introduces the third and fourth steps. The third is to let organizations borrow or raise money privately, or from an arm's-length provider of capital. (Government could even become a bank for lending to public-service-type organizations.) The fourth step is to announce that new providers are free to compete for the annual budget for services on terms level with existing suppliers.

The reforms taken together free the public sector from the constraints imposed by politicians, most notably the rationing and control of capital investment. And they impose the new constraints of the private capital market. Organizations are no longer rationed in how much capital they can have, but they have to pay for the capital they use. Once such a change is made, organizations are effectively under something much closer to private-sector-type governance than traditional public sector governance, and competition can occur.

There are a number of implementation details not outlined here. The transitional arrangements, for example, are a nightmare, raising what might be called the Chelsea & Westminster problem. If you take a capital charge with one hand and give back a higher running costs budget with the other, then the average organization need be no worse off, and no better off. But not all organizations are average. Those who start their new capital-charged life with a lot of capital equipment may well suddenly find themselves dramatically worse off. For them, the extra capital charge will be higher than the compensating increase in running costs. This is the problem faced by the Chelsea & Westminster Hospital Trust – the most expensive hospital investment in the UK – which now (along with all hospital trusts) has to pay a capital charge, and finds the cost of its capital a heavy burden. It would not be unreasonable for Chelsea & Westminster to argue that it would never have chosen all that capital if it had known it was going to have to pay for it.

Another implementation issue is what will these new organizations look like? Who will own them? (Are public libraries going to become shareholder-owned organizations?)

Neither of these issues is easily answered in brief, but neither provides an insurmountable obstacle to the creation of the full purchaser–provider split. The real implementation problems arise from trying to persuade a sceptical public, and a sceptical Treasury, that the reforms are worthwhile. In particular, the challenge is to overcome two particular arguments used to attack the idea that private capital can be used in public services.

The Challenges of Reform

Bankruptcy

If government is to really leave its hands off the capital stock, it has to allow the possibility that organizations providing public services will go bankrupt. This is for two reasons. Bankruptcy is integral to the process of change in the privately governed world, releasing capacity for new, superior providers to expand. And anyway, if government is not going to let suppliers go bankrupt, it cannot let them raise their own capital, for then they would face no downside risk in borrowing. And lenders would face no downside risk in lending.

In practice, there seems to be a deep sense of unease at schools and hospitals, for example, closing down. Even though many private bankruptcies do not lead to liquidation, merely to refinancing and a change in management, there is a worry that lives will be more disrupted if there is instability among the providers of, say, health and education, than among the providers of holidays or fridges. In particular, there seems to be an aversion among the public to children being turfed out of their school midway through their education (even though this is a familiar experience in the private school sector).

Even in the least sensitive industries, getting bankruptcy arrangements right is tricky. There are two major concerns in the design of bankruptcy law, and they often conflict. The first is that you want to devise arrangements which salvage any organization which is worth salvaging. Firms that have over-borrowed – that are worth less than the money they owe, but which are still worth more than nothing – should not be closed down and liquidated. Instead, they should be refinanced and set back on course. There is no point in closing a firm down, however big its past mistakes, as long as it is capable of covering any future costs it incurs. If you have lent money to a bankrupt but salvageable organization, your best bet is just to write it off, and let the organization carry on. This argument suggests bankruptcy legislation should be gentle on those who have over-borrowed, and supports the idea they should be protected from an unseemly scramble to liquidate their assets and parcel them out to creditors.

But at the same time, bankruptcy law has to ensure that when people take out loans they do so responsibly, and for this to be the case, people must know that over-borrowing will not go unpunished. If executives think that there is no penalty to over-borrowing – because the sensible lender will just write off his debts and let the organization carry on – then the lending market will not work.

These factors are more complicated in the case of sensitive organizations in public services, like hospitals and schools. Banks may be very loath to close them down if they default; knowing that, executives may not be disciplined in their borrowing; and knowing that, banks may not choose to lend to them. In short, getting a quasi-bankruptcy arrangement sorted out is vital to the project of getting government's hands off capital generally.

What is needed is a smooth, rapid, and standard procedure – a procedure entirely set out in advance. To remove any obvious and unpleasant associations with the option of bankruptcy, it might be called 're-establishment'. But what should it consist of? First, in order to foster responsible borrowing, it has to entail mandatory personnel changes at the top of an organization so that those responsible for over-borrowing suffer a personal penalty. Secondly, at the same time, it probably has to make provision for an organization's existing service to be maintained. The most favoured liability of the organization would surely have to be the rights of existing customers to obtain a continuing or alternative service of a reasonable standard. And thirdly, any arrangement would have to allow some transfer of the organization's future income to be diverted to the creditors, away from the core of running costs. The amount of income diverted should be the maximum that is just compatible with the organization meeting its service obligations.

Writing the legislation for 're-establishment' would not be easy, and cannot guarantee that no organization will ever go to the wall. Sometimes even rather good organizations – perhaps ones that have been spending too much or whose financial management has been poor – will have to disappear. And fundamentally, that means many people will feel a kind of repulsion at the whole idea. This is just one of those dilemmas: if we want more freedom for success in the public sector, we have to be willing to tolerate more freedom to fail.

Who Would Lend at What Cost?

Another great problem with the pure purchasing route to reform is that the private sector tends to require large profit margins. The amount you have to pay private companies to invest is a much higher percentage of the total investment than you have to pay to someone in order to persuade them to lend to government. It would be far better, it is argued, to let the public sector do the investing, exploiting its unique power to raise money cheaply.

Why is the public sector able to borrow more cheaply? The fact that it is held to be able to do so is one of the most common arguments against the more extensive use of private ownership in public services. A historical study of US financial data from 1926 to 1981[1] found US government bonds paid an average nominal return of 3.1 per cent (just 0.3 per cent after inflation), while company bonds paid 3.7 per cent

1. R.G. Ibbotson and R.A. Sinquefield, *Stocks, Bonds, Bills and Inflation: The Past and the Future*, Financial Analysts Research Foundation, Charlottesville, Virginia, 1982, quoted in *Principles of Corporate Finance* (second edition), by Richard Brealey and Stewart Myers, published by McGraw-Hill, 1984.

and company shares paid 11.4 per cent. The typical company uses a mix of shares and bonds, so averages at a much higher rate of return than government. To quote a more recent year, in 1996 the average corporate return on capital was 12.5 per cent in the UK; the long-term government bond rate was 7.8 per cent.[1] Apparently governments can borrow more cheaply than anyone else.

But we should treat the idea that ownership of a project affects its cost of capital with suspicion. After all, do we think that government can procure stationery much more cheaply than large private sector buyers? The stationery market is highly competitive, there are unlikely to be huge margins to trim down. But if government cannot get stationery cheaply, why can it borrow capital cheaply? If a project uses a certain amount of capital, and it uses it to a given level of efficiency, then the fact that it is owned by government should not make it cheaper or more expensive. Indeed, one of the simple rules of finance is that a project's cost of capital is determined by the project, and not by the person doing the borrowing.

So how on earth does government apparently save so much in capital costs relative to the private sector? There is a simple, fallacious version of the argument which suggests government can save a lot; and a more complicated, correct, version which suggests government can save a little.

The simple version says that government can reduce the risk investors face, because within reasonable limits, it cannot go bankrupt as it will always be able to raise taxes to repay debts. So, within reasonable limits, governments do not have to pay a bankruptcy risk premium on the debts they take out. This argument is seductive, but in fact deeply misleading. Of course governments can save the bankruptcy risk premium – but only at a cost: by covering loans that in the private sector would be written off. The cost of the latter almost precisely offsets the saving of the former.

To understand why this simple version of the argument is wrong, suppose we build a public library. We expect it to do well, but know there is a 10 per cent chance that it will fail to deliver sufficient benefits to have made it worth building. There is a 10 per cent chance that we will regret putting up the initial capital for the library. Now, in the world of the private sector, that 10 per cent chance is a chance of bankruptcy: it is the chance that the library fails to deliver sufficient revenues to service or repay its debt. In the traditional public sector, there is no equivalent of bankruptcy, and hence nothing happens when the investment decision transpires to have been a mistake.

In the private sector world, the 10 per cent chance that the initial loan will not be repaid has to be factored into the cost of the loan. In the public sector world, it does not have to be as the loan will be repaid in any event. But how much has the public sector really saved? The answer is nothing, because although the cost of the loan is cheaper in the public sector world, the taxpayer has to continue payments on the library's loans even when those loans were mistaken. So there is a different distribution of risk, but no reduction of risk, in the world of public borrowing. Of course, if the private lender to the public sector does not have to bear the risk, he will not charge for it. But that doesn't mean the risk has gone away.

In principle, to discover the true cost of public sector borrowing, you would have to add to the public sector interest rate the cost of repaying debt on projects that would have gone bankrupt had they been in the private sector.

But there is a more subtle correct version of the argument, and it does explain how the public sector can have a lower cost of capital, albeit not as low is it might appear: the essence of the argument – normally attributed to economists Kenneth Arrow and R. C. Lind – is that it is cheaper for the public to share the risk of a project, than to impose on it a small number of investors. If the total losses of a project are the same under public or private ownership, the *suffering* created by the losses is smaller, the greater the number of people over whom they are spread. Underpinning this is the idea that a lot of small losses are less bad than one big loss of the same total magnitude.[1]

---

1. There is a good reason for this, which is the so-called diminishing marginal utility of money: we value money more and more, the poorer we are. So absorbing the first pound of a loss is relatively painless; absorbing the second pound is a little more painful and the thousandth pound gets quite painful indeed. It is thus cheaper to ensure that everybody suffers a small loss, than that a few people suffer a big loss.

If this is true, the risk premium that government has to pay to borrow is smaller than the premium paid by private entrepreneurs. So there is a case for government to do the borrowing, and to eschew the idea that private finance should be brought in everywhere. But in an advanced economy, with a sophisticated capital market, the saving should be tiny, too small to abandon private allocation of capital.

So the popular argument is based on the idea that government suffers less bankruptcy than the private sector, but this is really just a mistake based on the fact that government doesn't place much stress on working out whether projects lose money or not. The subtle argument is that for a given level of loss, government can minimize the effective burden imposed. This latter argument – in a world of widely diffused institutional investments – cannot possibly explain the difference between the apparent 8 per cent rate of government borrowing and the 13 per cent return on capital in the private sector, let alone the 30 per cent return demanded by some venture capitalists. Most of that is explained by the hidden costs to the taxpayer of financing failure that would otherwise be borne by the private sector.

Risk is not the only reason why government may apparently save money relative to private investors. The second concerns spare capacity. One of the advantages of co-ordinated control of an industry – rather than messy competition – is that slack can be avoided. It is an interesting feature of most government services – health and prisons being the most obvious cases – that all capital is run very close to capacity. Hospitals and prisons work very hard and do not have much in the way of idle assets. Among schools, there have been a lot of 'surplus places' – left after a bulge in the childhood population – and the Treasury was able to use its co-ordination power to prevent new schools opening in those areas where surplus places existed. (Indeed, the eradication of surplus school places appears to have been something of an obsession of policy-makers in recent years, on a par with improving standards; it has merited its own table in the Department for Education and Employment's Annual Report.) In this way, the traditional public sector minimized the spare capacity used, and thus effectively economized on capital.

Now this is a genuine saving. We could exploit it in other industries: the state could pass a law saying that no one could open a cinema when there are spare seats at other cinemas nearby; or no one could open a hotel when there is spare hotel capacity nearby. Undoubtedly, that would be welcome to hotel and cinema owners, who would find costs reduced as capacity usage would be higher. They could lower their prices as a result. Should we exploit that power? Should we prevent new entry into an industry on the grounds that there is spare capacity already there? Of course we should not. It is a penny-pinching saving in the short term, that protects incumbent suppliers at the expense of better new entrants. The only new firms tempted to enter a market characterized by surplus places are those that think they are better than the incumbents. It seems a bit short-sighted to deprive them of the right to demonstrate that.

There is a third reason why the use of private capital may sometimes cost more than public capital in public services: any private provider may face a big risk in having one effective customer, government itself. If you build a prison, you are to some extent a prisoner of government policy yourself. If you build a supermarket, you face no such risk, as you have thousands of potential customers to attract. Supermarkets cannot be taken hostage by any one customer in the way that a private prison operator could be. This is a serious problem. Where government is itself the risk, it is tempting to argue that government should bear the risk. That would minimize the temptation to government to let the risk of a policy change actually materialize. It certainly supports the need for long-term contracts in those areas where there cannot be a multiplicity of buying agents.

But in general, it is clear what government should do about the apparently high cost of private finance. Pay it. It may look expensive, but it is not nearly as expensive as it looks, and that it is worth paying is obvious from the fact that we cheerily pay it in every other sector of the economy.

Existing Government Reforms

The last government appears to have understood that private-sector-type corporate governance has certain advantages over the traditional public sector. It attempted to reflect this in its approach to the reform of public services. The privatization programme and the use of market testing and compulsory competitive tendering do involve the transfer of assets from the traditional public sector to the full purchaser–provider split model, and they do so even where publicly owned contractors have won contracts. More recent reforms, however, have been more modest. Let us appraise them in light of the above discussion.

Internal Markets

The most controversial public service reform the last government introduced was specific to one sector: health, where the divide between providing and purchasing was formalized with the creation of trust hospitals on the one side (still publicly owned) and on the other, district health authorities and fundholding GPs financed through a capitation formula. The trust hospitals face a regime ostensibly rather like the full purchaser–provider split. The trusts are charged 6 per cent on their capital, and produce reports and accounts rather like those of private companies.

But we need to recapitulate the argument so far: the purchaser–provider split is primarily useful for taking government out of the management of capital. The purchaser–provider divide is not itself a sufficient condition for full long-term improvement. Under this account, it is privately allocated capital which actually generates long-term benefits by leading to processes of adaptation and progress.

Unfortunately, what is needed in the health service is not so much an internal health services market, but a new health capital market. This was not – emphatically not – built into the health reforms. For example, the required rate of return on NHS capital has been only 6 per cent, less than half the rate competing private hospitals would expect to deliver. And the trusts have had to apply for permission from government to invest new capital, so capital is effectively allocated centrally. Trusts have not been able to borrow to invest themselves (they have been defined as 'inside the PSBR'). Private providers have not been free to compete at existing prices, even were it possible to compete against that public rate of return.

Moreover, the trusts have not been allowed to increase their prices in response to a shortage of capacity, so they have never been able to raise extra cash merely as a result of being more popular than rivals. Anyway, they have been encouraged to sign block contracts which do not closely relate outputs to reward. The government has always maintained control over hospital capacity decisions – effecting closures for example (Barts) and maintaining openings (Edgware). There has never been a takeover market in hospitals, despite the apparently large economies that insiders believe are possible. And as if to emphasize the last government's own confusion when it set up the internal market, hospitals have always been ranked on their waiting list performance, when in any normal purchaser–provider world, it would be the purchaser (the GP or district health authority) who should be blamed for not providing an adequate service to their patients. (Long waiting lists should result in purchases being made from alternative, non-capacity-constrained providers.)

Finally, there were always complicated transitional arrangements in the reforms. As a result, it has not altogether been as one might have hoped, that the requirement to earn profits (even at 6 per cent) was matched by an increase in the local purchasing budget to finance the profits. The profits have been ploughed back into the NHS and thus have increased the purchasers' funds in aggregate, but some redistribution between purchasers occurred in the process.

All in all, it is quite clear that in any meaningful sense, the health service was always entirely under public governance. On this basis, the purchaser–provider split – along with internal market reforms elsewhere, such as at the BBC – is likely to lead to some improvements in productive efficiency (there is evidence for this having occurred) but not to the longer-term dynamic benefits of private governance.

The Private Finance Initiative

No reform has the appearance of extending private governance of capital more clearly than the Private Finance Initiative (PFI). Introduced in the aftermath of the pound's exit from the ERM, it was a relaxation of various Treasury rules, with the effect that investments traditionally under the responsibility of government could be financed by the private sector.

For example, one old-style Treasury rule that was abolished under the PFI had prevented the private sector building a project – like a toll road, or a new government office – as long as the public sector could provide it more cheaply. The rule was designed to prevent costly private speculative investors building things when government could borrow money for them at lower cost. But the rule, somewhat perversely, forbade the involvement of the private sector *even if the public sector had no money to build the project, or intention to do so*. Although the rule would have made sense if the Treasury were rational and found cash for every worthwhile project (by worthwhile, one means a project that it is worth finding cash for), the Treasury was not rational and the rule was primarily only useful in providing an amusing reflection on the values of the most important department of state. It was abandoned by Norman Lamont.

The PFI is – very much in line with the argument here – about turning the cost of new investment into a flow of annual payments. It is a form of procurement in which the government does not buy a piece of equipment, it buys the services the equipment delivers. The scale of projects can range from a kidney machine to a new railway line. The idea – like privatization – has become popular worldwide, and in Britain it has inaugurated bipartisan talk of 'public–private partnerships'. The way the PFI works is quite simple – a public agency (London Transport, the BBC, or the DSS, for example) simply signs a contract with a private firm (or consortium) for the private firm to deliver some service at a specified cost. The private firm is responsible for the investment necessary to support that service. The capital provided is risk capital and does not have to be paid back by government if it all goes wrong. In most cases, however, PFI contracts specify enough business for the provider that there is not the usual degree of commercial risk attendant on a speculative project.

At the time of its introduction, the PFI was seen as a means of stimulating public investment without burdening government finances. There was talk of all PFI investments being 'additional' to the normal capital spending of government. As another benefit, it was suggested that private management would be superior to public management.

The PFI was slow to get going. But even in advance of it leading to any new investment, the conception of the PFI crucially changed. It was to be less about stimulating investment, and more about the introduction of privately governed capital for any type of government investment. Chancellor Kenneth Clarke – approving of private-sector-style governance of capital, and keen to keep the initiative alive – explicitly changed the 'additionality' provision, to one that said all big capital projects had to seek PFI funding before government would consider them.

We have to recognize that the PFI has not, in practice, delivered much in the way of investment. Total contracts agreed amounted to almost £5bn at the end of April 1996. Half of that was the troubled fast rail link to the Channel Tunnel. Almost £1bn of the remainder is a complicated leasing arrangement for Northern Line trains that looks rather like a sophisticated old-style procurement arrangement. In the vast bulk of cases, building work will be spread over several years, so the PFI has probably so far generated construction worth about one-sixth of 1 per cent of GDP over the period it is so far affecting.

Under the incoming Labour government, the PFI has been reviewed and in effect slimmed down. The Paymaster General, Geoffrey Robinson, decided it was better to focus it on a few deals that might actually happen, rather than waste time considering the PFI for deals that would not happen.

So how should we look back upon the PFI? A good idea, needing more time? A good idea badly implemented? Or a bad idea? In fact, of course, all three have an element of truth.

It is a good idea to substitute privately governed capital for publicly governed capital. The PFI does that, and is thus to be commended, even if one sometimes feels the motive is far from noble – more to do with depressing the PSBR in the short term rather than effecting long-term gains.

The PFI is also a vastly better way of buying things than the traditional procurement route followed by government. Because under the PFI government buys services, rather than capital equipment, suppliers are free to be imaginative in the equipment supplied. That is their risk. Innovation is more likely.

Also, under the old procurement route, the supply of services was split into the supply of capital, the supply of parts, the supply of maintenance, and so on. Under the PFI, where one deal covers the lot, the supplier has the incentive to ensure the equipment works and is properly maintained. There is no incentive for the provider of capital to economize on quality, for example, if he is to run and maintain the capital as well. Keeping ownership in the private sector, and bundling all aspects of production into one contract, improves incentives more effectively than the alternative – a set of complicated contracts for each component, each with penalty clauses, etc., to ensure the optimal level of quality.

For the good effect, though, there is a substantial implementation problem: the very high cost of negotiating contracts. It turns out that they are all very complicated, because to get the benefit of private governance, much of the risk of a project must lie with the private governor. But defining those risks is no easy task. Now, there is a good reason and a bad reason for this. The good reason for it is that it is just another manifestation of the same old difficulty of defining outputs in sectors that are not subject to obvious market valuations. Much of the tiresome public–private negotiating is about specifying quality and output standards that can be monitored, and tied to returns. That is bound to be difficult. The bad reason for complications in implementation is that government agents are by and large unaware of the going rate of speculative capital, and have been reluctant to finance it at the going rate. So transferring risks to the private sector is always possible at a price, but government is quite simply unable to believe how much it costs, relative to the apparently cheap price of riskless capital.

The contract-based nature of the PFI raises a second problem: it prevents the scheme being used to open up the supply of services. There is still to be a designated supplier, who provides a monopoly supply in the market for the specific contract. Now this is entirely understandable where the supply is specific to one department and by essence has to be monopolistic. Installing a computer system for the DSS, for example. Or building a specific road. A large number of the PFI deals are in this category. But not all of them, and for those like prisons, health services and schools, why engage in this tortuous debate about contract terms in advance: why not just specify a tariff for different forms of output? Of course, guaranteeing someone business for seven years makes it cheaper to buy from them, but in many cases this is not worth it, and the saving is outweighed by the lack of effective competition engendered.

In addition, the PFI is inevitably very modest, limited to *new* capital, and not to the management of existing assets. It really does nothing to bring about a switch to private sector governance of public sector assets. We know the capital assets of government are valued at about £360bn. Even if there were £5bn worth of new PFI contracts a year, it would take about sixty-four years before PFI accounted for a stock as big as government's current assets. But only by liberating all capital, can new capital and existing capital assets be pitched into competition with each other on a level basis.

All in all, public-private partnerships make room for some entrepreneurship; they extend private governance of capital and often lead to pragmatic improvements in services. But in truth they represent the triumph of ad hoccery in the management of public services. The PFI is a small step towards the purchaser state, but that is all it is.

Resource Accounting

Resource accounting is an important change inaugurated by the last government and endorsed by this one. Indeed, with the production of the National Asset Register in 1997, it is arguable that resource accounting has been advanced under the new administration.

Resource accounting is simply another basis for producing public accounts; but it puts them on a vastly better footing, in particular treating capital as a flow of resources rather than as a one-off up-front payment. In doing that, it aligns the accounting treatment of capital with its actual use, and it fosters the possibility of charging for capital in the public sector, very much as this chapter suggests.

In these respects, it is welcome. But there are several drawbacks of resource accounting in the absence of a more comprehensive programme of arm's-length purchasing. At what rate should capital be charged? In the NHS, where trusts have already been exposed to capital charging, the rate is 6 per cent. As mentioned above, this enshrines a low return into the purchasing mentality of health purchasing authorities and would render it almost impossible for a genuine private operation to compete were they invited to.

Another problem is the initial valuation placed on the assets for which charges are introduced. This is akin to the problem that was described above of measuring outputs – the value of an asset in the private sector is usually taken as being proportional to its effect in creating an output, and the value of that output. In the absence of output measures, it is not clear what an expression of the value of a public sector asset really means. Even though brave attempts are being made to introduce output measures as part of the move towards resource accounting, they face formidable difficulties, and many in government have expressed a doubt that 'staring at the numbers' generated will provide a robust guide to social welfare. These measurement problems are compounded by the absence of any competition to provide services to government in many of the areas where resource accounts are being introduced. Competition at least provides some benchmarks to costs, and hence values.

But once these problems have been overcome, there is every reason to believe that resource accounting makes the purchaser–provider split a far more obvious route to adopt. Transparency in the accounts is not, in itself, a major reform. But transparency can be an important spur to other changes which do constitute major reform. For advocates of the full purchaser–provider split, it is the most hopeful sign there is.

Resource accounting notwithstanding, this discussion suggests that we have yet to witness a reform programme in any public service that is likely to stimulate the kind of change and adaptability fostered by long-term private capital markets. One can be sympathetic to the lack of action, because if there is one message from this discussion it is that reforms have to be very radical to work. You cannot introduce them in an entirely piecemeal fashion. A host of risky reforms need to be introduced simultaneously – paying by outputs; the purchaser–provider split; public-service capital markets; bankruptcy and takeover. Few governments are keen to tread down such a hazardous-looking road, whatever the view at the other end.

Additional Reading

Davis, Evan (1993), *The Importance of Resource Accounting*, Social Market Foundation Memorandum No. 2, SMF, London.

Glennerster, Howard (1994), 'Health and Social Policy' in *The Major Effect*, ed. Dennis Kavanagh and Anthony Seldon, Macmillan, London.

Kable, (1996), *Resource Accounting and Budgeting – an Independent Progress Report*, Kable Publishing and Research, London.

Organization for Economic Co-operation and Development (1994), *The Reform of Health Care Systems, A Review of Seventeen OECD Countries*, Health Policy Studies, No. 5, OECD, Paris.

11 What Can Be Cut?
Redefining the scope of the state

> His is the search for a diverse yet egalitarian socialist individualism.
>
> DAVID MILIBAND writing, without apparent irony,
> on Gordon Brown, in *Reinventing the Left*.

Shrinking the State

The previous two chapters have looked at reforms on what might be called the supply-side of public spending. But we should not ignore the alternative agenda, concerned with the demand for public services – how much, who pays, and with what money? Indeed, in answer to the question, 'How big should the state be?' most people who express an opinion are concerned with the amount we spend, not what we get for it. And often the debate is not very intelligently conducted. A popular mode of discourse is to think of an arbitrary percentage of GDP that the state should take in taxation, and then rigidly stick to that as the desirable size of the state.

There are 50-per-cent people, like Roy Jenkins (writing in 1976). There are 40-per-cent people, like the former Chancellor Kenneth Clarke. There are 35-per-cent people, like the former Chief Secretary to the Treasury, William Waldegrave. And 30-per-cent people, like Lord Skidelsky, Chairman of the Social Market Foundation. Then there are the 15- or 20-per-cent people including, according to some reports, the former Governor of Hong Kong, Chris Patten, enamoured of the Asian tiger economies.

In fact, this picking of arbitrary numbers is a dubious process because participants feel no compulsion to specify what the state should cut in order to achieve their favoured percentage. To enjoy the 'fantasy league redesign of the state' game, your first move should not be to think of the percentage of GDP the state should raise, followed by your hilarious attempts to shape the state to the number you first thought of. Your first move should be to think of sound principles for determining what the state does, followed by the application of those principles to the state's spending.

How far can the demand-side agenda go? There is undoubtedly some shrinking of the state that is possible – but the purpose of this chapter and the next is to show just how large the obstacles to that route are: it is strewn with political difficulties; administrative challenges; and economic doubts.

Even if we adopted the broadly sensible principle that taxation should not finance anything direct user charges could finance efficiently, we could probably get public spending down by only about £50bn a year, equivalent to about 6 per cent of GDP. There are potential additional cuts in social security that may take public spending down further, but it is pretty obvious that we should spend *more* on certain items, and all in all therefore, it seems the maximum desirable cut in the level of state spending takes us from about 40 per cent of GDP on a conventional measure, to between 30 and 35 per cent, and probably somewhere nearer the top end of that range. Scaling the state back that far would involve it reverting to as small as anything we have known since the Second World War. It would mean that UK public expenditure is as small as that in the United States, except that ours would include a health service more comprehensive than the public service over there.

Cuts of £50bn sound huge – it's just enough to abolish VAT, or National Insurance. But this is not to say we the public would be £50bn richer. Well over half that total cut would come from removing the state from the provision of retirement pensions, a reform which would take a minimum of one working life-length to introduce, and we would all obviously have to make more alternative private provision to compensate for the loss of the state pension anyway, so there would be no real change left out of the tax cut eventually made possible by the policy. Like any reconfiguration of the state's role, that particular example is sensible not because it cuts taxes per se, but simply because it is slightly more sensible for us to finance pensions directly than it is for us to pay taxes in the expectation of a government pension.

Along with the state pension, to get to our £50bn saving, we would have to cut state support for agriculture (about £4bn); about half of the state budget for public housing (about £2bn); the national and local roads budget (about £6bn); about half the budget of the Department of Culture, Media and Sport (another £1.5bn); and most of the higher education budget (say, £2bn). Note that most of the items on this list do not primarily go to the poor or vulnerable. University students, farmers, motorists and art lovers are not prominent on the list of society's down-and-outs. But that is not to say they would welcome the removal of their enshrined rights.

But the most important point to note is that it is terribly difficult to shrink the state in a practical, equitable and efficient way. To demonstrate the point, in this chapter we can take a superficial and sweeping look at a few important areas of collective provision, and survey some of the factors involved in designing a less collective system. Above all, though, we can focus on the large residual role of government that would inevitably hang over any area where such an approach was to be made feasible.

Pensions

It does not always seem to be the case, but in principle probably the easiest, and biggest, potential cut in the role of the state is in the provision of pensions. Until 1994, pension payments were the biggest single item of government spending (the NHS has overtaken them since then), and they are an item in which it is hard to discern any very good reason whatsoever for the state to have a role. We know that in some areas – notably higher education and even education – the state may sensibly want to act as a kind of bank, lending money to those who would not be able to borrow it but who have good use for it. But in the case of pensions, the state acts not as a lending bank, but as a kind of savings bank. Yet, if there is one thing that capitalist institutions are good at, it is investing our savings. There are plenty of good reasons why people are not able to borrow; there is no underlying market pathology that says some people will be prevented from saving.

All one can say in defence of the state is that at the time it became involved in this area, pensions were a very much smaller affair than they are now.

Despite this being the biggest area for a potential withdrawal of the state's role, there are a number of reasons why the government may not put pensions at the top of its list of reforms. One perfectly understandable reason is that while the state pension has no good justification, it equally does rather less harm than most items of spending. There is almost nobody for whom the basic state pension is an ill-designed product, because it is so basic – it is barely imaginable that anyone would rationally subscribe to a smaller pension.

Another reason, less persuasive, is that pensions policy has to be tailored to three different groups: those already of pensionable age; those in work; and those who have yet to start their career. Starting from where we are, policy needs to distinguish between the rights and expectations of these different groups. Unfortunately, that inevitably means we have to do virtually nothing in the short term as existing pensioners are what costs a lot, and existing pensioners are the ones we cannot reasonably interfere with. Governments have little incentive to take controversial measures designed to reap modest benefits in forty years' time.

Perhaps the best reason for not doing much to privatize pensions is the performance of the private pensions industry. It is a sad reflection on market forces, but they do not appear to have delivered everything we might have hoped. Their administrative costs are high. The government and press have given a great deal of attention to the selling techniques which led a large number of people to make the wrong choice of pension in the 1980s. That was a scandal. Less publicized, and in fact a far greater scandal, is the fact that until the government intervened in the eighties, most people were given no choice at all, and were forcibly sold a product that was in a large number of cases quite inappropriate – a pension based on salary at the time you leave your job. These pensions had the effect of taking money from short-term servers, and passing it via a rather opaque route to long servers, particularly those (like company directors) who can enjoy a steep increase in earnings in their last year of service. Although the industry gets very sensitive and defensive when this criticism is made, it has always dragged its feet in reforming itself. The attention heaped on the problems of personal pension mis-selling has by and large distracted people from the much bigger problems of occupational schemes. Incidentally, these final-salary schemes have stultified the labour market at the older end of the spectrum, making it more expensive to employ people over fifty, whose contributions are much higher.

Innovation, diversity, choice – all the apparently positive attributes of markets – appear not to have emerged in this one. It is a pity that any reform of the state pension has to rely upon an industry that has served us so badly in the past.

A final reason why we might limit our enthusiasm for pensions reform is that since the last government introduced its policy of indexing the state pension to prices, rather than earnings, everybody has tended to feel as though the issue of the state pension will gradually fade, as it becomes a smaller and smaller proportion of average earnings.

There is still a case for acting more systematically, however, rather than letting reform occur by stealth. Indeed, it is quite a strong case. For one thing, it is not clear the public have quite understood the responsibility that falls on them with the diminution of the state pension. It is true that the state instructs us to make a compulsory contribution to a private pension, worth 4.6 per cent of our salary and if we fail to make that contribution, the state takes the money from us in the form of extra National Insurance and puts it into a separate state scheme. But it is not clear that the compulsory minimum contribution is enough. At any rate, it is only payable for that part of your salary between £62 and £465 a week, and that is indexed with prices, so it too is becoming more and more nugatory. If people fail to take discretionary action for themselves, then an awful lot of us are not going to have an adequate living in retirement. If policy-makers fail to understand the impending crisis of pensions adequacy, then it is unlikely the public will either.

Indeed, one worrying aspect of our behaviour in this area – perhaps not appreciated by policy-makers – is that there appears to be a great deal of herd-like behaviour. *My* decision over saving and spending should in principle be a reflection of my personal desire to trade off consumption now and consumption later when I retire. But in practice, my spending now is heavily influenced by everyone else's. If my friends want to eat at expensive restaurants, I find myself doing the same; and it is possible that societies do get caught up in a culture of consumption even though a large number of rational individuals might prefer to draw their spending back.

The second reason for reforming pensions is that the state scheme is unfunded – there is no pot into which savings go, in order to pay tomorrow's pensions. Private schemes do not have to be funded, but mostly are. Indeed, funding them is the best way of securing them. This is not the place to argue for or against funding, other than to say that in general funding imposes a welcome discipline on the pensions debate, confronting each generation with its own trade-off between income while at work, and income in retirement. Rather than letting us impose an obligation upon our children that we have not upheld towards our parents, everybody can simply decide for themselves how much pension to have, based on the true cost of saving for that pension in work.

There is a common supposition that once you are in an unfunded, pay-as-you-go, world, it is hard to escape from that: in such a world, the first generation save nothing, but collect a pension in their retirement; the second generation pay the pensions of their parents, and take a pension themselves; and every subsequent generation follows in that path. Reforming that system requires one generation to atone for the sin of the first generation, and to pay for its pensions twice: that generation is the transition generation – it has to pay its parents' pensions under the old, unfunded rules; plus it has to save for its own pension under the new, funded rules. This problem of the generation which has to pay twice is a severe one. And it is certainly true that we are now, as far as the state is concerned, in a world of pay-as-you-go. Surely we are stuck there?

The answer is not necessarily. What is perhaps less understood than the problem of the generation that has to pay twice, is the fact that shifts in the age structure of the population imply more or less funding as generations come and go. In particular, the existence of a bulge in the age structure – deriving from, say, a baby boom after a long war – implies that the effective unfunded liabilities of the state increase as that generation passes through the workforce. A bulge implies that each individual has to work rather little to pay for the pensions of the older generation; but each of their children has to work rather hard to pay for their pension. As we are currently enjoying a modest bulge in the workforce, if ever there was a time to convert from pay-as-you-go to funding, now is it. What is absolutely certain is that you cannot make the generation which pays twice the one following a bulge.

So how might we reform pensions if we wanted to? The best practical scheme came from Peter Lilley, with Basic Pension Plus, in the run-up to the 1997 election. It was simply a bargain to be struck with those who had yet to start work: we will give you £9 a week while you are at work; we will not give you a state pension. The £9 was the amount the government's actuaries calculated you would need to invest over a working lifetime to get the basic state pension in retirement. Of course, people would be compelled to invest the £9; but the government was confident enough of the caution of its actuarial assumptions to underwrite the investment and guarantee a basic state pension on retirement.

There was one real advantage to the Lilley scheme: because everybody would have a personal pension fund of one sort or another, with a contribution of at least £9 a week to put in it, it was then going to be very easy for people to top up their contributions, without having to go through a great administrative nightmare to open a new pension account specially. This would mean the state top-up pension (SERPS) could be abolished as well, as that is little more than an earnings-related pension for those too poor to make contributions to a private scheme worthwhile.

The other clever thing about the Basic Pension Plus system as proposed was that it overcame the problem of the generation who has to pay twice by making two generations pay one-and-a-half times. Existing workers would end up paying extra tax for the £9 per week rebates going to the young, as well as paying for their parents' pensions. Similarly, the generation getting the £9 a week would in fact have to contribute to that £9 a week itself through extra general taxation (the money doesn't come from nowhere) and it would also have to pay for the pensions of the generation ahead of it, whose state pension rights were still intact.[1]

---

1. Indeed, if the government allowed itself to borrow more than it otherwise would have to finance the rebates, it could effectively pass some of the cost on to a third generation.

Peter Lilley demonstrated that it was possible to abolish the state pension in a broadly fair and equitable way. But how practical and advantageous was the result? He demonstrated that we would have to replace a state pension with some form of compulsory saving. And in one view, most propounded on the right, compulsory saving is barely distinguishable from taxation, so there is little to be gained by it.

This is a point that will undoubtedly re-emerge in every discussion of welfare state reform. In support of it is the observation that in order to keep the administrative cost of private pensions – or private insurance – down, it is inevitable that the government ends up specifying a standard, homogenous pension product that everybody buys. Low cost and homogeneity go hand-in-hand, and it is not clear that the vast bulk of us are willing to pay the true, substantial market rate that we would need to in order to have better-tailored products and more choice. Once the diversity of a true, free market in private provision has been eradicated by regulation and compulsion, what have you achieved by removing taxation from the scene?

Those supporting a real withdrawal of the state from pensions would have to argue that there should not be compulsory saving, at least not beyond the point that ensures you would never have to come appealing to the state for a safety-net income when you grow old. This is superficially appealing from a libertarian perspective, but the first genera-tion of impoverished pensioners would lead to irresistible pressure to drop the idea. In any event, for good reason or bad, the public have been trained to expect the state to do quite a bit of their financial planning for them, and it would be a bit irresponsible to release us all back into the wild without rather better preparing us. Anyway, in as far as consumption decisions are made collectively, or culturally; in as far as people strive to maintain some relative consumption as well as absolute consumption, there is a case for some collective discussion and policy to steer us towards an agreed level of consumption. Government might be the object of that collective nudge.

The idea that compulsion and taxation are the same do not, however, quite ring true in any event. There is a big difference between a personal pension, with your name written on it, which rises and falls with the stock market, which you can top up to your heart's desire, which you know will be yours on retirement; and a system of taxation which loosely promises to pay you a pension on retirement.

As it happens, the Lilley scheme was defeated neither on the compulsory saving element, nor on the argument about funding. It helped contribute to the Conservative election defeat, because it was rather easy for Labour to imply the government was going to remove the state pension from existing pensioners, a proposition that almost nobody has ever discussed. It is a pity because the opportunity to reform pensions is a short-lived one: when the babyboomers hit retirement, it will become very much harder for decades to follow. But the brief life of Basic Pension Plus in political debate demonstrates that even where the arguments in favour of trimming the state's role are by and large persuasive, the practical route to doing so is fraught with genuine difficulties.

Housing

Governments rarely leave housing alone. In almost all countries, even the United States with its apparently naked free-market psychology, housing is not left to unregulated transactions between consenting adults. The provision of low-income housing in some form or other is an important dimension of housing policy almost everywhere. Rent control; direct state provision of social housing; housing benefit to subsidize rents for those on low incomes; and planning requirements that stipulate certain categories of housing should be built in some proportion to a general development; all have been used to support the low-income housing sector.

Policy in the UK, however, evolved very dramatically under the last government: rent control has gone; state provision of social housing has diminished; and instead housing benefit has grown in importance. In 1995, a total of 198,832 new dwellings were built in the UK; of those very few (3,208) were built by local authorities. Nevertheless, intervention in the UK is still extensive. About 15 per cent (29,262) of all new dwellings in 1995 were built by housing associations, which are not that distinct from municipal providers. Moreover, in 1995–6, the government spent £5.6bn on housing.[1] Of that, £1.6bn subsidized the ongoing (or current) costs of public sector and housing association provision. Some £4bn went on capital spending, mainly to housing associations and local authorities for building or renovating housing. Included within this was a substantial sum on grants to improve private property. And at the end of the long period of evolution, in 1995, there were still some 23 per cent of households in the social sector: 19 per cent in council houses, and about 4 per cent in housing association property.

This all raises the specific question of whether our interventions in the housing market are well designed, well costed, and properly subjected to normal controls over public resources. More generally, we have to ask whether the whole pattern of – fairly substantial – intervention is justified. Is it really the case that in order to ensure everybody has a home, we directly house a quarter of the population? Is it right that five million people should receive a social security benefit tied to their housing cost?

In addition to the mere extent of housing support, there are some specific reasons for questioning the complexity of housing finance in the UK, and the sometimes rather opaque and haphazard way in which subsidy is provided. Take the example of the Oxo Tower, on the South Bank of the Thames. It is a housing co-operative, without a profit-making objective, designed to act as social housing. Not a penny of its cost has ever shown up as public spending, primarily because it was financed out of a car-parking concession granted in the last days of the old Greater London Council. With the proceeds of that concession, the co-op built some of the most desirable property in London.

There are other reasons for thinking housing policy needs to be reviewed: when we house someone on a low income, we do so for life, not just for the duration of their hardship. This inevitably means we end up housing a large number of people whose conditions no

---

1. The source for this figure is the Annual Abstract of Statistics, 1997 edition, Table 3.6. Because government accounts are rather opaque, this headline figure takes into account neither the credit to government revenue from council rents, which reduces the true size of government intervention, nor the cost of government capital tied up in housing, which dramatically increases it. Nor does it include support to owner-occupiers through mortgage interest-rate support, or tax relief.

longer merit much help. It may not be decent to throw people out of a home because they have enriched themselves; it may not be conducive to stable communities to turf people out of them when they no longer require social support for their housing needs. But giving someone a subsidized house for life because they were poor for a few years, while there are poorer people queueing up for homes, seems manifestly unjust.

There is another potential problem with social housing, and that is that there are no clear, well-regulated criteria for determining who gets it. This is not just a problem with council and housing association property; it is a problem in other countries with rent-controlled property too. A desirable lease is desirable to the rich as well as the poor, and it is very hard to prevent the rich getting desirable leases without relatively tight policing. (It seems difficult to see why any single, prime-age male of able body and mind should ever be granted social housing.)

Finally, there is another problem with the existing extent of social housing, and that is that it ghettoizes and stigmatizes those who live in it. Oddly, the idea of food stamps for the poor is generally considered rather demeaning, whereas housing for the poor is considered vital.

All of this argues against the direct provision of housing at all, and in favour of limiting government intervention to the subsidy of rents for the poor. In fact, it takes you to the policy we are increasingly adopting. It is possible to have stricter rules as to eligibility; it is possible to 'turn the benefit on and off' more flexibly as circumstances change, without turning people out of their home. Of course housing benefit does not guarantee that people would obtain any, or any acceptable, leases in the private sector, but it would not be impossible to devise a standard lease, with generous security of tenure, to which benefit recipients would be entitled. If the lease was expensive, housing benefit would obviously have to cover the cost.

But how well does the housing benefit system really work? It has had a bad press. It was revealed by the National Audit Office that about 10 per cent of claims are fraudulent in one form or another. Housing benefit is complicated, and it encourages landlords and tenants to conspire with each other to exploit the state.[1]

---

1. Of course these problems are not unknown in the direct provision of low-rent housing as well, where sub-letting sometimes occurs, and is in effect a form of fraud.

To really judge the effectiveness of the cash support for housing, as opposed to the other possible forms of interventions, one is inevitably drawn back to the question, what is the intervention trying to achieve, or what problem is it attempting to overcome?

One simplistic answer is that the market will never provide low-income housing, because high-income housing is so much more profitable. This should immediately raise your suspicions. Surely the builders would all build high-income houses, and find they are running out of high-income families to occupy them? At that stage it will become profitable to build low-income housing.

In fact, it is possible to discern two quite sensible and distinct objectives. Firstly, housing policy has to be aimed at helping individual families, ensuring that in a market that is rather thin and capricious, everybody can find a place to live. It is clear that reliance on normal transactions leads to problems at the lower end, because one's housing costs probably bear little relation to one's housing living standard. To just expect people on benefits, for example, to pay for housing directly out of their weekly cash – even if that cash were quite generous – would mean that some people would be left homeless, while others would have plenty of spare cash left over.

In terms of dealing with this first problem, in particular with regard to the problems of households outside the labour force, direct provision of social housing seems unnecessary. Housing benefit copes admirably. It might be improved, reformed, it might even be that the state should actually find accommodation for people before paying their rent with housing benefit. (The local authority might have a housing rental agency that negotiates the rent, settles the lease and then pays housing benefit on normal terms.) But that housing benefit is in principle the right form of support seems indisputable. The state's role in housing as far as this group is concerned can be cut back to merely providing cash; and perhaps doing so in more judicious quantities than at present.

There is a second proper objective of housing policy, though, and that complicates this picture. It is not so much aimed at helping individual families for whom homelessness is a potential problem; it is about helping communities, and ensuring they function efficiently and economically. In this regard, it is a proper function of policy to ensure that each district has a reasonably balanced population. This would not need to be a concern if there was unlimited room to build housing in each community, because then there would no rationing of space. But in practice, in many areas there is rationing of space, and in desirable areas like Kensington, or in Kent villages, that would tend to mean the poor get squeezed out and the rich take over. That imbalance may have detrimental effects on the local labour market. Indeed, when you hear Kensington residents complain they can't get a cleaner, it is precisely because the local population is not balanced. It is a problem not just for the Kensington elite, but also for the person without a job in Merton, who would happily take one as a cleaner in Kensington.

We need to be quite clear on the source of the problem here. One might blame it on the fact that government itself restricts the supply of housing through planning regulations. The reason that the poor may not find a home (in the way they can pretty well always find food) is that there will be a shortage of supply. That is because in some areas, such as Kensington or Kent villages, no new homes will be built if the local people have any say in the matter. If new homes *are* built, they will be snapped up by rich, aspiring residents of Kensington or Kent villages. Only if there is an absurd amount of new building will space be found for the poor. But it is quite undesirable that whole areas should be ruined in order to maintain a mixed population within them.

The market allocation of a rationed supply of housing, though, is not efficient in the way that a market allocation of an unrationed product would be. When a rich family chooses to reside in Kensington, at the cost of a home for a poorer person, the rich family's decision has an impact on the other rich people in the community who might have used the labour of the displaced poorer family. Yet that impact – probably detrimental – is not reflected in the price of the Kensington property.

In dealing with the problem of balanced populations in travel-to-work zones, it is not clear that housing benefit works terribly well. The rules are cumbersome to apply to working households: they put on them very high marginal rates of benefit withdrawal with serious disincentive effects; and in any event, the incomes of working households, while sometimes insufficient to afford housing in expensive areas, are too high to qualify for housing benefit. It is thus quite arguable that direct provision of low-income housing for low-paid employees in any expensive area will always be inevitable.

The question then arises as to how much housing the state should provide. Could it not limit direct provision to those areas where rents are, say, 20 per cent more expensive than the regional average; could it not offer, say, six-year tenancies, rather than lifetime ones; and could it not limit social provision to a more modest proportion of the housing market?

It is, in conclusion, very unlikely that after a long transition period, a rational housing policy would end up looking nearly as extensive as the existing one. But it is pretty clear that any review of housing provision would have to enshrine existing tenants with existing rights, if only to avoid a huge political battle that would ultimately threaten any reform itself. It is also likely, given the complexity of factors at play, that a rational housing policy would involve both some housing benefit, and some direct housing provision.

Roads

Of all items of public provision, the free use of road space is perhaps now the most troublesome. There are so few good reasons to tolerate steamy, noisy, dangerous, congested roads it is amazing that we continue to do so. The only good news on this front is that the problems of urban congestion are now getting bad enough to provoke serious discussion of alternative policies.

The case of roads differs from most of the other areas discussed here. The primary problem is that roads are much in demand and free at point of use, so that use has to be rationed by some other limitation on the quantity consumed. Indeed, one libertarian thinker has likened the traffic jams so common in the West to the food queues in the former Soviet Union. The problem with queues is that they are a highly inefficient method of rationing demand. If we ration demand by pricing people off the roads, at least the rest of us benefit from the money raised. If we ration demand by making it unpleasant to drive, there is no corresponding benefit to the rest of us from that unpleasantness. It is a deadweight cost.

The other point about road pricing is that it counters a profound and quite underestimated source of selfish behaviour. Road users create inconvenience for other road users to a degree of which they are quite unaware. This is from the extra seconds of journey time they add to the journeys of the many other drivers they encounter en route. These seconds add up to an extraordinary total. According to traffic experts, in a city with an average speed getting down to 10 miles per hour, a driver on the road for one hour adds more than one hour to other road users' journeys.

It is clearly desirable to let people know the true cost of their behaviour by charging them for use of the road, and to incorporate that cost into their decision to use a car. Indeed, once those decisions were properly priced, there would almost certainly be a miraculous reassessment of the value of public transport.

The other most effective measure for controlling the car – making it almost impossible to park – is not to be dismissed. It is usually easier to implement, but unfortunately it comes at the cost of distorting a secondary market – the market for car-parking spaces – that would otherwise work perfectly well on its own. It can also give an undeserved windfall gain to those who can overcome it (owners of car-parking space); it unfairly hits those who need and want to park, without hitting those whose driving habits do not require parking.

Other restrictions on car use – such as limiting urban access on alternate days to cars with odd or even number plates – can also undoubtedly be useful (although this scheme imposes an unnecessary cost on people with occasional, valuable journeys who have the wrong number plate on the odd day on which they wish to travel). Restricting access by pedestrianization can also help limit traffic, but not necessarily to the desirable level. It might be that a road would ideally have *some* traffic, but the choice we tend to make is that it has lots or none, as it is difficult to allow, say, every second car into the street. It might be that speed bumps or narrow access gates are desirable to limit speeds. But when they are installed simply to make a driver's journey irritating, they are a deadweight cost to the drivers who persist in driving over them.

This is surely one of those cases where what are loosely termed market forces – i.e., individual choice in the context of accurate price signals – is the right way to allocate shares of a scarce right. Those price signals would necessarily vary enormously by road, time of day and perhaps type of vehicle. So why do we not jump at road pricing? The answer in this case relates to practical difficulties, and principled reluctance.

The practical difficulties relate to the need for a technology that makes paying for car use less irritating than the problem being dealt with. Tollbooths are more trouble than they are worth, and smart card technology is the only flexible and effective method of charging. Smart cards are no panacea however. In major urban areas, where pricing is most necessary, a huge number of overhead gantries or equivalent devices would be needed to monitor movements. The existing unsightly spectre of mobile-phone transmitters would undoubtedly be nothing compared to the plethora of road-readers necessary. Even once they were installed, there is the problem of national coherence in driving policy. Much of the country, indeed most of the country in terms of surface area, need not have any system of road pricing as the requisite prices would probably be too low to merit the investment in technology. But people who drive quite reasonably do expect to be able to travel outside their own locality. This means, for example, that people in Ipswich have to be able to drive in London, which means that Ipswich residents would have to be equipped with a London smart card, even if their need for it was rare.

Many of these practicalities have been thought through. The consultants MVA, based in Woking, were paid several millions of pounds to design a road pricing scheme for London. They did so quite successfully. It is worth looking at some of their conclusions:

We tested a range of charge levels and structures . . . One of the more extensive schemes ('three cordons plus screenlines') had three concentric cordons . . . the outer two were divided into sectors to form a total of nine charging zones covering Inner and Central London.

. . . the 'medium' charge level tested was a £2 charge on the central London cordon in both directions, £0.50 for crossing each of the two outer cordons in the peak direction with lower charges at other times, and £0.25 for crossing a screenline in the peak and less at other times.

. . . traffic in Inner and Central London, as a whole, would decrease by 7 per cent and CO_2 emissions by 14 per cent, while speeds would rise by about 10 per cent.

. . . the implementation costs for the three cordons plus screenlines scheme using read-write tags would be £240m, and the annual operating costs would be £150m, assuming that 4 million vehicles needed to be equipped. The use of smartcards could increase the implementation costs to £335m, and the annual operating costs to £155m.

. . . The three cordons plus screenlines scheme would produce £90m of net annual benefits, after allowing for operating costs. The cumulative economic benefits would be likely to exceed the implementation costs within two years.

. . . The main risks would lie with the reactions of the public, the reliability of the technology, the complexity of the administrative systems and the adequacy of the enforcement. Congestion charging could, however, significantly reduce congestion and the environmental impacts of traffic and could provide a rapid return on investment in both financial and economic terms.

These are persuasive conclusions, although they leave open the possibility that it may still be worth waiting to see whether better systems for implementing road pricing come along.

The other set of objections is based on dislike of the principle. It is argued that the poor would be driven off the roads, which is at best only true up to a point. In compensation, though, they would benefit from some of the revenues earned from the rich road users. And in fact, the real poor are not car users at all, and they would almost certainly benefit from the inevitable improvements to public transport that would follow from any scheme that took drivers off the road.

There is a second argument, though, and that is the balance of gains between drivers and non-drivers. The problem is that while society overall benefits enormously from the imposition of road pricing, drivers taken as a group on their own are likely to be losers. Drivers end up paying the charges, and even though they stand to benefit from the clearer roads that result, calculations of net benefits and costs show that they are losers overall, unless the revenues deriving from road pricing are given back to them. In practice, it is possible to give them a lot of money back – cheaper vehicle excise duty for example, or lower petrol taxes. But it is not really possible to give it all back, because that would involve upsetting some of the incentives the policy would be trying to improve. Without compensating drivers through reductions in other taxes, road pricing is unlikely to be very popular; indeed, until drivers believe they will benefit from it, the queue may well remain the least politically dangerous form of rationing. The key question for road pricing is whether enough revenues could be returned to drivers for them to benefit en masse from road pricing, without undermining the price signals given to them.

Again, therefore, the state can potentially introduce charges where once taxation was the norm, but it will not do so quickly or easily.

Higher Education

Higher education is the most significant area in which the traditional public sector model once applied and is in the process of being withdrawn. But this is not to say the state is removing itself from the sector.

The most important way in which provision is being curtailed is in tax-financed maintenance and tuition of graduates. On a means-tested basis, the state used to pay both; then it paid for fees; now it is set to retrench further, and collect payment for some tuition as well.

The government has not extricated itself from a financial role altogether, however; it knows that the capital sum involved in obtaining a higher education is larger than most people can afford without borrowing against their future earnings; it knows that the capital market is particularly reluctant to lend against future earnings; and it thus lends money to finance student education.

In 1996–7, prior to the report of the Dearing Committee on the future of higher education, and the implementation of its main findings, the extent of government involvement was about £3.3bn in direct grants to higher education institutions; and about £2.7bn in loans (net of repayments) and grants. We have been told that government cannot afford to finance the expansion of higher education, and this accounts for the increasing switch to loans from grant awards. In fact, this is open to doubt. We could probably have afforded to stay where we were. The number of full-time equivalent students is about 1.2 million, implying that about one person in three goes to university; a number that has doubled since 1979. Almost all of the growth occurred after

1988. While public expenditure on the sector did increase substantially over that period, the worst was over; similar growth would not continue, and the delayed incoming revenues from loan repayments had not yet caught up with the growth that had occurred in student numbers. Much of the expansion was financed through an increase in 'productivity' of the higher education sector. It simply spent a great deal less on each student. Over the 1990s, official projections had the real unit cost of higher education falling by 28 per cent.

The problem was *not* simply financing this level of activity in the sector; the problem was the inappropriateness of the old style of funding. For one thing, it is manifestly unjust to force non-graduates to pay for graduates, particularly when the economic evidence suggests that rates of return from an investment in higher education are high. (Indeed, widening pay differentials suggest that they may be increasing.) Ian Walker and Colm Harmon estimate the return at about 15 per cent per year of education,[1] although other estimates are lower.

The second problem – perhaps one that people feel embarrassed to talk about – is that when levels of participation get as high as one-third, society really wants to make sure that everybody going to university is really committed to benefiting from it. On the grounds that anything free tends to be consumed rather carelessly, there is a strong case for asking students to bear a large part of the cost of going to university to ensure they really do want to go.

The third and perhaps most important reason for refinancing higher education is that while apparent productivity has risen (because greater numbers of students are passing through, at less than proportionate extra cost), there has been some worry that this is merely a statistical artifact caused by the fact that quality is not properly measured in the university sector, and that quality has diminished as fast as quantity has increased. This is not to join the chorus of complaint that courses are lacking in academic rigour – because it is inevitable that a doubling of student numbers requires a different configuration of higher education products. The decline in quality that matters is that in teaching: if lecturers have too little time to keep up with their subject; if graduate

---

1. 'The Marginal and Average Returns to Education', presented at the Royal Economic Society's 1997 Annual Conference in Stoke-on-Trent.

students now teach where lecturers once did; and if teaching is based around bigger groups and less personal contact, then the whole population of graduates suffers.

For all these reasons, plus the fact that if yet more students did want to go to college in future, the state would end up with a yet bigger bill, the move towards shifting a greater proportion of the burden of higher education on to the recipients was probably inevitable.

In reaction to plans to retrench from the old public sector model of delivery, there were cries of betrayal from the old left (and, in fact, unpredictable cries of betrayal from the Conservative opposition). However, the argument that loan-based finance would mean many worthy students would skip college to avoid debts rather missed the point: college education has been rationed already, year after year, by the state limiting the entry numbers to universities in order to keep costs down. The whole point of liberating the sector from the annual public spending round is to *stop* rationing education, or to stop rationing other than by a willingness to hand over your high future salary to pay for it.

So with the Dearing Committee's proposals that students should contribute to their tuition costs using publicly supported loans, is the university sector now a market-led one? The answer is 'no'. One area of continuity between the old world of universities and the new one is a tight, and simple, form of price regulation. Universities are not allowed to charge what they want for a course. For the academic year 1997–8, the appropriate fees are: £750 for classroom-based courses; £1,600 for laboratory-based courses; and £2,800 for the clinical elements of medical, dentistry and veterinary courses. Oxford and Cambridge obtain a higher amount. Otherwise, these prices apply uniformly to the sector, regardless of the quality provided.[1]

So price regulation is simply a price the universities themselves have

1. In the past, these prices were not legally enforced. Universities always had the right to charge more than the recommended retail price, as long as they didn't expect the government to reimburse students for any top-up, and the universities were reluctant to impose a non-reimbursable burden on students. Under the new regime, the regulated prices are enforced through the expressed desire of the Dearing Committee and the Department for Education and Employment that top-ups should not be charged. Government has said it will act legislatively if the need to prevent top-ups arises.

to pay for government subsidy of the loan scheme. But price regulation in reasonably competitive industries like the university sector raises some particular problems. Most notably, it makes it difficult for providers to offer high-quality, expensive provision, even if students would be willing to pay extra to enjoy that high-quality provision. If University College London wants to install expensive teaching equipment on the grounds that it is helpful, we would like them to do so if they can persuade students it is worth them doing so. That kind of management decision is simply prohibited in the UK.

There are two bad reasons and one good reason for blocking variable pricing. The first bad reason – and probably the first in the minds of those imposing the policy – is that in the UK we maintain a polite fiction that a degree is a degree is a degree, from wherever it comes. Variable pricing would undoubtedly destroy the fiction that, for example, a first in car dealership at Loughborough is the same as a first in engineering at Imperial College. As that fiction in fact only apparently fools professional educational administrators, its demise would hardly be a disaster.

The other bad reason for making all prices the same is that all costs – most notably pay levels – are the same, because they too are regulated and nationally negotiated. That particular constraint is unnecessary, and while it has had the beneficial effect of encouraging better academics to seek supplementary income from consulting, it has meant that effective remuneration in the academic sector is rather capricious, and arbitrarily dependent on a talent, inclination, and opportunity to sell one's expertise commercially.

While these are bad reasons for imposing uniformity in prices, there is a good reason. Observation of unregulated educational sectors makes it clear that people will quite naturally pay not just for quality measured in absolute terms, but also for quality measured in relative terms. Indeed, the premium they are willing to pay to go to the best college or school, even where the best is not much better than the average, can be very substantial. It may even be that the absolute quality of the best college is no superior to that of many of its rivals, but as long as the college's reputation is better, rational students will queue to pay extra to get in. Their choice will be justified by the extra salary they will secure afterwards. And as long as the college chooses the best students from those queuing, its reputation will remain high, even though its teaching is mediocre.

This means prices in an unregulated education sector can be bid up to very high levels, unrelated to costs. Some capping of this escalation is desirable. Whether we need quite as rigid a form of regulation as we have; whether we could not adopt a more flexible system of banding of prices that allows universities to charge more than the average at the student's expense using a state loan, is open to question. That some kind of government hand in the market is necessary, is not.

Social Security: to Cut or Expand?

And then there is social security. This causes more concern and indignation than any other heading, and has a more distorting effect on general economic behaviour than any other government spending. This, aside from pensions, is the area of government spending where those wanting to act on the demand-side have the largest budget to cut, and can offer the most potential for reform and for cuts in state spending.

Social security, however, is not the problem it always seems. It is not the case that we cannot afford our social security system; evidently we can, as in fact we do. Over the long term, once the impact of the ageing population has been stripped out, and the impact of peripheral social-security-type subsidies added in, the cost has grown, but not as much as is popularly supposed. With benefits indexed only to prices in an economy which grows richer each year, the affordability of social security should improve rather than deteriorate in the next few decades.

There is another reason to be reticent about reforming social security. This is the piece of government spending where the ratio of value added – or actual production by government – is very low compared to the amount of spending involved. Most of it is transfer, rather than government production. To revert to the constant refrain of this book, if government value added is seen as more of a problem than government spending, you might well think social security is not a place to make a big fuss. In 1996–7 we spent about £3.5bn on administering the social security system. There is every reason to think that could be improved

Table 1: Social Security Growth
in real terms, excluding pensions and administration

1986−7	5.0%
1987−8	−1.8%
1988−9	−1.3%
1989−90	−4.9%
1990−91	1.2%
1991−2	18.8%
1992−3	16.7%
1993−4	9.4%
1994−5	2.9%
1995−6	−0.5%
1996−7	1.8%

Source: author's calculations based on official figures, mostly in ONS, *Annual Abstract of Statistics*, 1997 edition.

as much as any other piece of the public sector, and it would be no bad thing to reform the administration process in line with the suggestions in the previous two chapters. But it is very clear that high administration costs are not the pressing problem of the system. And the vast bulk of the budget, the other £94bn of it, is a transfer, not a piece of government value added. That can be cut, but only by making somebody poorer. It is not a deadweight loss.

Despite both these arguments, and the complacent impression they might yield, social security *is* in crisis, and desperately needs reforming. Not because it is unaffordable, but because it is not worth affording. We are spending money in quite the wrong way and dampening individual incentives for self-improvement very seriously. It is no wonder that the government has chosen to make welfare reform a centrepiece of its microeconomic programme.

Tables 1 and 2 demonstrate why we would should have our suspicions that the programme is failing. The overall budget, excluding most of the allocation for pensioners and administration, has jumped, particularly in 1991 and 1992. Although it has stabilized since then, it has ended up several percentage points of GDP above its level at the start of the last parliament. Part of that reflects a shift in the tax system from rates to

Table 2: Selected Social Security Benefits – Cost and Growth

	Cost 1995–6 £m	Real annual growth 1990–91 to 1995–6 %	Proportion of GDP 1990–91 %	Proportion of GDP 1995–6	No. of claimants 1991 000s	No. of claimants 1995	Growth in no. of claimants 1990–95 %, annual	Notes
Unemployment benefit	1,099	1.1	0.2	0.1	569.5	426.5	−7.0	
Sickness/invalidity/ disability benefits	17,724	13.3	1.4	2.4	1,479.5	1,987.7	7.7	1,2
Child benefit	6,292	2.2	0.8	0.8	7,024.4	7,222.2	0.7	3
Family credit	1,772	26.7	0.1	0.2	360.4	630.9	15.0	
Income support	16,650	9.4	1.6	2.2	4,683.0	5,896.5	5.9	4
Housing benefit	11,164	15.1	0.8	1.5	4,026.0	4,868.0	4.9	5
Total	54,701	10.8	4.8	7.3				
Money GDP	746,000	2.0						

1: Claimant figures are for sickness and invalidity only.

2: Costs include ICA, AA, Mob A., DLA, SDA, IIB.

3: Claimant families, not claimant children.

4: Includes pensioner claimants.

5: Figures for rent only.

Source: author's calculations based on official figures, mostly in ONS, *Annual Abstract of Statistics*, 1997 edition.

council tax, both of which are rebated to the poor, the former of which was paid by property owners and the latter paid by (the poorer) property occupiers. Part of it reflects a conscious effort to raise rents in the public sector, and allow rents to rise in the private sector, with a consequent impact on housing benefit. Part of it reflects a deliberate effort to get more people into work via family credit, and part of it is explained by the ups and downs of the economy. But there is still an overall effect of more benefit pay-outs.

Most worrying of all is the number of claimants. While it is understandable that there might be more housing benefit and family credit recipients in 1995 than 1991, it is hard to understand why there should be an extra half million sick people.

So let us take a look at the potential for reform.

Delineating the State's Role

Chapter 3 attempted to explain and justify the idea of social security by likening it to insurance against misfortune. It argued that the state had a role in providing a kind of insurance cover for bad luck that was uninsurable in private markets. If one accepts that general perspective, the first important decision to make is to delineate where private insurance markets could function. In general, for most risks, one might expect that private insurance, if it could be made to work, gives us more choice, more diversity, more innovation and a generally greater feeling of connectedness to our own contributions than state insurance.

On the other hand, it is not possible to have a totally individualized system of private insurance that also involves redistribution. The two aims are opposite in effect. Indeed, any system that satisfies the idea that people should feel 'connected' to their contribution is hard to reconcile with redistribution. Connectedness requires that there is a direct link between one's input and output; redistribution almost always requires that the link between input and output is broken. It is always going to be very difficult to replace the whole social security scheme with a private contribution-based insurance scheme.

The choice we appear to have made in the UK, is that the state provides insurance for all significant risks, and private 'top-up' insurance is used for risks not covered by the state, or undercovered by the state.

The government collects its 'insurance premiums' in the form of taxation (and a special form of taxation called National Insurance). This is not a bad way of running the basic package the state wishes to run, and it does sustain a broad measure of redistribution.

It does have one serious drawback, however: the existence of a basic state insurance package wipes out any market for private provision, even though the state package is rather modest for a high proportion of the labour market. As a result, the basic package is subject to little market pressure: the politicians decide upon it, the voters vote upon it, but there is no real test of whether the public themselves would choose to adopt it, and there is no mechanism by which the public could vote with their feet for a different or enhanced package.

There is an alternative that those proposing a trimming in the state's role might support. Under that alternative, the state would entitle everyone in the nation to basic insurance cover, but the state would not provide that cover at all. Instead, the state would give people cash to buy an insurance premium for themselves, or at least it would give them some of the cash they need to buy a premium, to ensure that everybody could at least obtain a basic insurance package equivalent to the cover implicit in the existing social security system. The insurance itself would be provided by competing private insurance companies, using actuarially determined premiums. As some people's premiums would be higher than other people's, and as the state would be picking up the cost of premiums, some people would get a bigger subsidy than others, so existing redistribution would not need to be affected.

In this world, the state would never actually pay any money out in the event of misfortune. The role of the state would be as the provider of 'basic insurance'; rather than as the provider of a basic income.

There is an important advantage to the idea of replacing a basic insurance package with the paying of premiums for a basic package of insurance. It is that once the cost of the basic insurance package for each individual has been ascertained, and once the state has seen how much it has to pay to secure that package for any individual, the individual could then be left to use the state premium to buy whatever package happens to be best. This may not be the basic state package at all. People who dislike the state's basic insurance policy might swap it for a better one (perhaps topping up the subsidized premium with their own income). Moreover, because the state premium could be combined with an individual top-up premium, and both thrown into one pot for one insurance package, it would be far easier for individuals to add to the state insurance system if they chose to. Such a system thus combines a little more flexibility with the basic redistribution on offer.

This system may still sound rather closer to some kind of theoretical ideal, rather than a practical option. But it would not be impossible to move towards a more competitive and innovative insurance system by simply breaking the existing social security machinery up into several parts, and asking them to compete for business with each other, along with private insurance companies. In fact, there is discussion of schemes for replacing parts of the social security system with private savings or insurance accounts. It does not all emanate from the right. Frank Field has been interested in the idea, and Dennis Snower of Birkbeck College has also devised what sound like practical schemes.

It remains to be seen whether any of these ideas prove attractive politically. Inevitably, they would be expensive to administer. The state will always have to cover those situations when an insurance company fails, for example. The state would also inevitably have to compel people to select enough insurance to avoid them falling into a state safety-net.

Most crucially, though, it should be noted that in as far as the state did pay everybody's premiums, they would be about as expensive as paying out basic entitlements instead.[1] Indeed, it might be argued that a system of broad, publicly funded private insurance is really not a policy of curtailing the state's role at all, but merely a policy for improving the supply of it; that the demand-side agenda of cutting the state is, in fact, not achievable and inevitably reverts to a supply-side approach.

Whether a particular policy should be described as demand- or supply-led, though, is not important. What is clear is that in any event, under the most radical imaginable reforms of social security, the state would always have an important role, and would also always have a residual insurance role.

---

1. If the state chose to save money by only paying premiums for the poor, there would be new incentive problems as poor people would find that as they got richer, they lost their premium subsidy.

Less Radical Options

That conclusion might reasonably lead us to investigate less radical options for reform – reform within the context of a broadly state-provided social security system.

Whether or not anyone finds the idea of re-basing social security into the payment of insurance premiums, rather than benefits, attractive, there is a purpose to discussing social security in that way. If we think of social security not as an unmanageable redistributive structure, but as though it were simply a form of state insurance monopoly, it allows us to focus on what a sensible competitively designed insurance package would consist of for most people. It allows us to ask, 'Would anyone who was neither subsidized, nor doing some subsidizing, choose to buy insurance of the form offered by the state in the social security system, at the price the state charges through the tax system?' I have to surmise that there are many pieces of the system on offer that people would not choose to buy, and that in a more diverse system, private choice would drive out some elements of the current system. In particular, there are deadweight costs endemic throughout it, and the expectation must be that if we did let individuals make a choice, there would be pressure for the system to eradicate those deadweight costs.

So, regardless of whether the state felt able to move towards a premium-based social security system, it is worth looking at the ways in which the state's own existing basic insurance package could be improved. This can be considered against one criterion: whether anyone would choose to buy different pieces of that structure at their existing cost if they were given a choice.

It is an interesting feature of consumer choice in competitive markets, that although consumers tend to get a better deal from it, there are many instances in which it actually imposes a discipline upon consumers themselves – a discipline that would otherwise be hard to impose. We might, for example, value our right to pay a gas bill late, and we might get angry when the gas company tries to get our money in a more timely manner. But if the gas tariff makes an explicit discount for early payment, suddenly it becomes less irritating to pay the bill on time. And in a competitive gas system, where one company demands early payment of bills, and is thus able to offer a modestly lower price for gas, consumers would not resent the discipline of early payment at all. Competition in this case acts as a constraint on the buyer as much as the seller. This is merely because competition sends price signals that invite the consumer to think carefully about what is taken up and what is not.

It is actually rather important that consumers of any product, be it health, baked beans or insurance, should face realistic incentives to purchase just the right amount in the right configuration. Allowing consumers to opt for the particular limitations that confront them should make those limitations more acceptable and more efficient, in the sense that just those limitations worth imposing end up being imposed.

The goal of reform in social security should be to impose those limitations on the insurance product we get from the state, that would, in a competitive market, be welcomed by consumers as worthwhile sources of saving on the price. Consider the following examples and ask yourself how much of a saving you would need in taxation, to accept these limits on benefit entitlements from the state:

Instead of receiving benefit pay-outs as at present, you would obtain half your receipts in the form of a loan, repayable once you were back in work.

Instead of receiving cash pay-outs as at present, you would receive tokens, which would be exchangeable for essential goods such as food and clothing.

Instead of receiving the same flat rate of benefit whichever part of the country you live in, you would receive a level of benefits based upon equalizing the amount you could buy given the prices in different areas.

These are examples of relatively modest ways in which insurers might save money, and hence by which they might cut insurance premiums (or taxation), were choice offered to consumers. Imposing any of these right now would make a government look rather mean. But when you consider them with the cost savings for the average member of the policy taken together as a package, they look more attractive. It might well be that by reconfiguring social security to offer both these discounts and these limitations, change would be welcomed by the public, and even the poor, as long as everybody could themselves enjoy the benefit of the 'insurance premiums' saved in the process.

If we were to design limitations on the pay-outs of our state insurance policy in line with the likely public preference for savings, just how far would those limitations go? Before looking at the details, we might consider some principles, by focusing on another, less emotive form of insurance, that against house burglary.

All insurers are aware of the problem, labelled 'moral hazard', that the existence of insurance increases the likelihood of misfortune occurring. Once insured, we are relieved of the incentive to take adequate precautions against burglary. Why go to the trouble of locking up, for example, if it is the insurance company that bears the cost of any burglary occurring as a result of our carelessness?

To cope with this problem, insurers take it into account by imposing restrictions in the design of their policies. The restrictions can neither be too tough, nor too relaxed. Insurers exempt themselves from paying out in the case of wilful neglect, for example. They have a deductible, to ensure we are always a little worse off being burgled than not being. They demand that our house has locks. But they do not demand so much of us that we might quite accidentally invalidate our insurance by our behaviour.

The trick is to design a policy that imposes just the right number of restrictions. The sensible policy towards moral hazard is to restrain people from behaving irresponsibly so that they don't simply pass the costs of their misfortune on to everyone else. But equally, not to deter people from buying insurance in the first place.

Now this has been where the state's social security policy has been at its weakest. It has attempted to combine high levels of permissiveness with high levels of protection. And the two together make for an uncomfortable mix. Either a society can offer protection against misfortune (like Singapore) – in which case it must regulate behaviour to minimize the risk of misfortune – or it can be permissive, in which case it needs to leave individuals to clear up their own problems, and thus minimize the risk of them. Combining permissiveness with protection has led many to question the whole system, precisely because most of the public do broadly view social security as a system of insurance, and it is a system that has imposed too few restrictions on behaviour.

Moving from generalities to specifics, what kind of reforms to the social security system would make it more compatible with people's tastes for insurance? The package currently pays out money in situations in which many of us would not choose to receive it, if we were paying the cost in an insurance premium.

This is not to criticize the bulk of cases of hardship identified: unemployment, long-term sickness, disability, even very low pay. But would we choose to insure against unemployment when there were jobs available? Of course, if the jobs were terrible, we might. Or if taking a rotten job gave us too little time to look for a decent one, we might want an income to allow us to search. Would we pay to cover ourselves against having to work as a waiter? The very rich might, but not the bulk of us.

Or what about single parenthood? It is clear we would all seek to insure against widowhood. Those for whom abortion is not an acceptable action might genuinely want to insure against accidental pregnancy. But to take an extreme example, would we 'insure' against a choice to carelessly have a baby that we cannot possibly look after? It is doubtful. We would choose not to have the baby, or to make arrangements in which we could look after it.[1]

Sickness, which has been one of the great causes of growth in recent social security claims, is clearly something we would insure against. The suspicion is that long-term sickness benefits have acted as a form of early retirement for those finding life in the labour market hard. Would we choose to insure against long-term unemployment in late career? Probably, but again, not if there were some reasonable jobs available instead.

This suggests a route of reform of the state social security system to bring it into line with what a well-functioning private insurance market would probably deliver: a focus on the eligibility conditions applying to benefits. The system would need to distinguish between what we

---

1. Note, most of us would choose to insure against the possibility of being born to a person unable to look after us, hence we do need to protect infants even if we blame their parents for their fate.

might see as deserving poor and undeserving poor; those who are unlucky as opposed to those who are unnecessarily careless, and those who are being unnecessarily demanding.[1]

The issue of identifying need more critically is a politically sensitive one. It is easy to appear mean in advocating a tougher approach, and it would be inappropriate to retrospectively change the rules as they apply to existing claimants. But there is an advantage to benefit payments to a smaller, more deserving core of recipients, and that is that the benefits can then be more generous.

There is another major advantage of tightening up the eligibility criteria: at the moment, because the system has become so unjudgemental in its allocation of entitlements, it has had to target benefits in relatively formulaic ways, based upon income. Means-testing has become a more and more important feature of our social security system since it was invented. This has exacerbated the problem of incentives, because means-testing implies that self-improvement necessarily involves a reduction in entitlement. The advantage of being more judgemental, therefore, and in restricting benefit payments, is that it should allow a reduction in the use of targeting via means tests.

The challenge of this approach is to find practical and enforceable means of discriminating between different categories of claimant. The welfare-to-work programme and other 'workfare' type devices are one effective means of doing that: only the very needy will jump the hoops necessary to claim once various hurdles to obtaining benefits have been put in the way. Other examples abound:

> More generous benefits to lone parents could be offered, and made conditional upon the parent having a reasonable expectation that the child could be supported before it was conceived, for example, via marriage.

---

1. This, in fairness, was the thrust of the reforms of social security under Peter Lilley. It explains the introduction of jobseeker's allowance, a benefit far harder to claim than the old unemployment benefit (especially after several months). It explains the introduction of incapacity benefit, with its harder eligibility requirement, to replace invalidity benefit. It explains the reforms of housing benefit to ensure that people did not live in unreasonably good accommodation.

Benefits paid to the unemployed or low paid could take into account the local rate of unemployment – more unemployment should reasonably lead to higher benefits, as it is obviously harder for each unemployed person to find a job in those circumstances.

Benefits for sickness could take into account the jobs people could still feasibly perform, rather than assume that they are unable to do anything.

Doctors awarding benefit to the long-term sick could be subject to random tests to ensure they are implementing the rules satisfactorily.

These ideas are simply designed to suggest rules that could allow benefit entitlement to be tailored more flexibly to the genuine needs of claimants.

All of this amounts to an agenda that would have been more familiar to the political right than the political left a decade ago. Since then, both sides have seen that a clumsy social security system helps almost no one in the long run, least of all many of its claimants. It certainly undermines state support for the impoverished. To some extent, the answer to the problem lies in the plethora of ideas and schemes arising out of the so-called 're-moralization' of the welfare state. This is simply a restatement of restrictions on the benefit pay-outs of a system that has been inefficiently tolerant of behaviour complicit in creating misfortune. Fortunately for those who find the moral agenda repugnant, it is also reasonable to view it as little more than a refinement of the principles of insurance necessary in a state which has created a monopoly of the vast bulk of insurance that exists.

Interestingly, though, it is a real problem with any insurance system – public or private – that true need is hard to assess. We all know there are people who could find a job but don't; who could live at home but do not want to; or who have been careless in bringing a child into the world without any visible means of supporting it. At the same time, we all know that there are really genuine cases of need in these categories. There is no easy answer to this problem. Attempts to impose change – such as the introduction of the jobseeker's allowance – have only achieved modest success.

And in conclusion (an appropriate conclusion to this discussion on the potential for demand-side reforms in the state system of collective provision of services), it may turn out to be the case that reform of the supply-side of the social security system – reform of the administration of it – is the active ingredient of change. If the administration of the existing social security rules could be improved; if a bureaucracy more willing to be tough and discriminating in the implementation of benefit allocation could be established in place, there are likely savings to be made. The demand-side agenda on its own – simply attacking categories of entitlements, or attempting to replace them with private insurance – ironically probably promises less in the way of savings than the reform of the state's delivery systems.

Additional Reading

Barr, Nicholas and Iain Crawford (1997), 'Funding Higher Education in an Age of Expansion', paper presented to the annual conference of the Royal Economic Society, Stoke-on-Trent, March.

Blow, Laura and Ian Crawford (1997), *The Distributional Effects of Taxes on Private Motoring*, Institute for Fiscal Studies, London.

Burchadt, Tania and John Hills (1997), *Private Welfare Insurance and Social Security: Pushing the Boundaries*, York Publishing Services, York.

Dolton, Peter, David Greenaway and Anna Vignoles (1997), 'Wither Higher Education? An Economic Perspective for the Dearing Committee of Inquiry', *Economic Journal*, May.

Magnet, Myron *et al.* (1998), *The Future of Welfare*, Social Market Foundation, London.

Miles, David (1994), *Housing, Financial Markets and the Wider Economy*, Wiley, Chichester.

The MVA Consultancy (1991), *The London Congestion Charging Research Programme*, Government Office for London, HMSO, London.

National Audit Office (1997), *Department of Social Security Measures to Combat Housing Benefit Fraud*, HC 164, London.

Seldon, Arthur (1994), *The State is Rolling Back: Essays in Persuasion*, E & L Books in association with the Institute of Economic Affairs, London.

World Bank (1994), *Averting the Old Age Crisis*, Oxford University Press, New York.

12 Better Budgeting

Allocating and controlling public spending

> It is remarkable how large a part of the art of living, from filling (or
> not filling) one's engagement diary to bringing up young children,
> consists of the ability to say 'no' and to stick to it; and how many
> people find the task beyond them.
>
> NIGEL LAWSON, *The Nigel Lawson Diet Book*, p. 16.

The demand-side agenda does not just focus on the withdrawal of the
state from specific areas of government spending. It also concentrates
on the potential for controlling the remaining areas of spending more
effectively; on the need for discipline in resisting unwelcome pressure
for excessive spending.

Not surprisingly, controlling and allocating money appears no easier
for nation states than it is for individuals. A non-negligible proportion
of them appear to get into financial difficulties from time to time, and
as we have discussed, there are plenty of reasons for believing the rest
are far from obtaining the maximum benefit from the spending in
which they do indulge.

The usual advice given to governments by proponents of the smaller
state, and indeed by international organizations like the International
Monetary Fund (IMF) or the Organization for Economic Co-operation
and Development (OECD), seems to be about as useful as that of the
Nigel Lawson diet book, essentially amounting to 'just say no'; sound
advice for someone overweight, but not in fact very helpful for someone
of normal stature who simply wishes to eat as pleasurably as possible
while remaining fit and healthy.

In this chapter we look at the task of controlling and allocating
spending not from the simple goal of getting spending down, but from

the more ambitious goal of getting it right – of spending where spending conforms to the public's taste for public services. We can look at various means governments might adopt for better aligning their decisions with public preferences; but just as in the last chapter, the discussion will inevitably have a rather inconclusive feel. There are things that can be done to improve the allocation of public money, but none offer the kind of revolution in spending decisions that, say, privatization or commercialization appear to have offered in the delivery of services.

Controlling Public Expenditure

Budgeting in Principle

'Budgeting' is simply the task of creating manageable decisions about spending (such as the amount to be devoted to a particular item) in the pursuit of a rather unmanageable ultimate objective: maximizing the long-term value obtained from all resources available.

In an ideal world, we would not need to budget at all. We would choose the very best value in spending by comparing every conceivable use of funds (within the long-term availability of resources) to every other conceivable use of funds (now or in the future) to ensure the absolutely best-value decision is made each time any decision is made. In this ideal world, we would also compare each potential piece of public spending against the value of private spending, to ensure we are not better off leaving money in taxpayers' hands.

In fact, this is rather impractical. Comparing every combination of spending possibilities across all time is computationally expensive. Even if we were choosing ten out of a hundred possible spending items arising once a year for ten years, we would have up to ten thousand spending comparisons to engage in. That's why we end up budgeting: taking simplifying sub-steps. These can break decisions down by time and by category. Rather than compare spending on every paper clip in the Department of Social Security with every bandage in the Department for Health, we make a broad allocation between Health and Social Security, and then refrain from comparing their spending any further; we let each department make its own decisions without regard to what the other does. We also limit the time horizons considered: instead of comparing spending on a bandage in 1999 with a bandage in 2002, we restrict ourselves to annual time periods only. Moreover, rather than compare every piece of public spending with the alternative of letting taxpayers keep more of their money, we set an overall limit to the level of spending within a year. We then attempt to spend as well as possible within that limit.

The simplified world of annual departmental budgets, and the theoretically ideal world in which every combination of spending items is rated against every other possible combination decision, need not generate very different outcomes if budgeting itself is sufficiently well handled. After all, you do not really have to compare every decision on health against every decision on social security to spend efficiently. You can simply compare the most marginal decision of each department to know whether there would be any benefit in taking money from one and giving it to the other. If the value obtained from the last pound spent by Health was higher than the value obtained from the last pound spent by Social Security, then we would do well to take money from Social Security and give it to Health. The same principle might apply to the allocation between public and private spending. As long as we compare the value we get from the most marginal spending in the public sector with the value of private spending, then we can ensure the annual spending total is 'efficient'.

Unfortunately, simplifying the computational steps does not solve the general problem of resource management. Real decisions labour under the additional problem that they are made in the absence of perfect information, so there may well be a deviation between the expected allocation of spending and the actual allocation; and between the expected achievable allocation and the actual achievable allocation. How can we approximate the ideal world of comparing every possible spending idea against every other, if we are not sure what spending is possible overall? Or how much different possibilities cost? For government, there is not only uncertainty over how much can be afforded over time; there is also an uncertainty associated with the level of demand for its services. How many AIDS patients will there be in 2002? What defence requirement will there be in the former Yugoslavia next year? How much will housing benefit cost this year? (The Treasury cannot always tell us how much we spent on different things *last* year, let alone what we will spend next.) If this sounds like a minor problem – after all, we could hazard reasonably intelligent guesses in answer to all these questions – imagine what it would really be like for a government if there were no uncertainty at all. It could set its budget across, say, decades rather than years. That would make it far easier to ensure consistency and balance over time. It could establish a policy – such as granting beta interferon to anyone with multiple sclerosis – and it would know the real cost of such a policy in advance. In fact, though, government obtains new information as time passes, and thus has to review its spending policies. All this creates a number of budgeting dilemmas. Here we focus on two.

Firstly, what time period should we adopt as our budgeting horizon? At the moment, we follow the cycle of the earth around the sun and use an annual budgeting period – a feature of life that feels so natural, many people could not conceive of a world with budgeting of any other duration. But could we follow the cycle of the rotation of the earth on its own axis, for example, and operate daily budgets? After all, the day is a period over which we can exert some degree of control and base decisions for it upon a fair degree of certainty. Unfortunately, a daily budgeting period would mean we refrained from comparing spending decisions taken on Tuesday, with those taken on Wednesday; yet typically there will be benefits from treating both days as part of one planning horizon.

What about using budgets for each generation? Durations of, say, twenty years? We would then in principle be able to rank decisions on spending in 2002 with other decisions in 2021. In principle, this makes it more likely we will spend well, as our decisions are unrestricted. In the NHS we could avoid the end-of-year running-out-of-money problem nineteen times compared to the existing annual budgeting cycle. But computationally, life would be far harder. One manifestation of this could be that the end of cycle running-out-of-money problem becomes very severe, or that many 'within budget' decisions transpire to be wrong, as information emerges during the budget period.

Uncertainty generates a second dilemma for governments concerning budgeting policy. Should the authorities make their overriding goal the overall level of spending over a particular time period; or the delivery of a particular level of services, with the overall level of spending varying year by year, in line with the costs of the chosen level of services? That dilemma is acute when we make a choice between setting spending in terms of a policy (we give beta interferon to anyone suffering from MS, for example) or setting spending in terms of a cash amount ('we will spend £200m on beta interferon this year'). In the former case, which is popularly described as allowing spending to be 'demand determined' (because once the rule is set, it is no longer in the power of government or the delivery agents to manage the volume of supply), there is no guarantee that spending will 'add up' to the total amount intended, because we do not know what the policy will cost. In the latter case – where we use cash limits – we have far more control over total spending, and are far more likely to get the right total amount of spending, but only at a cost: we do not ensure consistency over time. It might, for example, result in some people getting beta interferon and others missing out once the money has all been spent.

Government Practice

In practice, budgeting is an imperfect and clumsy process. Public preferences – which in principle should dominate the choices made – are held to be almost fully encapsulated in the advocacy power of departmental ministers, who argue their corner for more cash. The public's preference for lower taxes is held to be encapsulated in the Treasury's attempts to limit the overall amount of spending.

As for the inevitable dilemmas, governments in the past attempted to adopt budgeting procedures that delivered a given level of services; and have now switched to a system that attempts to deliver a total cash spending amount, regardless of the services that cash amount buys.

In the former system, dating from the Plowden Committee report of 1961, the budgeting horizon was taken as five years. Department budgets were set in volume terms – meaning that a certain amount of spending power was allocated to each department. If a particular department's costs rose more than the average, that department would be given extra cash. The planning process was revised year by year, as new information became available. This process was held to be the most rational possible basis for ensuring public preferences were taken on board in the spending allocation.

The system lasted in some form until the Conservatives came to power in 1979. At that point, it was felt that insufficient attention was being paid to the overall constraint of resources on government spending. The budgeting system was too indulgent of cost rises. So, to stop spending running 'out of control', budgets were then mostly set in cash terms. The horizon was changed from five years to four years, then to (in effect) one year, with indicative cash plans for a subsequent two later years. If a particular department's costs rose quickly, they had to be borne by the department.

That is where the system remains. The last government in the UK typified this process. Under the arrangements introduced in 1992, planning was turned into a twin-track, two-stage process: on the first track, that of the 'control total' (the vast bulk of spending – in 1996–7 it was 84 per cent), the cabinet agree the total level of spending and then, through the autumn, ministers, the Treasury and a cabinet committee (entitled EDX) allocate that total. Departments are allocated cash totals, and have no guarantee at all of obtaining extra cash should new information about costs come forth once the year is under way. There is no attempt to weigh up the benefits of extra spending at the margin, against the costs of higher taxes. When the overall spending total is agreed, ministers are not aware of what vital spending will have to be sacrificed or what extravagant spending will be financed as a result. For the control total, therefore, there is control of the total, but spending does not necessarily serve public preferences as ministers are restricted from weighing up marginal spending decisions against the raising of extra cash; and they make many of their decisions in the absence of perfect information as to what they will get for that spending.

But the policy does allow a second track, of about 15 per cent of spending, which is broadly demand-determined. This covers debt interest and the most cyclically determined parts of the social security budget – over which no attempt is made at control at all. For these items, there is no attempt to make spending add up to an overall total. There is no attempt to use changes to the control total to offset unexpected over- or under-spending from the non-control items.

The use of the control total – the imposition of a tight overall limit on spending as a device for ensuring that it does not escalate – has tended to be broadly supported by those who wish to curtail state spending. If we cannot trust ourselves to spend well, then there is merit in this approach.

Ideally, however, we would find more sophisticated ways to allocate spending than to simply squeeze all round. In particular, it might be desirable to let demand drive more of our spending decisions (without having to impose artificial constraints in order to control spending to a set level), if only we could trust demand to genuinely reflect our preferences.

After all, it does not appear to matter very much within quite a few billion pounds what the final spending figures are. Setting the overall limit is more important for people on the edge of bankruptcy, or to whom no credit is available. Most governments – the British included – are not in that position. Their reluctance to let preferences do the talking is more about a fear of the irrational forces that would be unleashed if they did. And certainly, we are better off as we are than we would be with a bad system of relaxed spending behaviour. Is it possible, however, that we could harden our spending decisions where they should be hardened, and relax them where they should be relaxed?

That is the challenge. *Can we find ways of setting the overall level of spending (and allocating that spending) that broadly contain spending within sensible resource limits, but which yield decisions that better reflect public preferences?*

Numerous suggestions of a more or less sensible kind have been made for controlling and allocating public spending along these lines. We can take a look at some of these techniques that offer an alternative to day-to-day political control. The chapter is inevitably something of a smorgasbord of different subjects, but all of them are essentially directed towards one question: not how much should we spend on different headings; but how should we choose how much we spend on different items.

Asking the Public

At the risk of stating the obvious, the starting point for making decisions that are consistent with individual preferences must surely be to ask people what their preferences are, and to use the resulting information in deciding how much to spend. Why not survey people, and ask how much they think we should spend on defence, for example, and spend that much? Then we could dispense with setting more or less arbitrary overall constraints on spending, in the sure knowledge that the public would constrain spending themselves in their natural desire to keep some of their hard-earned money for themselves.

There are many responses to this idea. You might object on principle. Surely politicians are elected to make that kind of decision? Yet it was political decision-making that allowed public spending to run 'too high'. And anyway, politicians are also ultimately responsible for agreeing the routes of bypasses, but it would be silly for them to plan roads without getting their officials to analyse traffic patterns. Obtaining information about consumer preferences is not so different in principle. There is no cast-iron law of democracy that says the domain of responsibilities for elected officials has to include executive decision-making on spending even if better methods of decision-making are available.

An alternative objection to the use of market research on public preferences to drive spending is that unless the public are sufficiently interested and informed, they are unlikely to yield any very interesting information about their preferences. And just imagine how much you have to know about something to make a sensible judgement on how much to spend on it: you have to know how much money you want to devote to it, but also, how much a given amount will buy. You have to know the price of baked beans before you can say how many cans you want, or how much you want to spend. An expression of preferences is more than a loose statement that you want more or less defence. It is a schedule of different levels of defence, each attached to a willingness to pay.

But perhaps more important than either of these reasons is that even if the public were informed enough to articulate their preferences, there is little reason to believe they would declare them honestly. If the government attempted to ask us how much defence we want, with a view to taking the average, what is to stop enthusiastic defence supporters overstating their preference by several hundred billions of pounds in order to drag the average up nearer to their preferred level? Tactical declarations of preferences would be very significant. Or for benefits-in-kind, like health, people will ask for more as long as they expect someone else to pay for it. We will not find it easy to discern their personal willingness to pay. So we cannot just ask people, we have to be a little more sophisticated.

Top-ups

Most attractive among the various techniques for decision-making are those based on honestly elicited preferences of the population at large. Government could relax its controls and let the public do the controlling for them. But how can this be done in a practical way?

We have already distinguished between two different types of spending: that which is genuinely collective in nature – items like defence; and that which is not collectively consumed, but which for any number of reasons remains collectively financed – health, social security and education being the main examples. The technique for eliciting honest preferences in both cases is to levy fees or charges that confront the public with some cost to their statement of preference. The first technique to consider therefore, for aligning expenditure with preferences, is that of setting spending in line with the public voting with their wallets.

The circle that has to be squared is how the government can both charge the public for a service, in order to elicit our genuine preferences, while maintaining general tax finance for a service.

For private goods, like education, one solution lies in *top-up charging*. By allowing schools to charge parents a fee of anything, say, between zero and £100 a year per pupil, we can deduce what the parents want by how much they choose to pay schools, by whether they cluster at the top end of the top-up range, or the bottom end. This has the merit of letting parents vote with their wallet for spending. It only works if parents can exhibit a genuine preference by facing a genuinely competitive market for schools in which their choice can be reflected. But if schools and parents, in the context of a genuinely competitive market for schools, all appear to be opting for £70, we know that the basic state funding is short of the parental willingness to pay by £70.

That information can be used in one of two different ways. Either we can attempt to set a new level of state funding, designed to reflect the new information we have about willingness to pay. Or we can continue to let the amount parents pay each year permanently reflect an element of personal top-up.

A similar top-up could be used for social security and health, if either were financed through a state insurance premium, rather than through state provision. And for health, we could charge a top-up fee for use of the NHS even if the more direct state finance that we have at present were maintained. We could apply top-ups for any service that is currently free at point of use, like library services.

Top-ups for these services have an advantage on top of that of eliciting information on the public's willingness to pay for services. By connecting the public with the services they receive, they might make the public more conscientious consumers of those services. People might become more demanding of their schools and doctors if they have to pay for them. And by making a charge for a service, even a small nominal charge, we ensure that users of a service do genuinely value it at more than zero before they choose to consume it.

At the same time, though, these top-ups do have a disadvantage: they can only confront people with a proper choice over the level of spending they wish to support by to some extent re-creating all the problems state finance was introduced to solve. In particular, in as far as state spending is designed to help the poor, top-ups inevitably hit the poor. If they are set at a level that is significant, that becomes a real burden. If they are set at a level that is not significant, they become a burden to administer.

They also give rise to a more subtle problem of equalization: schools provide a clear example of what this problem means. If schools genuinely compete, and parents can genuinely choose a service level from a local range, and if richer parents generally have a greater willingness to pay for schooling, albeit within a limited, narrow, regulated range, then expensive schools will attract children from richer backgrounds, whose parents may have a greater willingness to pay for their service. The outcome that one will end up observing is that rich children will cluster in better-funded schools, and poor children will cluster in the less well-funded schools. This may well not be acceptable, as it significantly undermines the purpose of state education funding. If price competition between schools does not result in this outcome, one has to be suspicious that it is genuinely effective in demonstrating parental willingness to pay for education in the first place.

To overcome this problem, it is tempting to have income-related top-ups: schools would be allowed to quote a top-up, but whatever amount they quoted would be paid in differential amounts by parents of different incomes. For example, a school charging a £100 top-up might actually receive £50 from poorer parents and £150 from the richer ones. That would give schools a clear advantage to attract pupils from rich backgrounds, in order to pocket the most money possible for a given level of top-up. If the government attempts to preempt this by subsidizing the top-ups of the poor, and taxing the top-ups of the rich, then the state creates a distortion to the willingness-to-pay decision the top-up is designed to reflect.

In short, top-ups can only reveal true willingness to pay if they are set at a flat rate, in which case they work in as far as society is willing to tolerate inequalities in provision of service. In sensitive services such as education, our apparent willingness to tolerate inequalities is very limited, so use of this technique will inevitably be rather limited too.

Preference Charging

There is an alternative, and it can work for spending on both private services like education and more generally for genuinely public services like defence. It requires rather sophisticated forms of market research or even referenda, in which voters express a preference between different options, but in order to elicit honest preferences these are tied to choices between different levels of personal tax. These schemes are designed as rather clever 'lie-detectors': if you set the voting system and the taxes correctly, people will have no incentive to overstate or understate their preferences at all, and yet a level of spending can be derived for a uniform, tax-financed service.

These voting systems have not been tried on a large scale before, although more than a few economic tracts have been written about them. They are usually attributed to two economists, Edward Clarke and Theodore Groves, who saw the potential for taxes as a device *not* for actually financing services, but as a signal of people's true preferences.

Here is how these systems might operate: the public are confronted with a limited number of options of different service levels and costs attached to them. On health, they might be given a choice of several different service levels, with overall tax rates attached. One might be a cheap option, that excludes coverage of expensive drug treatments, and allows longer waiting lists; there might be two or three other options, with more extensive coverage of drug treatments, and different allowable waiting lists. Voters are asked to choose between these options. However, they do *not* put a cross next to their favourite option (because that would lead to all sorts of tactical voting, and would not reflect willingness to pay); instead, people declare a price in pounds and pence that they would be willing to pay for that option to be selected, relative to the minimal option. There is no limit to how much voters can attach to the option of their choice.

When votes are counted, the option that wins is the one that has the highest total value of willingness to pay voted against it. But that is not the end of the story. Voters now have to face the consequence of having cast their votes as they did. They do not have to pay the amount they voted (that would in fact encourage people to understate their true willingness to pay in the hope that others might bear the cost of voting for their preferred option). Instead, each individual pays an amount based on how the voting would have gone in their absence. If, disregarding their vote, the outcome would have been no different to the actual outcome, the individual pays nothing. If, however, their vote was decisive in achieving a particular outcome – if the price they declared was high enough to tilt the result – then they actually have to pay the amount of their vote that tipped the outcome to the one they wanted.

It is best to illustrate it with an example. Suppose we offer people three options for provision of a health service:

A: Current tax rates; current health service, with maximum hospital waiting time of eighteen months.

B: Increase in basic rate of tax of 0.2 pence in the pound; a maximum hospital waiting time of twelve months.

C: Increase in basic rate of tax of half a penny in the pound; a maximum hospital waiting time of six months.

All we have to do is ask people to vote with their wallet on preferences B and C: how much would you pay for that option to be adopted over and above option A? The option chosen is the one that has the highest value attached to it when we add everybody's votes together. In order to obtain honest preferences, however, we tell people that if their vote is decisive in swinging the result (i.e. if the amount they put down against their favoured option is larger than the margin by which that option wins) then they have to pay the difference between their vote and the winning margin of their favoured option. In other words, if I vote for Option C with £60; and if Option C wins by a mere £50 – then I have to pay £10.

Of course, if Option C wins by £100, then my vote has not in fact been decisive – Option C would have won even without my vote. The clever trick is that either my vote is not decisive, in which case it doesn't really matter how I cast it because it will make no difference to the result. Or my vote *is* decisive, in which case I am charged a fee equivalent to just how decisive it was. There is no incentive to lie about my preferences because either my lie will be indecisive (and irrelevant) or if it is decisive, I risk paying out more in support of the winning option than it really means to me.

The elegance of this kind of voting has impressed economists. It is an example of a system that can be described as 'incentive compatible'. Everybody has an incentive to tell the truth, and reveal the true value they attach to a particular option.

Given the theoretical elegance of this and similar systems, the question is why do we not use them in selecting the level of provision of public services? Perhaps it is the complexity. Perhaps it is the administration of charging people. Perhaps it is that there are one or two blemishes in the design of them. (Most disturbing is what we do with any money raised, a decision which might affect how much people put down when they vote.) Whether we would feel able to set the annual spending total or its allocation in this way is doubtful – and anyone suggesting a national referendum along these lines would probably be laughed out of Whitehall. But while preference charging is probably not a solution to our problem of letting public preferences play a larger part in spending decisions, it may be an aid. Indeed, it would not be impossible to use this type of technique on small sample focus groups.

Market Research

For reasons already discussed in Chapter 4, broad surveys are not likely to yield any very interesting public preferences. But the fashion in British political circles now is not for broad surveying, but for the use of more intensive, small-scale surveying – so-called 'focus groups'. Focus group analysis unfortunately suffers a significant drawback: it is taken as given that participants know what they think, and the goal is simply to draw their views out of them. In fact, there is no reason for many people to be carrying their preferences in ready-articulatable form with them. Instead, the goal should be to offer competing visions in detail to the participants; to explore the consequences of those visions and to then hear the participants' reactions. It should not be unheard-of to give them some time to think about their response.

The form of market research that this implies is most desirable, is that of the 'citizens' jury'. This involves the appointment of a small panel of lay-people to make some public decision, guided by experts and advocates of different points of view. The idea is that the small number of people involved can attach sufficient weight to the problem in order that a sensible decision is reached, without having to poll the public at large (who have no reason to devote much time to thinking about it), or leave it to elected officials.

It is certainly an appealing idea. Unfortunately, the range of problems to which a citizens' jury is the right way of finding a solution is probably rather narrow. Any issue that can be resolved by individuals making their own personal choice, should surely be left to individuals themselves. 'Should there be a new school in our locality?' is a question which primarily affects those wanting to run the school, and those wanting to go to it. They should be allowed to make the decision. On the other hand, when it comes to important and familiar *collective* decisions, the jury may not be sufficiently representative to be a legitimate authority. Table 1 simply lists the probabilities that a randomly selected panel of twelve will come up with the underlying views of the public under varying assumptions. It demonstrates the difficulty of establishing a jury process that is both decisive and ensures the representative result with a reasonable probability. One either demands the jury reaches a verdict with an overwhelming majority (say, ten votes out of

Table 1: Finding a Representative Citizens' Jury
the chance of a randomly selected jury of twelve reaching a particular verdict, given the underlying preferences of the population.

Underlying public preferences FOR:AGAINST a proposition	50:50		60:40		70:30	80:20		90:10	
Probability of a randomly selected jury having a majority AGAINST	39	%	16	%	4%	0.4%		0.01%	
Probability of a randomly selected jury having a majority FOR	39	%	67	%	88%	98	%	99.95%	
Probability of a randomly selected jury having at least ten votes FOR	2	%	8	%	25%	56	%	89	%
Probability of a randomly selected jury being unanimously FOR	0.02%		0.2%		1%	7	%	28	%

twelve), in which case there is a 45 per cent chance it will not reach any verdict at all even when the public's underlying preferences are overwhelmingly in favour of a particular proposition; or one eases the requirement for the jury to agree to reach a verdict, applying, say, a simple majority criterion. In this case, however, there is a non-negligible probability of the jury reaching a verdict opposite to the one the public generally would themselves choose.

In the case of simple collective decisions it seems better to leave them to a non-random selection of panelists. And it is hard to see a better non-random selection than that of an elected panel. Call them government, parliament, local council, or mayor, they provide the best citizens' jury in town.

The other problem is whether one would truly trust a jury – taking one issue on its own – to fully take into account all the accompanying hidden costs and benefits of the decision. In short, could we be sure that anything approaching a sensible total level of spending would be achieved? Or would juries have a tendency to say 'yes' too often?

In conclusion, the idea has its place, but that place is rather limited:

the jury works where there is likely to be a broad public consensus on an issue, but where that issue is sufficiently complicated that the broad consensus is far from obvious. It is clear that if the jury is not itself reasonably united on the issue, the public are unlikely to be either, in which case the jury is an inappropriate method of selection. Could we use juries definitively to set the level of public expenditure in different departments in the way the Monetary Policy Committee sets interest rates? Probably not. In contrast to the MPC, it would be unacceptable for the jury to come up with a level of spending that imposed serious political problems on a government, because it has neither representative or expert legitimacy. The jury is simply too arbitrary a method to stand up to serious attack.

The idea is therefore probably better suited to more local decisions about, say, priorities in spending. Or as a form of non-binding guidance for politicians who might sensibly seek the public's views in this way, while retaining responsibility for decisions themselves.

Localization

If government is in the business of delegating its budgetary decisions, it doesn't have to yield to market research organizations or the public at large; it can instead always knock them down to a lower-level authority or jurisdiction. If Westminster cannot decide how much or where to spend its money, why not delegate the task to local authorities? Pretty obviously, this does not actually solve the budgetary dilemmas, it just re-creates them elsewhere. But by turning one large national dilemma into a lot of small local dilemmas, it removes the opportunity for one large set of national mistakes. And local government might – being closer to its population – better reflect public preferences than national government.

There are several different ways to localize spending. The 'full monty' would be to deconstruct the nation state into a set of smaller nation states – each taking their own decisions on matters such as public goods, or at least some public goods. An alternative halfway house would be to maintain national funding and tax collection, but to hand over power on how the budget is spent to local authorities. The halfway house would simply involve replacing health, social security and local government support with the disbursement of a single cheque to each local area, for spending as that area chooses. Or a third, minimal form of localization would be to take individual areas of national spending – most notably social security – and make them the entire or partial responsibility of local government.

Where to Localize: Subsidiarity

Ideally, we need some principle to guide us as to where local decision-making should prevail. However, working out the principles of when any kind of localization is likely to improve the match between spending and preferences is itself a complicated business. The overarching and most appealing principle in this field is *subsidiarity*, which says that decisions should be delegated to the lowest level authority possible that just includes all the interested parties. It is appealing because it means the jurisdiction making a decision has the incentive to take into account all the effects of its decision – covering all interested parties – while remaining as close as it can to the people the decision affects. The idea does not just apply to the relationship between central and local government; it has been much promoted in Europe by the British, in the hope that it justifies the maintenance or repatriation of decisions to national governments.

There is, however, a troublesome thing about subsidiarity: it invites us to ask whether the decisions for the lower level authority in question are decisions for governments at all. In most cases people talk about, under the subsidiarity principle itself they are not. For example, at what level authority does subsidiarity tell us drugs policy should be determined? The answer is that it should be up to the individual, not the local council, nor the national government, nor some supra-national government. Under subsidiarity, if I want to take drugs, my dealer and I are surely the relevant interested parties. Subsidiarity fairly clearly indicates that we should between us decide whether I do take drugs or not on a particular occasion. Mutual free trading will deliver the right result in terms of subsidiarity. Indeed, subsidiarity for the vast bulk of our material provision is a simple restatement of market liberalism. After all, individuals are the lowest level jurisdiction around.

And this means subsidiarity is not very helpful in telling us who should make what spending decisions, as most of the controversy in those decisions is really about just who the interested parties are. At its crudest, subsidiarity prescribes that national government should make decisions on national public goods (like defence); that local government should decide on local public goods (like parks) and that individuals should decide on the rest (presumably, like health and education).

For good reason, however, government has chosen to take a more subtle view of who the 'interested parties' are in decisions concerning things like health and education, and these have thus been thrust into the government domain to some extent. Clearly, society at large has an interest in, say, health and education levels, and also likes to sustain some forms of redistribution. But if that is so, it is clearly society at large that is the interested party in these areas, and national government which is thus the relevant authority. Beyond providing parks and road signs, it is very hard to find issues – particularly spending issues – which seem genuinely local. Most of our decisions appear to be naturally either national or individual.

This is terribly important. If we consider education to be an important collective institution, and we are unwilling to sanction the idea that people should pay for their own, or opt out of it, or economize on it; if we are unwilling to let individual market choices yield diverse levels of provision, then why should we allow varied levels of provision across different localities?

Anecdotally, the public appear to accept this logic, and rarely does the idea of local variation grab the public's imagination. Typically, it seems unjust to people that someone living in one area should have, say, better schools or hospitals than those living in another area within the same country. The Social Fund – a social security loan scheme – is handled locally and has been much criticized for being capricious and inconsistent. Quite frankly, people think nationally, and act nationally. They consider it unfair that where you live might determine your benefit level, for example. Indeed, in the summer of 1997, when Frank Field, the minister responsible for social security reform, thought out-loud about the potential of giving control of budgets to local authorities, he was rapidly forced to beat a retreat. Ask people whether there should be different rules governing benefits, or different rules governing the rights of police to plant listening devices; or whether health and safety at work, or employment rights, should be determined locally; or whether the national curriculum should be a matter for local councillors, and you invariably get the answer that these are matters for national government.

The Problem of Equalization

If subsidiarity ironically often augurs *against* localization, there is another major problem with handing powers down to local government: it's that old problem of equalization again. Do communities pay for their own services as under the 'full monty' option? Or does national government pay for them under the halfway house scheme? Neither option is ideal.

In principle, we would expect communities to make the best decisions where they have to pay for their own services. But if the locals pay for their own decisions, they need their own tax base to do so. Yet there is no tax base that works very well at a local level in the UK. Taxing buildings *is* rather effective, because they do not tend to migrate across boundaries very often. But there is a limit to how far you can appropriately tax them. Try taxing anything major – people, their incomes, their purchases – and all raise substantial problems of cross-border distortions and enforcement. More importantly, with any local tax (interestingly, with the exception of a poll tax), authorities have different taxable capacity within them. Some are poorer than others. The value of property in different areas differs widely. A £50,000 flat in Newcastle is a different property from a £50,000 flat in Kensington, for example. To raise the same amount of money per head, Newcastle has to charge more to its £50,000 houses than Kensington does. And that means any given individual is bound to be better off living in an area where they have rich neighbours, because the neighbours will pay more tax, and hence deliver more local services. A poor person living in Kensington will thus be better off than a poor person living in Newcastle. Indeed, a rich person living in Kensington will quite possibly be better off in terms of what local services they get for their money, than a poor person in Tower Hamlets.

There are no satisfactory solutions to this problem. If government is to give money to poor districts in order to equalize their spending power relative to the rich areas, should it assume that either authority is high-spending or low-spending? If it chooses to give more money to those poor authorities that choose to spend more than the average, then obviously those authorities have an incentive to spend more – more, indeed, than their own willingness to pay. If, to avoid this problem, government finances services in their entirety, or caps the variation in service, then local authorities can only be responsible for allocating spending, and not for setting it in line with local willingness to pay. Moreover, if there is a flaw in the formula national government uses to determine its support to local authorities, there will be unintended variations in service quality.

These are not obtuse policy details. The whole area of local government finance in the UK has been plagued by such considerations and caused endless headaches for national and local politicians alike.

The problem put simply is that localization is merely a halfway house to individualizing spending (i.e., removing government from it altogether) and hence in as far as localities differ in terms of their income and wealth, localization has the same implications for redistribution as individualization.

The only way this can be avoided is by adopting a policy – like the halfway house – in which government pays for everything, or sets a standard spending level that can only vary by a rather limited amount. This is where we are on local spending in the UK. It just functions adequately, but it precludes much localization acting as a means of setting spending levels. The council is primarily an allocator of spending, rather than a determiner of it.

Indeed, localization can never both set a level of spending to reflect a local willingness to pay, and also preserve an equality of services received for different taxpayers. As soon as local areas deviate above or below the amount the national government gives them, there is a differential effect across areas of different incomes.

Localization: Other Problems

There is a third reason not to pin too much hope on localization as a means of bringing spending closer to preferences. Because the people who vote in local elections are a self-selecting minority, the only thing we know about them is that they are not quite normal. Self-selecting samples are notoriously unreliable indicators of public attitudes; indeed, a self-selecting sample of five million is inferior to a randomly selected one of five thousand. Whatever one's attitude to the indifference of the non-voting majority, it still implies that the local election is a sub-standard test of local taste. As a pragmatic addendum to this argument, one might note that local government is a layer of government that almost tops the league in the public's impression of badly-run organizations. It seems an odd way to inspire more faith in public spending, to hand it over to the least popular layer of authority in the nation.

Do these arguments taken together rule out any extended role for localizing spending decisions? Is there a role for 'second-best subsidiarity' – something short of individualization of spending headings, but a layer down from national government?

The key argument unfortunately has to rest on an empirical finding – as to whether tastes differ very much by area. If they do not, then there is little merit in building a complicated set of different jurisdictions to solve the inevitable problems that arise, because eventually all the jurisdictions will end up allocating spending uniformly. It is not obvious how far tastes do differ between different geographic areas – although it is clear that any variation in tastes will be much smaller than it is across individuals. Grouping individuals together in council boundaries inevitably pulls them towards the average.

Although existing local spending does differ by area quite widely, usually those differences are a reflection of obvious local need that could be fully taken into account by a national government. Areas replete with old people need more money for old-age homes; those cluttered with children need more schools. The fact that such variation exists is not to be taken as an argument that our existing forms of localization reflect local variations in tastes. That there is local variation in voting behaviour does imply some variation in tastes. But again, not as much as you might think. Much of that voting behaviour can be accounted for by factors other than taste for public services.

There is one jurisdiction in the United Kingdom where it *is* plausible to argue that a difference in tastes exists and where it is plausible to have a local tax base, and that is Scotland. Devolution to some form of

Scottish parliament does not seem a bad way of improving the allocation of spending, even if the creation of a Scottish parliament has never really been motivated by a need for spending decisions to be improved. The primary difference between a Scotland/England comparison and, say, a Kent/Surrey one is that in the former there is a general acceptance as a matter of history that differences between the regions are natural. There are different legal and educational systems, to start with.

Otherwise, it is not clear that local government does provide much of an answer to spending control. While local authorities are bound to have responsibility for local public goods, and for implementation of national policy, they do not seem to have any extended role in taking over national decision-making. If anything, the tendency has been in reverse, not just because greedy national politicians have snatched away decisions that can best be taken at the local level, but because high profile national policy issues tend to produce a single national policy.

Our efforts are probably best devoted to improving the efficiency of delivery of the budgets already allocated to local government, rather than allocating yet more.

Hypothecation

An alternative to the delegation of budgetary authority to market research or members of the public as a means of making spending decisions is simply to remove political discretion from the spending process, and to abide by one or more well-designed budgetary rules.

Of course, rules are unlikely to take us close to solving what has been identified as the fundamental problem: the small role accorded to public preferences in determining spending levels. Rules imply a degree of arbitrariness, because they dictate how you behave, regardless of any information that your discretion might have at its disposal, telling you otherwise. Despite the clumsiness of rules in comparison with discretion, some economists have argued in other areas of government behaviour that they can improve decision-making where that decision-making is subject to irrational or short-term pressures. In particular, Milton Friedman has long argued that governments should run their monetary policy on the basis of rules, to avoid the political temptation to inflate the economy. Similarly, the European Union has subscribed to the idea that fiscal policy should be subject to rules – in particular that government borrowing should not exceed 3 per cent of GDP in a reasonably normal year.

What form could rules take in the spending sphere? It is possible to imagine caps on spending; or caps on the growth in spending; or allocations between departments based upon formulae, rather than inter-departmental negotiation. Unfortunately, each of these takes us further down the route on which we have already embarked – away from preferences, towards achieving a modest overall level of spending. These do not constitute solutions to our budgetary problems.

One particular rule has merited extensive discussion of late. It was originally promoted by the right, and then reincarnated in the UK by Geoff Mulgan, the director of the fashionable and quirky think-tank, Demos, in a report entitled *Reconnecting Taxation* (co-authored by Robin Murray). As Geoff Mulgan now works in the Downing Street Policy Unit, it is an idea whose time may come. The idea (known as 'hypothecation') is to tie particular sources of revenue to particular forms of spending, thus removing that spending from political control, rather as already occurs with the allocation of lottery revenue.

The most obvious question about hypothecation is simply 'why bother?' The real answer is that it can bind government to spend a certain amount of money on headings that merit cash, but for one reason or another are liable to be squeezed in the annual spending round. Capital spending, for example, does appear to suffer in the spending control process; by deciding a particular source of revenue is for capital spending only, one might hope to protect it. That is not, however, an example normally proffered by proponents of hypothecation. Indeed, the normal examples mentioned earmark revenues for spending on popular items like the NHS, which does merit cash but which is hardly ignored each year in the political allocation of funds.

The merit of hypothecation in these cases, then, is to separate the tax and spend decisions on specific items, from tax and spend decisions generally. This might allow taxes and spending to rise without evoking fears that generally unpopular spending headings are growing. Hypothecation reconnects the public to the spending they actually want.

Certainly there is a problem to which this might be a partial solution.

As we discussed in Chapter 4, the public may want more health spending, but will not vote for higher taxes to pay for it out of fear the money will be wasted on other items. Hypothecation can overcome that: we can attach a segment of income tax to the NHS, and then raise that segment specifically, thus reassuring the public that their extra tax is going where they want it to go. Hypothecation can also enable a government that has fears being seen as a 'tax and spend' government to raise health spending without ruining its image.

Hypothecation is almost like a collective charge for the service in question. But there is a second important question to ask about any proposed scheme. Is it real or phoney hypothecation? Real hypothecation is a situation in which the money raised from a particular revenue source entirely finances a particular spending heading. In this case, there is a genuine connection between what you pay, and what you get. Phoney hypothecation is where the money raised from a particular revenue source is 'topped up', or even 'top-sliced', so that in fact what ends up going to the spending heading in question is not really what has been received in revenue. The National Insurance system is a form of phoney hypothecation, as the amount spent on National Insurance benefits can rise and fall year by year with little regard to the amount raised by National Insurance premiums.

Phoney hypothecation appears to have few merits, and seems simply to be a form of public relations. It cannot be overstated that it would be a deeply cynical act by a government to establish an NHS tax, and then to use revenue from it for other headings. The lottery itself is a form of phoney hypothecation, because one spending heading financed by it (the arts) also receives other government support. Buoyant lottery receipts thus allow government to trim its general arts subvention without the arts industry losing by it, and hence the lottery implicitly aids general government finances.

Unfortunately, real hypothecation has its own problems in that it really does remove from government all control over the amount spent on things, with consequent problems where discretionary policy changes might be desirable. If we finance schools by a sales tax, if sales are low the schools suffer, even if government has money pouring in elsewhere. Only by allowing politicians the right to top up (and in unnecessarily buoyant years, the right to draw money out), can flexibility be restored.

Indeed, if there is no flexibility, how can governments cut spending in areas that are overfunded? The economic consensus – propagated by international institutions such as the International Monetary Fund – has been averse to hypothecated taxes precisely because they can entrench undesirable public spending. You cannot really combine the advantages of a rule-based allocation of spending with the advantages of flexibility and discretion.

While governments are beginning to view hypothecation as a means of making taxation popular, it is probably not possible to slice up very much of the spending total in this way. Indeed, if governments choose to do so, as they did with the lottery, it is only a matter of time before they choose to change the rule and use discretion to reallocate spending – as they did with the lottery. Like some of the other topics in this chapter, hypothecation probably does have some place in the UK, but not a revolutionary one. It is perhaps best used for one-off changes, or major capital projects, where it can be combined with a referendum, market research, or a citizens' jury, and a specific proposal financed by a specific tax change can be put on the table.

Challenge Funding

Another idea for allocating and controlling public spending is to increase the proportion of spending that is awarded by open contest. This is the so-called 'challenge funding' principle, first used in the single regeneration budget for urban improvement schemes. Under this principle, an amount of spending is kept aside from the normal political allocation. It is then awarded on the basis of an open contest. Bidders make applications for funds which are then allocated on merit.

The principle is already applied in many areas of UK public spending – research awards by the funding councils for science and social sciences, for example. The allocation of lottery money within each of its funding titles is another example of the challenge principle. Perhaps less obvious, but far more extensive and general, is the allocation of the contingency reserve. This is an amount – about £3bn a year – that is in principle kept aside for unforeseen spending needs that arise during the financial year. In practice, however, it is not just allocated to the unforeseen; it is also awarded to meritorious spending, for which all that was unforeseen was that we could afford it.

One suggestion for budgetary reform would be to shrink the contingency reserve slightly and restrict its use to the genuinely unforeseen; and to establish a new, much larger fund, that is allocated in advance of the financial year on a more open, contestable basis. This special fund could be in the hands of a committee – or a citizens' jury, for example – and could be handed to taxpayers in the form of a tax cut in the event that proposals forthcoming were of lower value than private spending in the hands of the public. The special fund would have to be financed from cuts in the automatic allocations to departments. It would amount to a requirement for departments to bid for part of their budget each year – an analogy is the occasional requirement that some companies impose that staff should re-apply for their jobs.

It has a neat theoretical attraction. In principle, it ensures that cash is awarded to different spending items or to tax cuts in order of merit.

An additional advantage of the idea is that it creates a mechanism for changes in spending: private bidders, charities, groups of civil servants, could all be allowed to bid for money. Indeed, it might encourage entrepreneurship in the public sector by creating a vehicle within which multi-departmental projects could be funded.

Administering a special fund would take some work. For example, one problem with the idea is that departments might save their most valuable spending for the challenge – in the knowledge it would win some cash – and use their normally allocated funds for their more marginal ideas. The challenge principle would fail if the NHS chose not to finance heart operations out of the ordinary health budget, and applied for challenge funds to finance them instead, in the sure knowledge that heart operations would win a challenge against most likely contenders. Measures would have to be taken to ensure that only the most marginal departmental spending was entered for the scheme.

In general, though, the challenge principle is one that should be taken further. A target that maybe 3 per cent of government spending – say, £10bn – be allocated in this form would be desirable, and would genuinely focus public debate on spending issues in a constructive way.

Criterionization

Complementary to the idea of challenge funding is another principle that might be helpful if infused into public spending decisions: the use of targets, performance indicators, and success criteria to determine whether spending on an item, once committed, is maintained. The principle would simply be to attach to spending commitments – particularly new commitments – a set of criteria that would have to be met in order for that programme to be deemed a success. By setting out such criteria in advance, proponents of the programme would have far less incentive to exaggerate the potential benefits, for fear of setting insurmountable hurdles to the project's continued funding. There would be a similar reluctance to set targets too low, for fear that the programme would fail to attract funding at all.

Wise People

Another possible way of allocating and controlling spending would be to use panels of wise people to determine the level of spending on particular headings. At the moment, we use wise people to allocate budgets – such as support for the arts – but we do not primarily use them to set budgets. The fear of letting them do so is the potential for capture by those with an interest in the budget for which they are responsible. Would you really want the Arts Council to have a right to determine how much was spent on the arts, as well as where it was spent?

Nevertheless, were one to identify areas where this problem could be dealt with, charging an expert panel with the task of setting a spending level outside the government's own control total, might be attractive, in much the same way that using an expert panel to set monetary policy is attractive.

The area where this idea is to some extent already applied is in public sector pay, where review bodies are instructed to determine pay levels for different public sector employees. Review bodies cover a third of the total public sector, applying to doctors, nurses, dentists, teachers and the armed forces. Unfortunately, as pay is counted inside the control total, government has every incentive to ignore the review bodies' findings, and squeeze public sector pay (or at least delay implementation) anyway. There is a strong case for putting the whole public sector pay bill on the same footing, and removing it from the control total. The politicians would have ultimate control over levels of spending, but the power to influence spending would be exercised through their power to set the number of employees, rather than the remuneration that each employee enjoyed. Adopting this idea may not affect the overall budgeting process, but it would at least improve the workings of the labour market, and remove the incentive for government to exploit its market power in certain sectors (in education and health, for example).

Another possibility would be for an expert panel to draw up a provisional budget allocation, rather than for the politicians to do so, and for the government itself to draw up a final budget in terms of deviations from the expert panel's own budget. That would be rather like the American Office of Management and Budget (OMB), and it would at least focus the government's efforts into some form of rationality, and force the politicians to answer for their decisions more clearly. The existence of a 'benchmark budget' against which the actual budget could be compared would again focus public attention on spending in a far more intelligent way than the current spending round possibly ever can.

Some Conclusions

No one ever said it would be easy to think of systems of controlling public spending. The Treasury thinks of new ways of organizing the spending round every few years, and sometimes appears to believe that changing the system is helpful in preventing departments finding ways round the control mechanisms. None of the ideas outlined here will revolutionize the way we control spending. However, together they might constitute a small uprising. Introducing a benchmark budget; hypothecating, say, one major item of spending; using the challenge principle to impose cuts on the automatic budget allocation of each department; putting all pay decisions into the review bodies; and using citizens' juries with sophisticated voting methods to determine public preferences might allow us to reduce the authority of the control total in setting spending.

Whether the proponents of a smaller state would find the adoption of many of these devices desirable is a different matter. It is not clear that aligning spending more effectively with the public's tastes wouldn't increase state spending, particularly if other ideas for improving the delivery of services were adopted as well.

Additional Reading

Blow, Laura, John Hall and Stephen Smith (1996), *Financing Regional Government in Britain*, Institute for Fiscal Studies, Commentary No. 54, London.

Chartered Institute of Public Finance and Accountancy (1996), *Councillors' Guide to Local Government Finance*, CIPFA, London.

Clarke, E. H. (1980), *Demand Revelation and the Provision of Public Goods*, Ballinger, Cambridge, Massachusetts.

Corry, Dan (ed.) (1996), *Public Expenditure: Effective Management and Control*, Dryden Press, London.

Groves, T. (1979), 'Efficient Collective Choice when Compensation is Possible', *Review of Economic Studies* 46, April.

Heclo, Hugh and Aaron Wildavsky (1981), *The Private Government of Public Money* (second edition), Macmillan, London.

Hennessy, Peter (1990), *Whitehall*, Fontana Press, London.

Jones, Rowan and Maurice Pendlebury (1992), *Public Sector Accounting*, Pitman, London.

Jordan, Grant (1994), *The British Administrative System*, Routledge, London.

Lawson, Nigel (1992), *The View from No. 11: Memoirs of a Tory Radical*, Bantam Press, London.

Mulgan, Geoff and Robin Murray (1993), *Reconnecting Taxation*, Demos, London.

Teja, Ranjit S. and Barry Bracewell-Milnes (1991), *The Case for Earmarked Taxes*, Institute of Economic Affairs, London.

Some Conclusions

The Big Three

There are obviously plenty of good ideas around for reforming both the supply of services and the way in which they are 'demanded', or financed. What you have not had here is a department-by-department guide as to how government money should be spent, or a masterful blueprint of potential reform strategies. In order to summarize some themes, it is worth taking a very brief look at the main decisions that need to be taken in management of the 'big three' spending areas: education, health and social security. In particular, there are four key decisions on which attention has to be focused.

The first decision clearly relates to how far the supply of services should be liberalized: to what extent provision should be in the hands of private, and quasi-private, operators. My own view is that aside from specific examples like the blood donation service, traditional public governance of services is very rarely necessary. It can alleviate pain in the short term by postponing tough decisions, particularly on closing failing providers; but in the long run, it is hard to identify any reason for it. Indeed, the ferocity with which early opponents of privatization deployed their arguments – talking as though privatizing any sector from telecommunications to water was touching on core functions of the state – has only emphasized that the successful models of delivery for telecoms and water might also be useful in core sectors of the state like education and the NHS.

The second decision is what form any liberalization should take. Should consumers be able to 'purchase' services directly, using state funds; or does there need to be an intermediary? To what extent should consumers be allowed to choose the intermediary who purchases on their behalf? What kind of contracts should govern the relationship between a purchaser and a provider?

The third decision is whether existing state obligations in the finance of services should be preserved. Do we want as much state finance of items like education, health and social security? It is a commonly held precept that any reform of any service at all will be far less politically controversial if existing obligations are preserved. On the other hand, many critics of the state argue that existing entitlements are often the problem and that it is only by attacking them that reform will have any effect. You cannot counter a dependency culture by preserving benefits.

Which of these views to uphold in any particular case depends on precisely whether the problems in that case are those of poor supply, or uncontrolled demand. Generally, the biggest obstacle to reforming supply – for example, liberalizing the schools or hospital sector – is a pervasive suspicion that the 'next target' will be state finance for these services. I do not think there is any hope whatsoever for reform of education and health without some kind of cast-iron commitment to continued state finance. In social security, the problems are rather more complicated, but clearly relate to demand as much as supply. Some attempt to restrain entitlements seems inevitable in any reform programme.

The final decision is how far the state should go in liberalizing the market for 'top-up' services. Should people be allowed to buy better health care through the NHS? Or pay more to their school for education than the normal state subvention? Or replace their state social security entitlements with alternative or enhanced provisions? The idea is now broadly accepted in the area of pensions – but how far should it go elsewhere?

We can take a brief look at these decisions as they relate to the big three spending headings.

Education is an area where the purchaser–provider split could be implemented in a number of ways. Local education authorities could become purchasers, buying services from schools governed on essentially private terms. Alternatively, probably more attractively, parents could be the purchasers, possibly using vouchers, or 'virtual' vouchers, under which schools received a payment from the state for each student attending. There would only need to be a minimal residual role for the LEA in terms of being purchaser of last resort, finding schools for children within its jurisdiction unable to buy a place at the existing state rate. There would obviously have to be a national inspectorate to ensure schools receiving state money were actually schools serving the ends of the state's support for that sector. There would probably need to be a minimal state curriculum to that end. There would be a significant state role in providing standardized tests and exams so that the world outside might interpret what each child's ability and knowledge consist of. There would be an important state role in providing standardized information on school performance, in order that parents may make an informed decision. There would be an important state role in regulating price competition, in order to prevent parental attempts to buy a good education *in relative terms* spilling over into huge profits – quite unrelated to costs – for popular schools. There would have to be new procedures for the 're-establishment' of bankrupt schools; these might well have to involve the local authority.

This might all sound rather radical, but in fact enacting this kind of system would not be terribly difficult. We already pay the bulk of school fees on a per capita basis. We would simply have to pay the entire fee in that form. Schools would obviously have to be freed from the constraints of public sector control, and be allowed to borrow on their own account. We would have to allow schools to opt out of the existing LEA support facilities (the existing LEAs could still function, selling their services to those schools which wanted to buy them). We would have to liberalize new entry into the sector, so that new providers could offer competing services; we would ideally arrange a takeover procedure so that there was some market in the management of schools. Otherwise things could carry on very much as they are. Parents would choose schools, children go to them, teachers teach in them.

The only possible addition to this system might be to make it permissible to charge a modest – regulated – top-up fee. This would make parents fussier purchasers than otherwise, and would give the state some information as to the willingness-to-pay of education consumers.

Health is a very different type of sector, because it is a sector where there is no standardized consumer need. A flat-rate health voucher would be far bigger than some people need to spend and far smaller than others need. There inevitably has to be some intermediary between the individual and the health provider. That intermediary will be a fundholder of sorts, who will end up buying services on the part of its membership. That intermediary may be a private insurance company, or a state purchasing agent such as a fundholding GP, or a health authority.

A reform of the NHS, then, would have to consist of two strands: firstly, liberalizing the actual provision of health care – taking NHS hospitals out of the public sector, and letting them borrow freely, and compete for business rather as GPs, dentists and aged-care homes do now. The second strand would potentially consist of liberalizing to some degree consumer choice over which fundholder to subscribe to. The consumer might have a voucher or virtual voucher to take to a private insurance company, to a fundholding GP, or to a health authority of their own choice.

Again, this is not so different from the existing system. Obviously, it would mean allowing public purchasers the option of buying health services privately. It would obviate the need for complex PFI-type contracts for the building of NHS hospitals; it might engender a more efficient sector, because spare capacity in the private sector (of which there is apparently quite a lot) could then be turned over to use by the NHS. At the moment, the state does give a per capita grant to health authorities for each patient on the books. There is no very good reason why patients should not be allowed to choose the authority to which they belong. Neither is there any very good reason why individuals should not be allowed to top up the state's contribution to their health care with their own money, if they felt they wanted an entitlement to more health care than the state was willing to buy for them.

The third major area is social security. Here there is a very good case for separating pension provision, which is not really an insurance-based service, from the rest of the budget, which is. There is a case for replacing the state pension with a compulsory obligation to save, with the state subsidizing those unable to afford their own contributions. On the non-pension side, there is a good case in principle for fragmenting the huge state system into a small number of competing systems, each compelled to provide basic insurance cover for anyone who wants it or offering alternative insurance policies to those who want something different. This is not as radical as it sounds, however, as it is almost inconceivable that if the state chose to go down this route, it would not end up paying for the insurance premiums of those unable to afford them.

More likely, in practice there is the option of simply reforming the way the existing system is run, with maybe several organizations competing to administer the system, ensuring in particular that it does not pay out benefits to those who do not truly need them. The distinction between the supply-side and demand-side approach – the distinction between a system of private insurance with state-financed premiums, and public insurance privately administered – is a rather blurred one.

Technocrats, Values and Politicians

A final word directed to those, on both the right and the left, who perhaps find the style of argument just outlined, and the likely vision of the state consequent upon it, objectionable. You are not alone. Many people share the view that in a democratic state, government and politicians exist to take decisions, an idea that is apparently an anathema to the arguments as presented here, which sometimes appear to think of politics as a problem rather than as a solution. Indeed, the latter chapters of the book, on the subject of reforms, all share a common approach – to remove political power from elected officials, and to bestow it upon agents and quangos, the capital market, wise people, and abstract rules. To those with more faith in the effectiveness of the political process than is demonstrated in this book, the arguments offered here are naive. They assume that 'policy wonks' can somehow run nations on rational principles; can distinguish right and wrong; arbitrate in our complicated social divisions; and drive historical progress with their over-sophisticated sense of public preferences.

Many reach a similar negative conclusion from the simpler premise that all this tortuous discussion of this criterion or that, by which one might determine the precise role of the state and the precise role of everybody else, is just more complicated than it is useful. Indeed, to this group, the book is almost miserly in its attempts to calculate exactly where a rational case for spending does or does not exist.

There is some merit in both these arguments, so it is worthwhile finishing with some thoughts on the role of technocrats, economists, lawyers and accountants in running public services. The new thinking on public services does place some stress on more dispassionate management of the public sector and public decision-making. But it is not about increasing the power of bureaucrats and administrators. Technocrats *can be* useful, but they do need to be kept in their place.

To see technocrats at their worst, hark back to the 1960s and the National Plan. Published in September 1965, it was 'a plan covering all aspects of the country's economic development for the next five years', and it was described by George Brown as 'a major advance in economic policy-making in the United Kingdom'. The Plan (always with a capital 'P') was in fact perhaps the most futile attempt at economic policy-making since records began. But that was not because it was performed by bad planners (the Plan in fact quoted an economist who subsequently won a Nobel prize) or because it was badly executed, but because planning at the level of detail involved was misconceived. Take the following examples of industry analysis in the Plan's 470 pages:

The wool textiles industry is affected by increasing use in the knitting industry of texturized man-made fibres which usually bypass the spinning section of the wool textiles industry. Nevertheless, it forecasts a reversal of the past tendency for output to decline and a check to the rise of imports. It also aims to increase exports, though stressing the importance of Government assistance in opening new markets.[1]

The rubber industry makes a wide variety of products, but tyres account for about 40 per cent of total output. The 4.9 per cent annual increase in output assumed by the industry is therefore closely linked with assumed rate of growth of production and total registrations of motor vehicles; it is somewhat low in relation to the assumptions about vehicles made elsewhere in the Plan.[2]

The National Ports Council's Interim Plan, published on July 28th, 1965, has been accepted by the Government as a basis for planning; the Council

1. The National Plan, HMSO, Cmnd 2764; p. 149, para 28.
2. Ibid. p. 156, para 64.

recommend major investment at 14 ports; much other investment will also be needed. The Council anticipate that investment will rise from a level of £18 million in 1964 to a rate of £40 million by 1967 and will total £234 million over the six years 1965 to 1970.[1]

The Plan also contained policy analysis:

> The problems of structural imbalance in the regions are deep-rooted and of long standing. The Government are tackling them by strengthening the controls on expansion in areas where pressure on resources is excessive and by taking more positive action to stimulate growth where it is lagging . . . One of the first decisions the Government took when they assumed office was to control the growth of office employment in London. The necessary legislation has now been carried through to control office development in London Metropolitan Region, and the control has been extended to the Birmingham conurbation. This will release labour for more essential uses and will help to prevent the over-concentration of office employment in the congested parts of the country.[2]

And it also contained a 'checklist of action required':

> Various industries, including machine tools, electrical engineering and wool textiles, will examine their structure to see where rationalization and larger units would increase competitive efficiency. Government will assist in the promotion of mergers which will have this result.[3]

> The Ministry of Technology will strengthen and co-ordinate the Government machinery for accelerating technological advance throughout industry.[4]

This was all obviously a complete waste of time. The technocrats' efforts should not have been devoted to a detailed assessment of micro-decision-making, but to a clear and intelligent delineation of principles on which progress would occur. In fact, the technocrats were so busy compiling industry submissions on a case by case basis, and checking the consistency of forecasts, that they didn't have time to draw up

1. Ibid. p. 132, para 31.
2. Ibid. p. 97, paras 42 and 43.
3. Ibid. p. 18.
4. Ibid. p. 19.

principles at all. There was no analysis of whether mergers actually do foster competitiveness, or what the role of the government should be in promoting mergers. There was no time to analyse why growth was occurring in London and Birmingham, or whether thwarting that growth was likely to help other areas of the country.

It is central to the case of this book that the traditional public sector way of organizing things is not too far from the National Plan way. Acknowledging the weakness of detailed planning by large offices of graduate economists is *not* to say that all policy analysis is a waste of time, however. What should the technocrats have been doing?

For one thing, there are certain situations in which central planning is inevitable, and detailed analysis appropriate. The deployment of troops, the forecasting of traffic, the assessment of a controversial merger by the Monopolies and Mergers Commission. In the private sector, it is reasonable for companies to employ boffins to assess whether productive capacity is likely to be able to serve forecast demand. These are entirely sensible activities, conducted in the right measure by the appropriate decision-taker, with an appropriate degree of flexibility built into the resulting actions.

Secondly, virtually all macro-decisions are best taken with a close regard to a sound description of the outlying scenery. In executing its role in the management of the economy, the Bank of England quite rightly looks at what business is saying, and what it is doing, region by region. That kind of analysis clearly animates decisions that have to be taken one way or the other. As long as description is offered as a check against the realism of actions, or against the relevance of principles involved, that is fine.

And thirdly in defence of technocrats, there are more and less intelligent principles on which to base decisions; there are criteria against which behaviour can be judged. And there is an intelligent allocation of responsibilities. It often takes people who might be considered to be technocrats to draw up principles, unearth interesting criteria, and allocate responsibility. Set them about the right task, and they might have a useful role to play. So it was with economic policy in the 1960s; so it is with public spending decisions in the decades that follow.

Social security and taxation provide perhaps the most extensively studied area, in which the ambiguous contributions of technocracy are on display. The Institute for Fiscal Studies has analysed policy in this area for years. At its *least* useful, it has engendered an obsessive preoccupation with the benefits and losses of different income groups and household types from different policy options; these are measured on the basis of survey data to the nearest penny per week, and it has been broadly accepted that a penny to a poor person is 'a good thing'. While this kind of analysis has its place as background to proposed changes of policy, it should not be used to distinguish good policy from bad. There are some benefit recipients who are not helped in the long term by being drip-fed another few pence, for example. We need principles to govern benefit allocation, as well as detailed tables.

On the other hand, the Institute for Fiscal Studies has contributed very extensively to a clear understanding of sensible policy in taxation. By pioneering the notion of 'fiscal neutrality' – the idea that the tax system should be designed to minimize distortions to private behaviour – it has provided a clear starting point for a discussion of any tax proposal. This is an idea which may have eluded a non-expert, but which is not so technical or detailed as to concern only an economist.

Contrast the professionalism, and well-researched findings, of the IFS with the amateurish attempts to redesign the social security system made by some on the right and the left, who think that 'all we need is a —', with no appreciation of second-round effects, side-effects, revenge effects, and unanticipated costs.

So technocrats, when restrained, can be more than useful, and their principles have a lot to deliver in the management of public money. Public spending should not be driven by ignorance and prejudice; but nor should it run without reference to broad principle. Our decision-making should be based around a value system, founded on a set of well-researched propositions.

Getting the principles right is particularly worthwhile if we are to *refine* the way that government operates. And this attempt at refinement seems the best way to steer a course between the two, rather broad and crude philosophies that dominate thinking among the broadsheet-newspaper-reading classes of the UK.

One such philosophy, the dominant one of the British post-war generation, is broadly compassionate, and rather collectivist in its instincts. For it, much of the writing here will appear unnecessarily tortuous; it is as though every little bit of state compassion has to be justified, designed, monitored and checked at every stage. 'Why make such a fuss about such small matters?' is a likely reaction.

The other reaction would emanate from the market-liberal right, which has tended to dominate all innovation in policy-making in the last two decades. They would ask why I have made so much effort to identify so many pernickety market failings, and used them to rationalize clumsy government interventions that are bound to cause more problems than they solve. Under this view, most of the welfare state and the public sector is built upon the simple mistake of believing that market failures are sometimes worse than government failures; and that compassion always has to be delivered in the form of a girocheque.

Does one have to adopt the view of one side or other in its entirety? The old left have forgotten that effectiveness of compassion matters at least as much as the intention of it. The liberal right have become so accustomed to – justifiably – defending market forces, they have lost the skill of understanding the importance of market failure. The reason that government got involved in the first place in the sectors of our lives that it did, was because people observed outcomes that were clearly not very satisfactory. Reverting to the naked forces of individual market transactions may well see us revert to the old set of problems in place of the existing set.

So there is no need for us either to return brutally to Victorian times, nor for us to carry on as though the old public sector model was a roaring success. There is no reason for us not to refine our interventions in ways that are easier to justify than the blunderbuss approach of policy in the post-war years.

Appendix

The Size of Government Since 1961

How big is government, and how much has it grown since 1961? The table overleaf provides an ultimate breakdown based on data from National Accounts.

all figures are percentages of GDP

	1961	1962	1963	1964	1965	1966
General government: crude spending total	36.2	37.1	37.0	36.6	37.5	38.4
minus capital investment	3.6	3.9	3.9	4.5	4.5	4.8
minus debt interest	4.3	4.2	4.2	4.1	4.1	4.2
plus implicit return to capital	4.3	4.4	4.4	4.3	4.4	4.5
General government: total current spending	32.5	33.4	33.2	32.3	33.4	34.0
minus basic state pension	3.0	3.0	3.2	3.2	3.6	3.6
minus core social security	3.7	4.0	4.0	3.8	3.9	4.0
minus peripheral social security	2.6	2.7	2.4	2.2	2.3	2.1
General government: total consumption of goods and services	23.2	23.7	23.6	23.2	23.6	24.2
minus purchased spending	7.9	8.1	7.8	7.5	7.6	7.8
General government: value added	15.3	15.6	15.8	15.7	16.0	16.4
of which . . .						
wages	9.9	10.2	10.3	10.2	10.5	10.8
capital: implicit return and depreciation	4.9	5.0	5.0	4.9	5.0	5.1
payments abroad	0.5	0.5	0.5	0.5	0.5	0.5

cont.

	1979	1980	1981	1982	1983	1984
General government: crude spending total	44.3	46.6	48.7	49.5	49.6	50.0
minus capital investment	2.8	2.6	2.0	1.8	2.1	2.3
minus debt interest	4.7	5.1	5.4	5.5	5.1	5.3
plus implicit return to capital	6.3	6.5	6.4	5.8	5.5	5.2
General government: total current spending	43.1	45.5	47.6	48.0	47.8	47.7
minus basic state pension	4.6	4.8	5.2	5.3	5.3	5.1
minus core social security	6.2	6.6	7.7	8.6	8.6	8.9
minus peripheral social security	3.3	3.5	3.5	3.2	3.4	3.7
General government: total consumption of goods and services	28.8	30.6	31.2	30.9	30.5	30.0
minus purchased spending	8.1	8.7	9.0	9.4	9.4	9.4
General government: value added	20.8	21.9	22.3	21.5	21.1	20.6
of which . . .						
wages	12.6	13.7	14.4	14.1	14.1	13.9
capital: implicit return and depreciation	7.1	7.4	7.2	6.6	6.2	6.0
payments abroad	1.1	0.8	0.7	0.7	0.7	0.7

1967	1968	1969	1970	1971	1972	1973	1974	1975	1976	1977	1978
41.7	43.0	42.6	42.2	41.4	41.3	41.2	45.5	46.8	46.9	44.5	44.1
5.3	5.5	5.3	5.2	4.9	4.6	5.2	5.4	4.9	4.5	3.5	3.0
4.3	4.5	4.6	4.3	4.0	3.8	3.8	4.3	4.0	4.4	4.6	4.5
4.6	4.7	4.9	5.0	5.2	5.5	6.3	6.6	6.4	6.1	5.9	5.9
36.7	37.7	37.6	37.7	37.7	38.5	38.4	42.4	44.2	44.1	42.3	42.6
3.7	3.9	3.8	3.9	3.7	3.9	3.9	4.3	4.4	4.6	4.7	4.6
4.6	4.9	5.1	5.0	4.9	5.3	4.7	4.9	5.2	5.5	5.7	6.2
3.3	3.9	3.9	3.5	3.4	3.1	3.3	4.9	4.6	3.9	3.3	3.4
25.2	25.0	24.8	25.4	25.7	26.1	26.6	28.3	30.1	30.1	28.6	28.4
8.5	8.2	7.8	7.7	7.4	7.1	7.1	7.6	8.1	8.4	7.9	7.9
16.8	16.8	17.0	17.6	18.3	19.0	19.4	20.7	22.0	21.6	20.7	20.5
11.0	11.0	11.1	11.6	12.1	12.4	12.0	13.0	14.5	14.1	13.3	12.8
5.2	5.3	5.5	5.7	5.8	6.2	6.9	7.3	7.1	6.9	6.6	6.6
0.5	0.4	0.4	0.4	0.4	0.4	0.5	0.4	0.3	0.6	0.8	1.0

1985	1986	1987	1988	1989	1990	1991	1992	1993	1994	1995	1996
48.9	48.1	46.3	43.3	42.5	43.4	45.2	47.8	48.3	48.0	48.0	46.4
2.1	2.2	2.0	1.5	2.1	2.5	2.3	2.3	2.1	2.0	2.0	1.5
5.5	5.0	4.8	4.3	4.1	3.7	3.3	3.2	3.3	3.7	4.1	4.1
5.0	4.9	4.8	4.9	5.0	4.5	4.1	3.8	3.5	3.5	3.6	3.8
46.4	45.9	44.4	42.4	41.3	41.6	43.7	46.1	46.5	45.7	45.5	44.5
5.0	5.2	4.9	4.5	4.4	4.4	4.9	5.0	5.0	4.8	4.7	4.7
9.0	9.1	8.5	7.8	7.2	7.3	8.5	9.9	10.6	10.6	10.5	10.0
3.1	2.6	2.3	2.2	1.9	1.9	2.0	2.1	2.2	2.0	1.9	1.9
29.3	29.0	28.7	27.9	27.8	27.9	28.3	29.2	28.7	28.3	28.4	27.8
9.1	9.2	8.8	8.4	8.5	9.0	10.0	10.4	11.6	13.1	13.5	13.4
20.2	19.8	19.9	19.5	19.3	19.0	18.3	18.7	17.1	15.2	14.9	14.4
13.4	13.5	13.4	13.1	12.7	12.8	13.2	13.4	12.1	10.3	9.6	9.3
5.8	5.7	5.6	5.7	5.7	5.3	4.9	4.4	4.1	4.1	4.2	4.3
1.1	0.6	0.9	0.8	0.9	0.9	0.2	0.9	0.9	0.8	1.1	0.7

Notes on Table

All figures are expressed as percentages of GDP, at factor cost. However, the GDP figure used is not equivalent to the official figure. The Office for National Statistics GDP does not include any element for the implicit return to capital of the public sector. As an estimate is made in the table of such a return, the GDP figure has been scaled up to include it.

General government: crude spending total is made up from data in National Accounts, Table 9.4. It consists of general government wages, other current spending, Gross Domestic Fixed Capital Formation (GDFCF), subsidies, capital consumption, debt interest, grants abroad, grants to the personal sector, and grants to private companies. Net lending by general government was excluded from the spending total, as were capital grants to public corporations and net acquisitions of company securities.

Capital investment is general government GDFCF, from National Accounts (ONS code AAYE).

Debt interest is drawn from National Accounts (ONS code AAXL).

Implicit return to capital is 0.07 times the fixed assets of general government (ONS codes EXHN plus EXHO).

General government: total current spending is derived from the previous four.

Pensions were drawn from the ONS (CSDG). For the years 1961 to 1965, estimates from DSS figures were used.

Spending on core social security includes all grants to the personal sector (ONS code AIIE) except those included as pensions.

Peripheral social security includes subsidies to producers (ONS code AAXJ) and capital grants to private companies (ONS code GTKH). The latter is frequently categorized as a form of capital spending. In fact, it does not contribute to general government net worth, so counts here as current spending. The variable for capital grants to private companies is only published from the mid-1970s. The earlier data – kindly made available by the ONS – is not certified to be of high quality. Any error is not likely to affect the general picture, however.

General government: total consumption of goods and services equals Row 5 minus Rows 6–8.

Purchased spending is drawn from National Accounts 'other' current spending (ONS code GTKG).

General government: value added represents Row 9 minus Row 10. It consists of all the residual items that were included in total government spending at the top of the table.

Wages (ONS code GTKF).

Capital: implicit return and depreciation is simply the sum of Row 4 and the National Accounts variable Capital Consumption (ONS code AAXG).

Payments abroad is typically the sum of overseas aid and payments to international institutions (ONS code HDKH).

Index

NOTE: **bold** page numbers refer to tables